Warfare
in the
Ancient World

Warfare
in the
Ancient World

Brian Todd Carey

Joshua B. Allfree
Tactical Map Illustrator

John Cairns
Regional Map Illustrator

Pen & Sword
MILITARY

First published in Great Britain in 2005, reprinted in 2007 by
PEN & SWORD MILITARY
an imprint of
Pen & Sword Books Ltd
47 Church Street
Barnsley
South Yorkshire
S70 2AS

ISBN 1 84415 173 5

A CIP catalogue record for this book is
available from the British Library.

Printed and bound in Great Britain
By CPI UK

Pen & Sword Books Ltd incorporates the Imprints of
Pen & Sword Aviation, Pen & Sword Maritime, Pen & Sword Military,
Wharncliffe Local History, Pen & Sword Select,
Pen & Sword Military Classics and Leo Cooper.

For a complete list of Pen & Sword titles please contact:
PEN & SWORD BOOKS LIMITED
47 Church Street, Barnsley, South Yorkshire, S70 2AS, England
E-mail: enquiries@pen-and-sword.co.uk
Website: www.pen-and-sword.co.uk

Contents

Preface and Acknowledgments

Researching, writing and illustrating this book was a seven-year odyssey. The idea of writing a two-volume survey of warfare in western civilization – *Warfare in the Ancient World* and *Warfare in the Medieval World* – came to me while doing a book-search for two undergraduate courses at the American Military University. Unable to find a suitable text, I decided to write my own. I soon recognized that my narrative required a visual component, and computer-generated maps were not my forte. Luckily for me, I was exposed to some wonderful maps generated by two of my best and brightest students. US Army Master Sergeant Joshua Allfree joined me as tactical illustrator early on and his abilities as both cartographer and military historian were invaluable. Later on we were joined by John Cairns, a physics major and professional cartographer, who was taking my one-hundred level western civilization course at Front Range Community College-Larimer Campus. His computer-generated maps of the Persian Empire, Hellenic Greece, and Imperial Rome knocked my socks off and he graciously agreed to assist Josh and me in this undertaking. Both of these gentlemen believed in my vision and this project years before a publisher was found. For that I will be forever grateful.

We could not have completed the project without the collaboration and support from a few notable people. We would first and foremost like to thank Pen and Sword Books, especially our managing editor Rupert Harding and our copy-editor Merle Read. Without their generous support and guidance this endeavour would simply have been impossible. Colorado State University history professors Jordan, Long and Knight each saw and commented on an early draft and their comments were greatly appreciated, as were the comments of Ken Danielson. Peter Glatz assisted with proofing the regional maps in a production environment, while Paul Wessel at the University of Hawaii and Walter H.F. Smith at NOAA provided the GMT mapping system. We would also like to thank Jona Lendering from http://www.livius.org for his assistance with plates. Finally, no labour of love is ever possible without the unwavering support from our family and friends. We robbed them of hours and hours of our time, and now they can see what it was all about.

Brian Todd Carey
Loveland, Colorado

Maps

Key to Maps

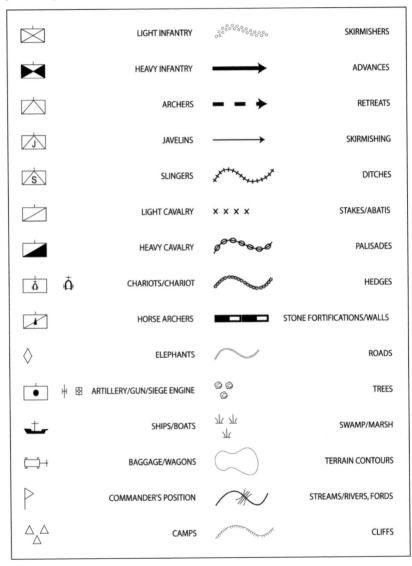

LIGHT INFANTRY	SKIRMISHERS
HEAVY INFANTRY	ADVANCES
ARCHERS	RETREATS
JAVELINS	SKIRMISHING
SLINGERS	DITCHES
LIGHT CAVALRY	STAKES/ABATIS
HEAVY CAVALRY	PALISADES
CHARIOTS/CHARIOT	HEDGES
HORSE ARCHERS	STONE FORTIFICATIONS/WALLS
ELEPHANTS	ROADS
ARTILLERY/GUN/SIEGE ENGINE	TREES
SHIPS/BOATS	SWAMP/MARSH
BAGGAGE/WAGONS	TERRAIN CONTOURS
COMMANDER'S POSITION	STREAMS/RIVERS, FORDS
CAMPS	CLIFFS

Introduction

Military equipment and tactical organization in pre-modern western civilization underwent fundamental changes between the rise of civilization in Mesopotamia in the late fourth millennium BCE and the revival of Europe in the seventeenth century of the Common Era. During this four and a half millennium span, the art of warfare reached a sophisticated level, with commanders fully realizing the tactical capabilities of shock and missile combat in large battlefield situations, situations where perhaps 150,000 men took the field at the same time along a narrow front. On a battlefield where the force-to-space ratio was so high, the ability to orchestrate tens of thousands of infantry and cavalry became necessary for ultimate victory. Modern principles of war, such as the primacy of the offensive, mass and economy of force, were understood by ancient, classical, medieval and early modern generals, and applied on battlefields throughout the period under study.

Warfare in the Ancient World is the first volume of a two-volume study. It surveys the evolution of warfare on the battlefields of the Near East and Europe between the beginning of the Bronze Age to the fall of the Western Roman Empire (*c*.3000 BCE–*c*.500 CE), while the second volume, *Warfare in the Medieval World*, covers the development of warfare from the rise of Byzantium in the early medieval period until the Thirty Years War (*c*.500–1648 CE). Through an exploration of fifty-four select battlefield engagements (twenty-one battles in volume one and thirty-three in volume two), it is this author's intention to survey the changing tactical relationships between the four weapon systems – heavy and light infantry and heavy and light cavalry – focusing on how shock and missile combat evolved on the battlefields of the Near East and Europe.

Overview of *Warfare in the Ancient World*

Warfare in western civilization began with the invention of civilization in southern Mesopotamia and Egypt in the late fourth millennium BCE, a date roughly contemporary with the beginning of the Bronze Age (*c*.3100–*c*.1000 BCE).

As the world's first city-dwellers, the Sumerians, organized into city-states in lower Mesopotamia, they applied the new technology of bronze to warfare, creating bronze maces, sickle-swords, socket spears and axes, and the defensive technologies of copper and bronze helmets, armoured cloaks, and bronze armour. Surviving artefacts suggest that as early as 2500 BCE the Sumerians waged war in close order, with heavy infantry massed in rank and file and protected by standardized equipment.

The Sumerians are also credited with inventing war chariots. Initially a large cumbersome vehicle drawn by teams of onagers, the war chariot would evolve into a light, manoeuvrable machine pulled by teams of horses. By 1500 BCE, the composite bow-wielding archer was placed in the improved chariot by the New Kingdom Egyptians, creating the dominant tactical system of the ancient world and initiating an age of tactical symmetry. During the late Bronze Age, Mesopotamian kings and Egyptian pharaohs sought battle on level terrain where they could employ their own expensive, prestigious and lethal machines against opposing chariots, or batter enemy infantry formations and hunt down fleeing footmen. Warrior pharaohs such as Thutmose III at *Megiddo* in 1458 and Ramesses II at *Qadesh* in 1285 used the chariot to great effect expanding Egyptian hegemony into the Levant (italicized battles are illustrated in multiphase tactical maps throughout this work and volume two).

But the invasion of a new wave of barbarians threw the eastern Mediterranean into a chaotic period known as the 'Catastrophe' lasting from roughly 1200 to 900 BCE. In the Aegean and Near East, Bronze Age civilizations declined or were completely destroyed by barbarian invaders using new military technologies (longer cut-and-slash swords and chariot-hunting javelins) and more sophisticated tactics. The 'Age of the Chariot' was over, replaced by an era where iron weapons, not bronze, ruled the battlefields of western civilization.

The beginning of the classical period (*c*.1000 BCE–*c*.500 CE) also witnessed the widespread domestication of horses by civilizations and the subsequent rise of cavalry. Though history cannot pinpoint the precise beginning of this unique and enduring relationship between human and horse, it is believed that nomads first domesticated ponies for riding on the Eurasian steppes some time in the late second millennium. The Eurasian steppes are an elongated belt of grassland some 3,000 miles long and 500 miles wide, bordered to the north by the Siberian taiga or subarctic forest, and to the south by a wide band of desert, reaching the Great Wall of China in the east and the salt marshes of Iran in the west.[1] Steppe warriors eventually married the skills of riding and archery, creating the signature martial art form of the region, light cavalry. Western civilization would contend with numerous waves of these horse archers, including Scythians, Parthians, Huns, Magyars, Turks and Mongols, by first employing steppe warriors as mercenaries, then developing their own cavalry corps, emphasizing heavy cavalry over light.

The proliferation of iron war-technologies in the first centuries of the first millennium BCE resulted in changes in the tactical organizations of two important early Iron Age civilizations: Persia and Greece. Both of these civilizations organized for war in a different manner. Achaemenid Persia was a willing student of the Assyrian experience and adopted and adapted many martial technologies and tactical organizations from Nineveh, and in turn leaned toward a limited combined-arms tactical system emphasizing light infantry and heavy and light cavalry. The Greek experience was quite different. Because of their geographic isolation, the Greeks in the archaic period (*c.*750–*c.*500 BCE) developed a tactical system emphasizing heavy infantry and tactical symmetry. Both civilizations developed cultural prejudices concerning how to wage war, specifically which weapon systems to emphasize and what technologies to adopt. The Persian Wars (499–*c.*469 BCE) brought these two civilizations into direct conflict.

When the Greeks and Persians met on the field at *Marathon*, Thermopylae and *Plataea*, both armies could not have been aware of the lasting impact this encounter would have on the development of classical warfare. During the next one and a half centuries, a profound exchange of martial ideas and technologies took place between the Greeks and Persians. The Greeks would learn from the Persians the value of light infantry (illustrated at *Sphacteria* in 425 BCE), cavalry and a well-organized logistical train. The Persians, on the other hand, would learn the importance of articulated heavy infantry from the Greeks. The military and cultural contacts between the Achaemenid superpower and Hellenic city-states offered lessons in how to wage more efficient war. Although Persia and Greece benefited from these lessons, it would be the Macedonians who put all of the elements of classical warfare together, resulting in a combined-arms tactical synthesis that dominated the battlefields of the Hellenistic world and challenged Rome for mastery of the Mediterranean.

The Macedonian combined-arms tactical system consciously blended the best Greek and Persian tactical developments. Philip II of Macedon added heavy cavalry, already used by the Persians, to the Greek art of war, creating the most sophisticated army yet fielded in world history. By the time of Philip's death in 336 BCE, the Macedonians had perfected a combined-arms tactical system and logistical train capable of meeting and beating the Persians on the battlefield. Alexander the Great proved this by leading his father's army to victory and empire when he crossed the Hellespont and defeated the armies of the Great King Darius III in the battles of *Granicus River*, *Issus* and *Gaugamela* and King Porus of India at the battle of *Hydaspes*. These spectacular victories were made possible by a combination of adroit battlefield leadership and a superior army. Though strategic and tactical genius was obviously present in Alexander, it was the training, organization and equipment of his Macedonian army that made victory possible again and again. After his death in 323 BCE,

Alexander's generals carved up his conquests and created the Hellenistic monarchies. These principalities would continue to use the Macedonian combined-arms tactical system, but the inclusion of elephants and the movement away from cavalry and towards infantry as the decisive arm changed its character, as illustrated by the battle of *Raphia* in 217 BCE.

About the time the Greek *poleis* and the Persian superpower were engaged in their epic struggle in the eastern Mediterranean, the small city-state of Rome was throwing off the yoke of Etruscan rule. Even before the founding of the republic in 509 BCE, the Roman war machine was constantly changing, taking on many of the martial characteristics of its enemies. Over the 500-year history of the Roman Republic (509–31 BCE) the legion evolved from a Greek-styled phalangeal infantry formation into a linear formation with unprecedented discipline and articulation. These changes led to the fusion of heavy and light infantry into one weapon system, the javelin-carrying legionary, and an emphasis on the sword over the thrusting spear as the primary shock weapon.

Roman commanders used this new tactical synthesis to defeat their enemies on the Italian peninsula, then turned their attention to Carthage, initiating the Punic Wars. Though they were defeated by the tactical genius of Hannibal Barca in the Second Punic War (218–202 BCE) at Trebia, Trasimene and *Cannae*, the Roman general Scipio Africanus' legions defeated Hannibal's veterans at *Zama*. Carthage later submitted to a punitive Roman peace, effectively ending its influence as a power in the western Mediterranean. The Romans next vanquished the last Macedonian dynasty in a series of wars in Greece. The Roman *gladius* proved superior to the Macedonian *sarissa* as legionaries waded into enemy phalanxes and carved up their Greek adversaries at *Cynoscephalae* in 197 and Pydna in 168 BCE. Greece was conquered, annexed and utilized as a staging area for further eastern penetrations.

The last century of the Roman Republic witnessed legions meeting and beating large Germanic invasions. The Roman consul Marius reorganized the legions, exchanging the smaller maniple for the larger cohort as the legion's manoeuvre unit. He also reformed Roman logistics and opened up the ranks of the army to the landless poor, paving the way for the rise of client armies and bloody civil wars. In an attempt to bring stability to late republican politics, Pompey, Crassus and Julius Caesar formed the First Triumvirate. Seeking military reputations, Crassus went east to battle the Parthians and Caesar went north to Gaul to make war on the Celtic and Germanic tribes. But Crassus and his veteran legions underestimated his steppe warrior enemies, and Rome suffered a serious defeat at *Carrhae* in 53 BCE at the hands of Parthian horse archers and lancers. Caesar faired much better in Gaul. His well-disciplined legions destroyed barbarian armies many times their size, as illustrated in the *battle against the Helvetii* in 58 BCE. Caesar eventually pacified Gaul and even made two forays into Britain.

When Caesar was asked to return to Rome in 49 BCE, he crossed the Rubicon River and initiated civil war against Pompey. These two political giants battled all over the Mediterranean, with Caesar bettering his rival at *Pharsalus*. Pompey's eventual defeat ushered in a period of brief dictatorship, one that ended in Caesar's assassination in 44 BCE by ardent republicans and closet Pompeians. A second round of civil wars culminated in the battle of Actium in 31 BCE and the rise of Julius Caesar's adopted son, Octavian, as first emperor of Rome.

Octavian Augustus reduced the number of legions and raised the enlistment to twenty years, creating a standing professional army that was unmatched in the classical period. But even his beloved legions were not immune to defeat, suffering a humiliating loss at *Teutoburg Forest* in Germania in 9 CE. This defeat pushed the Romans back across the Rhine River and set the northern border for the next 400 years. During the 200-year *Pax Romana* (31 BCE–180 CE), the Roman legionaries policed the regions around the Mediterranean, making the sea a Roman lake and ensuring a period of unprecedented peace and prosperity. Legions crossed the English Channel again in 43 CE and brought most of Britain under Roman hegemony. This occupation was not without its setbacks. Celtic tribes rebelled under the Iceni queen Boudicca, forcing the vastly outnumbered Romans to put down the rebellion at the battle of *Verulamium* in 61 CE, once again illustrating the benefits of Roman drill and discipline.

But renewed civil war and Germanic penetrations from the late second century onward took their toll on the Roman legion. The *esprit de corps*, discipline and battlefield articulation that had characterized the Roman art of war declined and Roman warfare experienced a profound transformation with the addition of Germanic martial practices and technologies. When Roman infantry fought the Visigoths at *Adrianople* in 378 CE, the Romans suffered a catastrophic defeat at the hand of barbarian cavalry. It was a harbinger of the role the horse would play in warfare in the age to come. Seventy-three years later, the Roman army that faced Attila and his Hunnic confederation at Châlons was barely distinguishable from the invading army. The infantry-based Roman army that had carved an empire at the expense of Carthaginians, Greeks, Gauls and Germans and kept the imperial provinces safe for an unprecedented 200 years had become, in the words of the fourth-century commentator Vegetius, 'barbarized'. By 476, the last of the Western Roman emperors was replaced by his Germanic bodyguard. The classical period was over.

Relevance of the Combined-Arms Tactical System
The history of combined-arms tactical systems in the western world witnessed a watershed event in the fourth century BCE. Warfare before the conquest of Persia by King Alexander III of Macedon was characterized by the limited use of combined-arms forces. Bronze Age armies in Mesopotamia and Egypt and the early Iron Age empires of Assyria and Persia did utilize limited co-operation between farmer-militia infantry forces and their chariot-borne

aristocratic masters. But for the most part, Near Eastern infantry levies were not trained to fully participate in effective offensive action against enemy chariots, and later against cavalry. Their role remained primarily defensive on the battlefield.

Across the Aegean in Greece, the invention of the heavy-infantry battle-square in the seventh century BCE witnessed for the first time a citizen-militia trained to fight collectively in an offensive manner. The Persian Wars between Persia and the Greek *poleis* exposed the light infantry and light cavalry of Asia to the heavy infantry of Europe, creating a new combined-arms synthesis. The conquest of the Greek city-states by Philip II of Macedon in the fourth century BCE fused the conqueror's strong tradition of heavy cavalry with the Greek world's new tradition of limited combined-arms co-operation. The victories of the Macedonian king Alexander the Great at Granicus River (334 BCE), Issus (333 BCE) and Gaugamela (331 BCE) represent a high point in pre-modern western warfare, with the Macedonians fielding heavy and light infantry and heavy and light cavalry in a fully integrated and balanced combined-arms army.

Tactically, utilizing a combined-arms system meant bringing to the battlefield the capabilities of both shock and missile combat. In the periods under study, this meant the ability to kill in close proximity in hand-to-hand engagements using hand-held weapons (shock) or at a distance using slings, javelins, spears, bows and, later, handguns (missile). Modern military historians describe tactical systems with shock capabilities as heavy, while tactical systems that utilize missiles are described as light. Heavy weapon systems, both infantry and cavalry, are considered heavy because of their protective factor. Because they wore more armour, heavy infantry and heavy cavalry were better able to perform their shock role, as well as being better protected against lance and arrow, even though this added protection sacrificed tactical mobility. Heavy weapon systems relied on collective effort to be effective, and collective effort required discipline and training. The degree of discipline and training determined the offensive capability or *articulation* of the units in combat.

Articulated tactical formations such as the Greek and Macedonian phalanx were capable of some offensive tactical mobility, keeping close order during an offensive march and then striking in a frontal attack. But the classical phalanx was not capable of attacking in all directions, nor could it protect its own flank and rear. Well-articulated tactical formations such as the Roman legion, medieval heavy cavalry *bataille* and Swiss battle square were capable of great tactical flexibility and responsiveness, wheeling and attacking or defending in many directions. Less articulated or unarticulated formations such as the Persian *sparabara*, Germanic *hundred* or Scottish *schiltron*, because of their lack of drill and discipline, performed poorly in offensive shock action, preferring to remain on the defensive in static formations. Hand-to-hand shock combat rarely lasted very long because of the enormous physical and emotional strain on combatants. Most engagements lasted only a few minutes, with total exhaustion setting in after only fifteen or twenty minutes of uninterrupted combat.[2] If a battle lasted an afternoon or longer, then multiple engagements took place, compounding the emotional and physical strain of the event on the combatants.

Light infantry and light cavalry weapon systems relied on a missile weapon system that dealt out death at a distance. These lighter units were less armoured than their heavier counterparts, and consequently had greater tactical mobility. Archers and javelineers, whether mounted or not, did not have to fight in close order to be effective: instead they usually fought in open formation where they could best use their mobility. Because of this tactical mobility, light units were often used by ancient, classical, medieval and early modern commanders in guerrilla roles and as physical probes (skirmishers) against their less mobile but better protected heavy counterparts. But this mobility did little to protect them when shock combat ensued. Unable to withstand hand-to-hand combat with enemy infantry and mounted shock troops, these light units often retired through the ranks of their heavier companions to act as flank and rear protection during the engagement.

Each weapon system had strengths and weaknesses that can best be illustrated in Figures 1 and 2, which explain the tactical capabilities of the four

Figure 1. Ancient Weapon Systems. An illustration of general rules of dominance in conflicts between different ancient weapon systems: (1) heavy infantry is generally dominant when defending against heavy cavalry; (2) heavy cavalry is generally dominant when attacking light infantry or light cavalry; (3) light infantry is generally dominant when defending against light cavalry; and (4) light cavalry is generally dominant when attacking heavy infantry. Dominance between heavy and light infantry varies according to the period and unit type involved in the action. Based on Archer Jones, The Art of War in the Western World *(Urbana and Chicago: University of Illinois Press, 1987), schematic 1.2.*

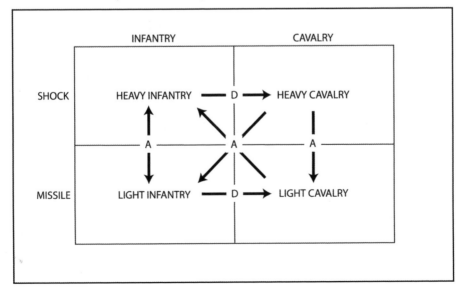

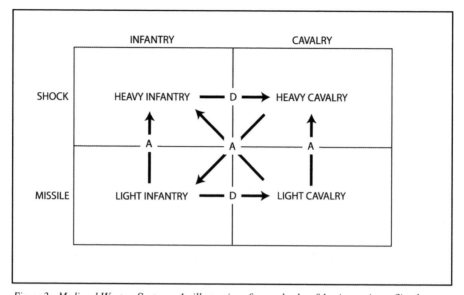

Figure 2. Medieval Weapon Systems. An illustration of general rules of dominance in conflicts between different medieval weapon systems: (1) heavy infantry is generally dominant when defending against heavy cavalry; (2) heavy cavalry is generally dominant when attacking light infantry; (3) light infantry is generally dominant when defending against light cavalry or attacking heavy infantry; and (4) light cavalry is generally dominant when attacking heavy infantry or heavy cavalry. Based on Archer Jones, The Art of War in the Western World *(Urbana and Chicago: University of Illinois Press, 1987), schematic 2.1.*

weapon systems in ancient and medieval warfare. With some or all of the weapon systems present and co-operating in a combined-arms synthesis, a general of the calibre of Alexander the Great, Hannibal Barca, William the Bastard, Batu Khan or Gustavus Adolphus proved irresistible on the battlefield.

Still, it should be remembered that the mere presence of a combined-arms army under the command of a general who had showed brilliance on the battlefield in the past did not guarantee victory. History is replete with examples of outstanding commanders who fell victim to what the Prussian military theorist Carl von Clausewitz called 'friction' in his seminal work *On War*, published in 1832.[3] Although Clausewitz was a student of Napoleon and his campaigns, his appraisal of what has been called the 'fog of war' holds true in any era. Friction refers to the accidents, uncertainties, errors, technical difficulties or unknown factors on the battlefield, and to their effect on decisions, morale and actions in warfare.[4] To Clausewitz, 'Action in war is like movement in a resistant element. Just as the simplest and most natural of movements, walking, cannot easily be performed in water, so in war it is difficult from normal efforts to achieve even moderate results.'[5] Friction, Clausewitz tells us, 'is the force that makes the apparently easy so difficult'.[6]

The great commanders who fought, won and sometimes lost the battles that shaped the history of western civilization understood the repercussions of friction when making war. They understood that the best strategies, bravest soldiers, most modern equipment and ingenious tactics did not always carry the day. Ancient, classical, medieval and early modern commanders recognized that each engagement carried the possibility of victory, with all of its spoils, or defeat and possible death, enslavement or the extermination of their soldiers and families, and loss of homeland. Warfare, to these men and their cultures, was more than, in the famous statement by Clausewitz, 'the continuation of politics by other means'.[7] Warfare in the pre-modern world was instead, in the words of the British military historian John Keegan, 'an expression of culture, often a determinant of cultural forms, and in some societies, the culture itself'.[8] And in the period under study here, a period without the Geneva Conventions and formal rules of war, the distinction between how 'civilized' and 'barbarian' peoples fought was often blurred, with all sides routinely killing or maiming combatants and non-combatants alike, and enslaving or ethnically cleansing entire populations.

This monograph is by no means comprehensive. It is the first part of a two-volume introduction to the development of the art of war during western civilization's ancient, classical, medieval and early modern periods. By pulling together both primary and secondary sources, it is my hope that this synthetic work will help my students at the American Military University and armchair military historians alike better appreciate the sophisticated nature of pre-modern warfare and the importance of organized violence in shaping western civilization's history and culture. This remarkable process begins over five millennia ago with the rise of civilization in Mesopotamia and north Africa.

Chapter 1

Warfare in the Ancient Near East:
The Bronze and Early Iron Ages

Warfare in Ancient Mesopotamia and Egypt:
The World's First Armies

The rise of the world's first civilizations in southern Mesopotamia and Egypt in the late fourth millennium BCE also begins the history of organized warfare in western civilization. The creators of the first Mesopotamian civilization were the Sumerians, a people whose origins still remain unclear. By 3000 BCE they had established a number of independent walled city-states in southern Mesopotamia, including the cities of Eridu, Ur, Uruk and Lagash. As the number of Sumerian city-states grew and expanded in the third millennium BCE, new conflicts arose as city-states fought each other for control of local natural resources or united against the persistent threat of barbarian raiding and invasion.

With the rise of civilization and organized violence came the experimentation with metal alloys in a search for harder, more lethal materials to make weapons. As early as 6000 BCE in Anatolia, Neolithic man experimented with copper tools and weapons. But it was not until the fourth millennium BCE that tin was added to copper to produce a superior alloy, beginning the Bronze Age. Roughly contemporary to the rise of civilization in Mesopotamia, the Bronze Age made warfare a much more dangerous activity than it had been before in the neolithic period.[1] From the back of their bronze-gilded war chariots, Mesopotamian kings and, later, Egyptian pharaohs made war and carved empires, bringing civilization to newly conquered regions.

The Sumerians are credited with inventing numerous military technologies, including the war chariot, bronze maces, sickle-swords, socket spears and axes, and the defensive technologies of copper and bronze helmets, armoured cloaks and bronze armour.[2] Many of these weapons, such as the mace, spear and axe, were present in the pre-neolithic and neolithic periods as stone weapons, but the Sumerians improved their lethality by making them out of copper and, later, bronze. In response to the increased lethality of metal weapons, personal body armour was developed, made first out of leather, then copper and, later, bronze. By 2100 BCE, bronze scale-armour had been developed, and by 1700 BCE was widely used by Mesopotamian and, later, Egyptian armies.[3]

The standard shock weapons in Sumerian armies were the long heavy spear, battleaxe and the dagger. The effectiveness of the heavy thrusting spear on the battlefields of Mesopotamia affected the tactical development of ancient armies more than any other weapon. If soldiers armed with the spear were to fight effectively in groups, they had to arrange themselves in close-order formation, giving rise to the first heavy-infantry battle-square in western civilization.[4] Unfortunately, historians know very little about ancient Mesopotamian military formations and tactics because kings used writing to commemorate significant military victories, not the manner in which the battle was fought. Occasionally, the same events were recorded in pictorial form. The most impressive of these early illustrations of the Sumerian army at war is provided by the Stele of Vultures from the city-state of Lagash, dating from around 2500 BCE.[5]

The Stele of Vultures commemorates a victory of King Eannatum of Lagash over the king of Umma and takes its name from a section of the stele depicting a defeated enemy whose abandoned bodies are shown being picked at by vultures and lions.[6] The battle scene shows the army at the moment of victory, marching over the bodies of their defeated and slain enemies. In the upper register the king leads a troop of heavy infantry, while in the lower register the king is shown riding in a four-wheeled battle chariot pulled by four onagers in the van of a troop of light infantry.

The Sumerian light infantryman is depicted without protective equipment and armed with a long spear in the left hand and a battleaxe in the right. It is not known whether these unarmoured light infantry used their spears for shock combat or as throwing weapons. The Sumerian heavy infantry are portrayed in formation, with the unnamed sculptor carving helmeted spearmen, organized six files deep with an eight-man front, with the front rank bearing large rectangular shields. What is interesting is the apparent standardized equipment and number of spears projecting between the shields. The common panoply and close order suggests that these soldiers were well trained, uniformed and equipped to fight as a corps, anticipating later Greek, Macedonian and Roman heavy infantry formations.[7] Still, without corroborating textual evidence it is unknown whether this early battle square was a common battlefield formation, if it was capable of offensive articulation, or if it served primarily as a defensive formation.

Eventually, the Sumerian civilization would fall to the inventor of imperium, Sargon the Great, around 2340 BCE (Map 1.1). During his fifty-year rule, the Akkadian king would fight no fewer than thirty-four military campaigns and carve out an empire that would include all of Mesopotamia, as well as lands westward to the Mediterranean, inspiring generations of Near Eastern rulers to emulate his accomplishment.[8]

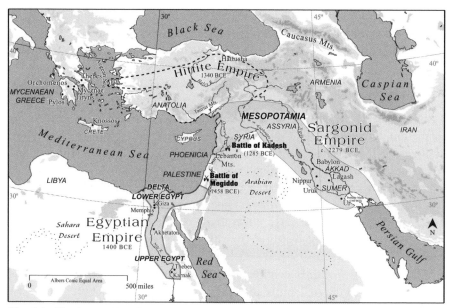

Map 1.1. The Ancient Near East.

During the Sargonid period (*c*.2340–*c*.2100 BCE) the Akkadians contributed another major innovation in weaponry: the composite bow. Although it is likely that the Sumerians utilized the simple bow in warfare, no textual or pictorial evidence exists to support this claim. The first evidence of the bow being used in collective warfare is found during the reign of Sargon's grandson Naram Sin (2254–2218 BCE), though it is possible that Sargon himself utilized the weapons in his own campaigns.[9]

The impact of the composite bow on the battlefields of the Near East was significant. While the simple self-bow (a bow made of a single piece of wood) could kill at ranges from 50 to 100 yards, it could not penetrate even simple leather armour at these ranges.[10] The composite bow, with a pull of at least twice that of a self-bow, could easily penetrate leather armour, and perhaps the bronze armour of the day.[11] The reason for this increased performance was the unique construction of the bow. The composite bow was a recurve bow made of wood, horn and tendons from oxen, carefully laminated together to create a bow of superior strength, range and impact power.[12]

Possibly invented on the Eurasian steppes and brought to the Akkadians by mercenary nomads, the composite bow quickly became an important asset on the battlefields of ancient Mesopotamia. Aiming against packed heavy-infantry formations, light infantry archers could fire withering barrages of arrows, causing gaps and tears and eroding the morale of the foot soldiers. Although we have no descriptions of Mesopotamian battles from the Bronze Age, it is safe to assume that the co-ordination of heavy infantry and light infantry archers working together on the battlefield represents a combined-arms tactical synthesis, perhaps the first in the history of western civilization.

Once created, the composite bow spread quickly to other armies over the next 500 years, appearing in Palestine around 1800 BCE and introduced to Egypt and the Aegean region by 1600 BCE. In New Kingdom Egypt (1567–1085 BCE), the improved archer was placed in an improved war chariot, combining for the first time a powerful weapon with increased tactical mobility.[13] Composite bow-wielding light infantry and cavalry would remain a persistent adversary to the heavy-infantry-based armies of western civilization for the next two-and-a half millennia (*c*.1000 BCE–*c*.1500 CE).

Perhaps no other single military invention is as closely associated with the ancient period as the war chariot. The military application of the wheel came quite early in the development of civilization, with the first chariot integrated into Sumerian battle tactics around 3000 BCE.[14] These early chariots were either of the two- or four-wheeled variety, were manned by a crew of two, and were pulled by a team of four onagers. The wheels were constructed of solid wood sections held together by pegs, while the placement of the axle either in front or in the middle of the chariot itself made the Sumerian war chariot heavy and unstable at speed. The absence of a mouth bit made controlling the wild asses very difficult, and it is unlikely that these machines could have moved at more than 10 miles per hour.[15]

Armed with javelins and axes, Sumerian charioteers used their weapons to deliver a shock attack, driving into opposing heavy infantry formations and scattering enemy footmen. The Sumerian machine, pulled by wild asses, was too heavy and cumbersome to offer effective pursuit. Still, the Sumerian chariot served as the prototype for wheeled shock combat for the next thousand years. In the early centuries of the second millennium BCE, two different innovations appeared in significant conjuncture to create a superior chariot: the widespread use of the domesticated horse and the new technology of lightweight, bentwood construction.[16]

Although horses were raised as food in central Asia as early as the fourth millennium BCE, it was only in the second millennium BCE that domesticated equines spread throughout Europe and the Near East.[17] At first too small to be ridden as a cavalry mount, the even-tempered horse was originally used as a replacement for the onager, harnessed to chariots, usually in teams of four. The development of bentwood techniques allowed for the construction of the spoked wheel with a rim of curved felloes and the manufacture of lightweight chariot bodies.[18] At the same time, the appearance of the horse bit improved the control of the animal teams at higher speeds. This lightweight chariot with spoked wheels drawn by teams of horses provided for the first time a fast, manoeuvrable chariot, one that could be used as a firing platform for composite-bow-wielding archers.

By the fifteenth century BCE, the Egyptians had modified the chariot into the finest machine in the world. The Egyptian chariot was made entirely of wood and leather and was so light that two men could carry the body over rough terrain. The Egyptians improved the control, manoeuvrability and speed of the chariot by moving the axle to the very rear of the carrying platform.[19] But manufacturing and maintaining a chariot corps was a very expensive endeavour, the prerogative of rich and powerful kingdoms. The chariots' presence on the battlefield was supported by the complex logistics of horse breeding and training, a small army of wheelwrights and chariot builders, bowyers, metalsmiths and armourers, and the support teams on campaign who managed spare horses and repaired damaged vehicles.[20] Moreover, the chariots' position as the pre-eminent weapon system in ancient warfare required continued access to strategic materials, specifically the light and heavy woods required for bentwood construction. In the case of Egypt in the late Bronze Age and Assyria in the early Iron Age, this meant access to the famous cedars of Lebanon. It is no wonder why both of these empires expended so much effort maintaining their presence in Lebanon, the chief source of wood for the armies of the Near East.

How chariots were employed in battle in the late Bronze Age (*c*.1600–*c*.1100 BCE) is a matter of some debate. One view holds that the Bronze Age kingdoms used war chariots as a thin screen for massed infantry formations, with chariots moving laterally across the front of their own infantry and the chariot archers shooting – at a right angle – their arrows against the enemy infantry.[21] A second view suggests that chariots were held in reserve until the infantry engagement reached a decisive point. At this moment, commanders would commit their chariots and win the day.[22]

A more recent interpretation has opposing chariot forces lining up in long, shallow formations, then hurtling toward each other as archers fired over their teams and into enemy chariot formations.[23] As enemy horses were killed and wounded, chariots veered, slowed and eventually stopped. At this time, friendly infantry 'runners' would finish off enemy chariot crews whose machines had been immobilized. Infantry may have also served as a cordon, a haven for damaged chariots to return to after battle. Because there is no evidence for a clash of close-order infantry formations in late Bronze Age warfare, it is believed the infantry of the period was lightly armoured and unarticulated, and was most probably used in direct support of chariot charges, to fight in terrain unfavourable to chariot warfare and to garrison cities.[24] During the Egyptian New Kingdom period these new chariots would help pharaohs carve an empire stretching from the Libyan Desert across the Sinai to the Orontes River in Syria.

The Chariot at War: The Battles of Megiddo and Qadesh
The Hyksos invasion and conquest of Egypt in the seventeenth century BCE introduced state-of-the-art military technologies from Mesopotamia to the people of the Nile for the very first time. The Semitic-speaking Hyksos were

originally from the Arabian peninsula, moving into northern Mesopotamia, Syria and Palestine in the first centuries of the second millennium BCE. The Hyksos infiltrated Egypt in the seventeenth century BCE, dominating much of Egypt for nearly 100 years. During their occupation the Hyksos introduced to the Egyptians new ways of making war, including the horse-drawn war chariot, a heavier bronze sword and the composite bow. Eventually, the Egyptians made use of these new martial technologies to throw off foreign domination, expelling the Hyksos and founding the New Kingdom in 1567 BCE.

During the period of the New Kingdom (Map 1.1), Egypt became the most powerful state in the ancient Near East. Palestine and Syria were occupied, and local princes were permitted to rule, but under Egyptian suzerainty. At times these client kings rebelled against their Egyptian landlords, precipitating military expeditions to deal with the uprisings. In 1458 BCE Pharaoh Thutmose III (1490–1436 BCE) decided to deal directly with the growing problems in Syria-Palestine that threatened the integrity of Egypt's north-eastern frontiers.[25] The ruler of the small kingdom of Qadesh hoped to take advantage of the change in leadership in Thebes by moving south from Syria, allying with local princes, and seizing the strategic city of Megiddo in Palestine. The strongly fortified site of Megiddo dominated the main line of communication overland between Egypt and Mesopotamia.[26]

To counter the king of Qadesh's gambit for Megiddo, Thutmose advanced rapidly north with his army in the hope of surprising and defeating the Syrians in a battlefield engagement. It took Thutmose only nine days to travel from Egypt to Gaza, a pace that rivalled Alexander the Great's marches and demanded a very lean and sophisticated logistical system.[27] When the pharaoh reached Aruna in the vicinity of Megiddo, he summoned his generals to discuss the final approach to the city. There were three possible routes to the fortress: through the narrow and steep Musmus Pass leading directly to Megiddo, and less difficult routes from the north and south. His generals argued against taking the direct route because it would be necessary for the Egyptians to march through the pass in column against a defending force waiting for them arrayed for battle. The generals asked:

> What is it like to go on this road which becomes so narrow? It is reported that the foe is there, waiting on the outside, while they are becoming more numerous. Will not horse have to go after horse, and the army and the people similarly? Will the vanguard of us be fighting while the rear guard is waiting here [behind] in Aruna, unable to fight?[28]

But Thutmose decided to disregard the advice of his war council and take the direct approach to Megiddo. This decision proved a sound one, for the king of Qadesh, believing the pharaoh would attack from one of the easier routes, split his forces to guard the other approaches and the citadel itself. As Thutmose neared the end of the narrow Musmus Pass, his generals urged him to halt the advance and wait for the column to catch up:

> Let our victorious lord listen to us this time, and let our lord guard for us the rear of his army and his people. When the rear of the army comes forth for us into the open, then we shall fight against these foreigners, then we shall not trouble our hearts about the rear of an army.[29]

This time the pharaoh heeded his generals' advice, concentrating his forces in column. The Egyptian army then exited the pass and executed the extremely difficult manoeuvre of deploying from column to line of battle without being attacked by the enemy (Map 1.2(a)).[30] It took seven hours for the end of the column to reach the mouth of the valley and deploy into position.[31]

Once on the plain of Megiddo, Thutmose divided his army into three divisions, sending his infantry divisions to take position in the north and the south, while arraying his war chariots in the centre, across from the main elements of the enemy encamped in front of Megiddo. There are no reliable estimates of the size of the armies involved in the engagement, but the battle of Megiddo stands as the first battle in western civilization where historians have a description of the general tactics involved.

The battle began at dawn, with Thutmose ordering his infantry on the right to stay in place behind the steep banks of the Kina Brook, while the rest of the army struck on the centre and the left (Map 1.2(b)). The Egyptian centre pressed its attack, pinning the Syrians against their own camp. At the same time, a chariot force penetrated between the Syrian right and centre, rolling the Syrian centre upon itself and its camp.[32] The chariot missile-shock attack was devastating, and the enemy army lost its integrity and routed all along its lines.

But Thutmose was unable to capitalize on his battlefield victory. Instead of pursuing the fleeing enemy as they scampered back to the safety of the walls of Megiddo, the Egyptian army, including the chariot corps, stopped to plunder the Syrian camp, providing time for the fleeing troops to be pulled up the city's walls to safety. The chance to crush the enemy coalition on the battlefield was lost, and Thutmose was forced to reduce Megiddo in a seven-month siege.[33] Still, despite the lost opportunity to bring the war to a rapid conclusion through a set-piece battle, the Egyptian victory at Megiddo guaranteed security and control over southern Palestine and extended the Egyptian frontier to the Orontes River in Syria.[34]

About 200 years later, another powerful pharaoh conducted a similar campaign to secure his north-eastern frontier. In 1285 BCE Ramesses II (r. 1279–1213 BCE) faced the expansionistic Hittites who had moved from their base in Anatolia into Syria (Map 1.1). Ramesses' target was the city of Qadesh

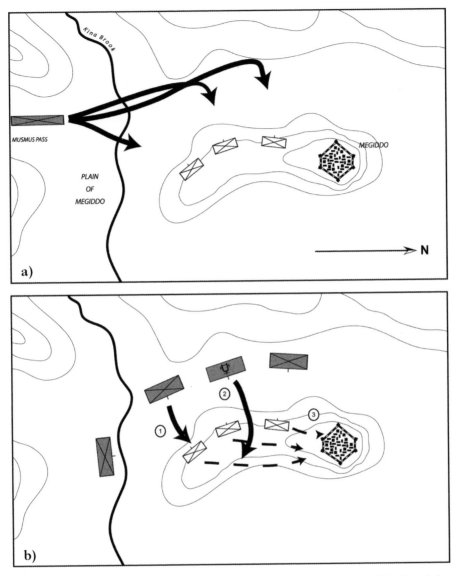

Map 1.2. The Battle of Megiddo, 1458 BCE. (a) Phase I: Thutmose concentrates his column before emerging from the Musmus Pass. The Egyptian advance column emerges onto the plains of Megiddo, deploying from column to line over a seven-hour period, yet the Syrians make no attempt to interfere. (b) Phase II: Thutmose retains an infantry force behind the banks of the Kina Brook, while his centre infantry press the Syrians back against their camp (1). The Egyptian chariot force then pierces a gap in the defences (2), and the Syrians rout to the shelter of the city (3). The Egyptians pause to plunder the Syrian camp and lose their chance to destroy the enemy army, and a seven-month siege ensues.

on the Orontes River, and his goal was to end Hittite interference in the Egyptian sphere of influence in Syria by defeating the enemy's main force in the field.

Ramesses' expeditionary army marched from Egypt to the city of Qadesh in one month, illustrating again the sophistication of the Egyptian logistical system. The Egyptian army contained perhaps 20,000 men, composed of four divisions of 5,000 each and some allied contingents. Each of the divisions consisted of chariots, archers, spearmen and axe-wielding infantry, and they were named after the gods Amon, Ra, Sutekh (Seth) and Ptah.[35] Almost half the Egyptian force consisted of chariots, suggesting that approximately 5,000 machines were brought to the battlefield. Defending the city of Qadesh was King Muwatallis II's Hittite army of 18,000 to 19,000 men, the largest combat force ever deployed by the Hatti. Hittite chariots numbered around 3,500 machines in a force of about 10,000 men (including support personnel), or about half the Hittite army.[36]

Egyptian chariots were served by a crew of two and were primarily a firing platform for archers, and accordingly were light and flexible. The Hittite chariots encountered at Qadesh were heavier, six-wheeled platforms crewed by three (a driver, shield-bearer and soldier) and presumably designed for shock attack, a combat mode that required a sacrifice of speed and flexibility for combat survivability.[37] But a newer interpretation suggests that perhaps the composite bow was the primary weapon in Hittite chariots as well, and that the heavier platforms were simply better protected firing platforms, and not moving battering rams.[38]

On the evening of 9 May, Ramesses encamped within 15 miles of Qadesh on a hill overlooking the city, near the smaller city of Shabtuna. The next morning he moved out at the van of the Amon division, hoping to seize Qadesh by the end of the day. After crossing the Orontes near Shabtuna, two Hatti 'deserters' were brought before the pharaoh, claiming that the Hittite host was still far away and had yet to encamp at Qadesh. Emboldened by the news, Ramesses moved ahead with his bodyguard to establish a forward camp north-west of the city while his army advanced in column from the south (Map 1.3(a)).[39]

As the first elements of the lead division of Amon reached the forward camp, two newly captured Hatti scouts revealed under torture that the Hittite army was hidden to the east of Qadesh near the ruins of the old town of Qadesh. Before Ramesses could react, the Hittite army quickly forded the Orontes and its tributary the Al-Mukadiyah from the south-east, emerging from the tree line and striking the exposed right flank of the Ra division. The heavier Hittite war chariots, perhaps 2,500 in number, pushed into the Egyptian files, killing and scattering the invading infantry (Map 1.3(b)). The Ra division broke in panic and fled up against the just-arriving Amon division, which as a result began to rout as well.[40]

The Hittite chariots pushed through the Egyptian column and, using the broad plains of Qadesh to turn their cumbersome machines, swung to the north-east and pressed their attack on the western gate of Ramesses' encampment. Although the lead Hatti units that penetrated the camp were dragged from their chariots by the pharaoh's bodyguard and killed, Ramesses was unable to hold the fort.[41] The Hittite army poured in and began to loot the camp, just as the Egyptian army had done at the battle of Megiddo two centuries earlier.

It was at this time, according to contemporary Egyptian accounts, that Ramesses mounted his chariot and rushed forward without his bodyguard into the thick of the battle (Map 1.3(c)). There, surrounded by thousands of chariots, he single-handedly defeated the Hittite army.[42] Though it is often dismissed as legend, there is perhaps a kernel of truth in the account. It is possible that Ramesses' personal display of courage rallied what remained of the badly outnumbered chariot reserve left in the camp, who sallied forth from the east gate, wheeled to the north-west and struck the Hittite flank while it was preoccupied looting the camp. Commanding his forces from the basket of his own machine, Ramesses led the assault, scattering the heavier Hittite chariots before him as his own infantry from the camp joined in the pursuit, chasing the enemy towards the river.

While the Egyptians began a concerted counter-attack against the fleeing Hittite forces, King Muwatallis acted, committing his remaining 1,000 chariots to the battle. This relief force forded the Orontes north of Qadesh and swung south to hit Ramesses in the flank. Unfortunately for Muwatallis, two events coincided to help the warrior pharaoh (Map 1.3(d)). Arriving from the north were reformed Egyptian troops (perhaps aided by allied mercenary warriors called to battle by the pharaoh), while at this same time the third of the Egyptian divisions, the Sutekh, approached from the south.[43] Just as the Hittite chariots spread out onto the plain and into line of attack, their right was threatened by the arriving rallied Egyptian forces from the north. To make matters worse for the Hatti king, Ramesses broke off pursuit of the Hittite chariots trapped between him and the river and, joining forces with the Sutekh division, turned north to intercept the Hittite relief force. Caught between the two converging Egyptian armies, the Hittite relief force was utterly destroyed. As the remnants of the first Hatti force escaped south of Qadesh across the Orontes, the final of the four Egyptian divisions, the Ptah, arrived on the battlefield, too late to join the mêlée.

Although Muwatallis' losses were perhaps 1,000 of the 3,000 chariots committed, a significant tactical and financial loss concerning the enormous expense of the war chariot, he still had his entire infantry force in reserve.[44] But without the assistance of heavy chariots, an all-infantry attack on the light and fast Egyptian chariots would have proven costly on the open terrain. Wisely, Muwatallis decided to garrison Qadesh and wait. Ramesses had won the battlefield engagement, but lacked the manpower or siege train to successfully attack the city.

Tactically, the battle of Qadesh ended in a stalemate. After a few days, Ramesses withdrew from Syria, leaving the Hittites in Qadesh. Strategically,

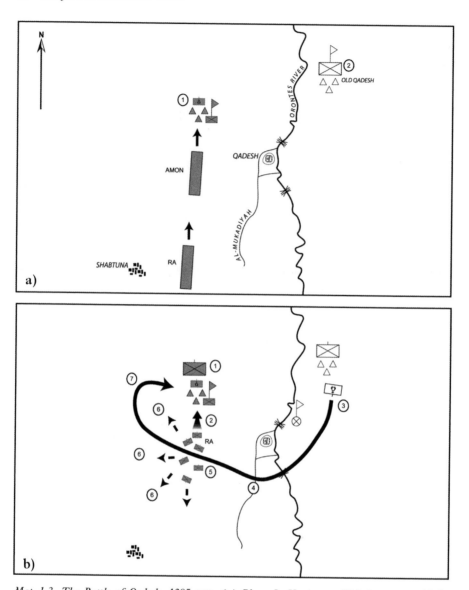

Map 1.3. The Battle of Qadesh, 1285 BCE. (a) Phase I: Having established a camp with his bodyguard and chariot reserve (1), Ramesses II awaits the arrival of his army's lead division, Amon. Screened from view by trees and brush along the Orontes River, King Muwatallis and the Hittite army (2) are camped on the site of Old Qadesh. (b) Phase II: As the Amon division arrives at the camp (1) and the Ra division approaches (2), a Hittite chariot force is dispatched to reconnoitre (3). As the chariots emerge from the scrub bordering the Al-Mukadiyah (4), they are unable to check their momentum and crash through the enemy division's flank (5). As the Egyptians scatter (6), the Hittite chariots wheel towards the camp (7). (c) Phase III: The Hittite chariots strike the Egyptian camp from the west and begin to loot (1). Ramesses rallies the chariot reserve, leads it out of the east gate,

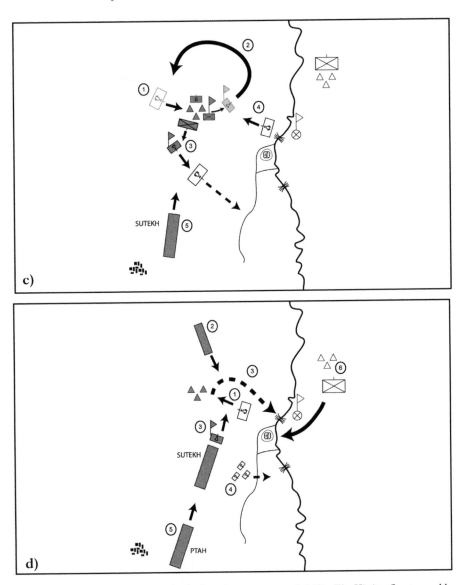

and wheels to strike the Hittites in the flank as they are preoccupied (2). The Hittites flee, pursued by Ramesses, who is now joined by infantry from the camp (3). Muwatallis dispatches a reserve to renew the assault (4), while the Sutekh division arrives from the south (5). (d) Phase IV: As the Hittite chariot reserve approaches the camp (1), its right is threatened by the arrival of allied Egyptian forces from the north (2). As the Hittite chariots begin to turn and fall back, they face more danger to the south, as Ramesses breaks off his pursuit and leads his chariots and Sutekh against the new threat (3). The remnants of the first Hittite force continue their retreat (4), as the remaining Egyptian division, Ptah, moves to join the rest of the Egyptian army (5). Muwatallis garrisons Qadesh (6). Lacking siege equipment and adequate forces, Ramesses is forced to break off the action.

the Egyptians had failed in a major military operation to end Hittite influence in Syria-Palestine. Over the next two decades, the Hatti would instigate revolts in Palestine, forcing Ramesses to respond with military action, but never again did the Egyptians threaten the Hittites north of the Orontes. Eventually, these enemies became allies in the face of a new regional threat, the rise of Assyria in northern Mesopotamia.

Warfare in Late Bronze Age Greece: The Mycenaeans

The dominance of the chariot in late Bronze Age warfare (*c*.1600–*c*.1100 BCE) extended to regions outside of the ancient Near East. In Greece the invasion of the Mycenaeans at the beginning of the second millennium BCE brought a chariot-borne aristocracy to south-eastern Europe. The Mycenaean Greeks were part of the larger Indo-European migrations that spread from their original location in the steppe region north of the Black Sea to India, Iran and Europe. The Mycenaeans entered Greece from the north and successfully challenged the Minoans, a civilization based on Crete, for mastery of the Aegean. By 1400 BCE the Mycenaeans established in Attica and on the Peloponnese a number of city-states especially noted for their fortified palace centres built on hills surrounded by large stone walls. These Bronze Age palace centres formed a loose confederation of independent states, including Tiryns, Pylos, Thebes and Orchomenos, with the city-state of Mycenae the primary hegemon (Map 1.1).

Historians know very little about Mycenaean warfare. What is known comes from a combination of pottery, bronze weapons, wall murals and limited textual evidence from the Bronze Age itself, supplemented by the remarkable epic poetry of Homer, written some time in the eighth century BCE.[45] Homer's *Iliad* stands as the beginning of European literature and as western civilization's most influential war poem. The origins of the *Iliad* date back to the Aegean Dark Ages (*c*.1100–*c*.750 BCE) and are in the oral tradition of reciting poems recounting the deeds of heroes in the Mycenaean Age. Homer made use of these oral traditions to compose the *Iliad*, his account of the wrath of Achilles and the war between the Mycenaeans and the Trojans.

Despite Heinrich Schliemann's revealing excavations of Troy and Mycenae in the late nineteenth century, the value of Homer's epic for the study of early Greek warfare remains controversial. Still, Homer provides some important information about Mycenaean warfare in the Aegean region, but because he wrote in the eighth century BCE, some 300 years after the fall of Mycenaean civilization, his accounts of battle reflect more the warfare in his own day in the early archaic period (*c*.750–*c*.500 BCE) than that of late Bronze Age Greece.[46]

For example, although Homer knew that Mycenaean warriors fought with bronze weapons and used chariots, his description of the chariot as merely battlefield transportation to bring the heroes of his epic together to engage in man-to-man combat clashes with what historians know about chariot warfare elsewhere in the ancient Near East. In late Bronze Age Mesopotamia and New Kingdom Egypt, it was the composite bow fired from a moving chariot, not the sword or spear wielded in hand-to-hand combat, that was the weapon most closely associated with kings and nobility. It is more likely that Homer's infatuation with individual shock combat in the *Iliad* mirrored the early archaic period's emphasis on individual warfare, where early Iron Age Greek aristocrats duelled with each other for control of Greece's limited resources.[47] This view is supported by Homer's absolute contempt for missile combat in the *Iliad*, a contempt perhaps generated by the elite warriors' fear of light infantry archers and javelineers in the poet's own time.[48] Aristocratic fear of an ignoble death from a distance was to be a prevailing theme in medieval warfare nearly 2,000 years later.

Although historians do not have any descriptions of Bronze Age Greek battles in contemporary writings, there is ample evidence for the war chariot being the centrepiece of Mycenaean warfare. Tablets written in Linear B (the Mycenaean Greek language) found at Knossos on Crete show inventories of fully equipped chariots along with chariot bodies, wheels, bridles, and other accessories, presenting the possibility of the Mycenaean Cretans fielding a force of perhaps 200 chariots.[49] The Mycenaean chariot was a light machine pulled by a team of two horses in the style of the Egyptian rather than the heavier Hittite models.

Mycenaean war chariots were most likely supported on the battlefield by both unarticulated heavy infantry armed with thrusting spear, sword and dagger, and light infantry archers and javelineers. The most common body armour consisted of linen shirts fitted with bronze scales, though excavations at Mycenae revealed a full suit of bronze armour with a helmet made of boars' tusks.[50] Shields are represented in the art of the period as either oblong, tower-like shields or the narrow-waisted figure-of-eight shields, both capable of covering the defender from chin to ankle. Battle itself probably took place on the handful of flat plains found throughout Greece. Here, engagements between war chariots and their supporting infantry probably unfolded like other ancient Near Eastern conflicts, but on a smaller scale because of the limited resources of the Greek city-states and the mountainous terrain involved.[51]

By the late thirteenth century BCE, Mycenaean Greece was showing signs of serious decline. Historians are uncertain whether this decline was precipitated by internal conflicts between Mycenaean kings or brought about by external invasion. But according to the Greeks' own legends, their mainland was invaded from the north by another wave of Indo-Europeans called the Dorians, though what actually happened remains a mystery.[52] Still, the archaeological record clearly indicates that Mycenae was torched around 1190 BCE, reinhabited, and finally abandoned around 1125 BCE. Other Mycenaean palace centres show similar patterns of destruction. By 1100 BCE the Mycenaean civilization had fallen and the Aegean region was plunged into a Dark Age lasting over 300 years.

From the seventeenth century BCE to the last centuries of the Bronze Age, the chariot ruled the battlefields of the Near East.[53] These expensive, prestigious and lethal machines were the dominant weapon system, and kings and pharaohs alike sought engagements on level terrain where they could employ their super-weapons against opposing chariots, or batter enemy infantry formations and hunt down fleeing footmen. But the chariot's dominance would be challenged in the closing centuries of the second millennium BCE, as the eastern Mediterranean and Near East entered a period known as the 'Catastrophe', lasting from about 1200 to 900 BCE. Throughout the Aegean, Anatolia, Cyprus and the Levant, dozens of cities and palaces were burned. In the Aegean and Anatolia, the Bronze Age civilizations of Mycenaean Greece and the Hittite Empire were destroyed by barbarian invaders using new military technologies and more sophisticated tactics. Egypt and Mesopotamia were mostly spared from the destruction, though Egypt declined as the major power in the region.

Historians argue about the exact reasons why late Bronze Age civilizations declined. Some champion famine-induced internal revolts, while others support the idea that earthquakes destroyed cities or made them vulnerable to attack by invading 'Sea Peoples' from the Balkans, setting off a domino effect of migration and invasion that affected most Bronze Age civilizations in the eastern Mediterranean world.[54] One historian postulates that it was perhaps mercenary infantry, recruited from outside the kingdom by the Bronze Age armies themselves, who eventually learned how to overcome the chariots of their former employers.[55] Barbarian light infantry developed and adopted new weapons and armour, specifically the 'leaf-bladed' cut-and-slash long sword, the chariot-hunting javelin, and the metal-reinforced leather corslet and round shield, giving them the tools to effectively challenge the war chariot's battlefield dominance.[56]

At the beginning of the Catastrophe (*c*.1200 BCE) there appeared in the eastern Mediterranean a superior cut-and-thrust sword known to archaeologists and typologists as the Naue Type II. It was a long bronze weapon (usually 28 inches from pommel to tip) with a parallel blade that slightly tapered about 9 inches from the tip, producing its signature 'leaf-shape'. This sword design quickly diffused to the Near East, the Aegean, Italy and as far north as Britain and Scandinavia. Although iron replaced bronze in its construction in the early first millennium BCE, the Naue Type II remained the standard sword design for these regions until the seventh century.[57]

The Catastrophe also witnessed the appearance and widespread use of the infantryman's corslet. Before *c*.1200 BCE, usually only specialized troops (chariot drivers) or aristocratic warriors wore metal-reinforced armour. But there is pictorial and archaeological evidence dating from this period of infantry in the Aegean and Egypt wearing waist-length corslets and leather skirts.[58] There is even some evidence of the use of bronze greaves.[59] But perhaps the most important defensive development was the adoption of the round shield. For millennia, Near Eastern and Aegean warriors used large body-shields of various shapes to protect against enemy missile fire. But after *c.*1200 BCE, there is evidence of widespread use of a symmetrical and balanced round shield. Held with a centre-grip and varying in size from less than 2 to more than 3 feet in diameter, the round shield sacrificed full-body protection for mobility, allowing the warrior to more effectively wield his sword or javelin.[60]

Deployed in skirmishing formations, the barbarians used their javelins to disable chariots by wounding horse or driver, and then finished off enemy archers with their superior 'leaf-bladed' long swords. Not intimidated by the social stature of the chariot-borne aristocracy and willing to close in and engage both horse and machine, hordes of barbarian light infantry javelineers swarmed through chariot formations and destroyed them. Barbarian infantry had similar success against civilized infantry, their longer cut-and-slash swords outmatching the shorter sickle-and stabbing-swords of the civilized world. By the first century of the first millennium BCE, the 'Age of the Chariot' was waning, to be followed by a new era in history where iron, not bronze, was the premier strategic material, and cavalry revolutionized warfare in classical western civilization.

Iron and Empire: The Rise of Assyria

Iron was first utilized as a technology of war around 1300 BCE by the Hittites.[61] By the beginning of the first millennium BCE, the secret of iron metallurgy and cold forging had spread to Palestine and Egypt by way of the nomadic invasions, and perhaps to Mesopotamia as well.[62] Iron weapons were superior to bronze weapons because they were heated and hammered into shape rather than cast, making them stronger, less brittle and more reliable than their bronze counterparts.[63] Within a few centuries the secret of tempering was discovered and diffused, and iron became the basic weapon material for all the armies of the period.

The invention and diffusion of iron smelting, cold forging and tempering created no less than a military revolution in the classical world. The importance of iron in the development of classical warfare lay not only in its strength and ability to hold an edge, but also in the widespread availability of iron ore. No longer were civilizations dependent on copper and tin deposits to make their bronze weapons. Five hundred times more prevalent in the earth's surface than copper, iron was commonly and widely available almost everywhere. The plentiful supply of this strategic material allowed states to produce enormous quantities of reliable weapons cheaply. In fact, a democratization of warfare took place, with most members of an army now being issued iron weapons.

Now almost any state could equip large armies with reliable weapons, with the result being a dramatic increase in both the size of battles and the frequency of war. The first people to take full advantage of the potential of the Iron Age were the Assyrians.

Assyrian monarchs had long understood the precarious strategic position of their state. Centred on the three major cities of Nimrud, Nineveh and Ashur on the upper Tigris River, in what is now north-western Iraq, Assyria was cursed with a dearth of natural resources and few natural barriers to keep out enemy invasions. Assyria lacked wood for constructing forts, temples and dams, stone for building walls and castles, and iron ore deposits to forge weapons. Assyria also lacked the large steppes necessary to support large horse herds, essential for chariotry and cavalry. If Assyria was to survive, it needed to expand at the expense of its more advantaged neighbours. Beginning in the fourteenth century BCE, the Assyrians successfully resisted Mitannian, Hittite and Babylonian expansion and subjugation to finally emerge as a regional power under Tiglath-pileser I (c.1115–1077 BCE). The empire created by Tiglath-pileser did not long survive his passing, and a new phase of expansion began in the ninth century under the reign of Shalmaneser III (858–824 BCE). By Tiglath-pileser III's reign (744–727 BCE), the Assyrians had expanded into Syria and Babylonia, securing their western and eastern frontiers.

The Assyrians quickly mastered iron metallurgy and applied this new technology to military equipment and tactics.[64] By the eighth century BCE, the Assyrians had used their large, iron-equipped armies to conquer much of the Fertile Crescent, and, for a short time in the seventh century, Egypt as well (Map 1.4). The general size, logistical capabilities, and strategic and tactical mobility of the Assyrian army were indeed impressive, even by modern standards, with the lessons learned by the Assyrians being passed on to the Persians.

As early as 854 BCE at the battle of Karkara (modern Tel Qarqur), Shalmaneser III was able to field a multinational army of over 70,000 men, made up of 65,000 infantrymen, 1,200 cavalrymen and 4,000 chariots.[65] By the eighth century BCE, the entire Assyrian armed forces consisted of at least 150,000 to 200,000 men and were the largest standing military force the Near East had ever witnessed.[66] An Assyrian field army numbered approximately 50,000 men and was a combined-arms force consisting of various mixes of infantry, cavalry and chariots which, when arrayed for battle, had a frontage of 2,500 yards and a depth of 100 yards.[67] Still, the Assyrian army, as large as it was, seemed small when compared to armies that appeared some three centuries later. For instance, by 500 BCE, a Persian Great King could raise an army of around 300,000 men from his vast territories, and Alexander may have faced a Persian army at the battle of Gaugamela of perhaps 250,000 men, including 20,000 cavalrymen, 250 chariots and 50 elephants.[68]

The Assyrians also recognized the need for increased specialization in weapon systems. With the exception of an elite royal bodyguard and foreign

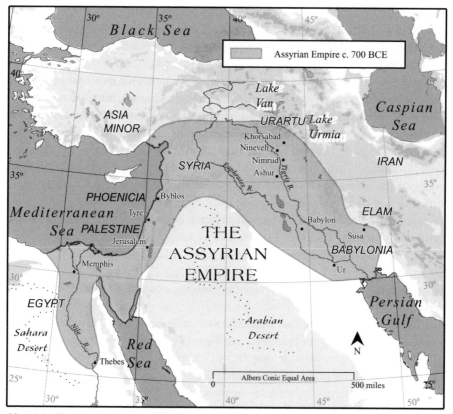

Map 1.4. *The Assyrian Empire, c.700 BCE.*

mercenaries, Assyrian kings relied on a farmer-militia raised by a levée en masse. But as these mobilizations increased in frequency, the Assyrians began to supplement their militia muster with an ever-growing cadre of specialized troops. By Sargon II's time (r. 721–705 BCE), the Assyrian army was a combined-arms fighting force of heavy and light infantry, cavalry, chariots and siege machinery supported by specialized units of scouts, engineers, spies and sappers.[69]

Assyrian heavy infantry were armed with a long, double-bladed spear and a straight sword for shock combat, and were protected by a conical iron helmet, knee-length coat of lamellar armour (a shirt of laminated layers of leather sown or glued together, then fitted with iron plates) and a small iron shield.[70] There is some evidence that can be gathered from the panoply depicted on stone bas-reliefs that the Assyrian royal guard was a professional corps of articulated heavy infantry who fought in a phalanx.[71] In battle, these Assyrian heavy infantrymen were organized in a battle square with a ten-man front and files twenty men deep.[72] But even if these troops were capable of offensive articulation, the financial resources, drill, discipline and *esprit de corps* necessary to field large numbers of these specialized troops was not a dominant part of the Near Eastern art of war, so if present, it was not the decisive tactical system that it would become under the Greeks. Instead, light infantry archers were probably the main offensive arm of the Assyrian army.[73]

Assyrian archers wore a slightly shorter coat of mail armour and the same conical helm as their heavy infantry counterparts, and are often depicted with a shield-bearer carrying a large, rectangular shield made of densely matted reeds covered with oiled skins or metal, similar to a pavise of the medieval period. The shield was curved backward along its top edge to provide extra cover from long-distance arrow or stone attacks and against missiles fired from enemy walls. Archers came from many regions within the empire, so bow types differed, with the simpler self-bow in use as much as the composite bow.[74] The Assyrians invented a quiver that could hold as many as fifty arrows, with some arrows fitted with special heads capable of launching combustible materials. Referred to as 'the messengers of death', these flame arrows were targeted at enemy homes or crops.[75] Slingers constitute another type of light infantry employed by the Assyrians. They are often depicted on stone bas-reliefs standing behind archers.[76]

Changes in technology also enabled Assyrian ironsmiths to design a stronger chariot, with builders emulating earlier Egyptian designs by moving the wheel axis from the centre to the rear of the carriage. The result was a highly manoeuvrable vehicle that reduced traction effort.[77] Still, the chariot suffered from terrain restrictions, unable to exploit its impressive shock capabilities on anything but level ground. Perhaps the chariot remained the dominant weapon system into the early Iron Age because of the sociology and psychology of the forces the chariot led and faced. In the Bronze Age the chariot was the weapon of the aristocracy, ridden into parade and battle by a social class culturally ordained as superior to the common soldiers who gazed upon these often excessively decorated weapons. It is possible that the utility of cavalry was not fully tested by the Assyrians because of a carry-over preoccupation with the Bronze Age domination of the battlefield by chariots. For over 2,000 years chariots were free to scatter formations of poorly equipped and weakly motivated infantry.[78] This preoccupation with a battlefield anachronism would continue with the Persians as well, until their final defeat in 331 BCE at Gaugamela by a Macedonian army unburdened by chariots.

Most significantly, Assyria was the first civilization in the west to exploit the potential of the horse as a mount. The introduction of larger, sturdier horses from the Eurasian steppes gave the Assyrians a new weapon system, the cavalryman. The first Assyrian cavalry were probably nomadic cavalry, perhaps Median mercenaries from tributary states across the Zagros Mountains on the Eurasian steppes. But not wanting to rely on foreign horsemen, the Assyrians began to develop their own cavalry corps, specializing in both light and heavy tactical systems. Assyrian light infantry emulated their nomadic neighbours, riding smaller, faster steeds and firing arrows from composite bows on the fly. It is notable that writers of the Old Testament called these Assyrian cavalrymen 'hurricanes on horseback'.[79] Assyrian light cavalry faced all kinds of opponents, including camels used as platforms for Arab missiles, with mounted archers sitting behind the beasts' jockeys back-to-back and firing at pursuing Assyrian infantry and cavalry.[80]

Assyrian heavy cavalry was in a state of continuous evolution. The original mounted lancer modified the equipment of foot soldiers to meet the needs of shock combat. The armoured coat was reduced to waist length and the shield was made smaller. Heavy cavalry were armed with both sword and lance, but the absence of a stabilizing stirrup meant Assyrian lancers, like their other classical-age counterparts, thrust out and loosened their spear at their enemy as they passed instead of riding through their target using the synergy of horse and rider.

Over time, the Assyrians developed their own cavalry corps and their own horse recruitment, acquiring specialized 'yoke' horses for chariots and riding horses for cavalry from as far away as Nubia and Iran.[81] It remains a mystery why this weapon system, far superior to the chariot in both strategic and tactical mobility, was never fully exploited by the Assyrians. Possibly the lack of the horseshoe made the use of cavalry in rough terrain too expensive in animals, or the Assyrians' preoccupation with chariots precluded them from sustaining large forces of both chariots and cavalry.[82]

The Assyrian Army at War: The Urartu Campaign

Sargon II's campaign in 714 BCE against the kingdom of Urartu on Assyria's northern and north-eastern frontiers illustrates the military and logistical capabilities of the Assyrian army. Urartu, the most powerful of Assyria's eighth-century adversaries, enjoyed the advantages of geography, nestled north of the Tigris River valley past the Taurus Mountains in what is now modern Armenia, a land whose rough topography has challenged foreign invaders for millennia. The two states shared hundreds of miles of common border, with the Assyrian capital of Nineveh just 30 miles away from the major mountain pass connecting the two regions.

Assyrian relations with Urartu became increasingly strained as both powers vied for dominance as the region's new hegemon. Decades earlier, in the 740s and 730s, King Tiglath-pileser III expanded in northern Syria in the west and Media (modern Iran) in the east, threatening Urartu's flanks. And though Tiglath-pileser never occupied the capital of Urartu on the shores of Lake Van, he did scorch the countryside and dismantle his enemy's fortifications, bringing the region under Assyrian control. His victory was short-lived, though, as local princes rebelled. Within twenty-five years, hostilities broke out again when Rusa, prince of Urartu, began to threaten the Assyrian northern frontier.

Sargon II inherited the Urartu problem when he came to power in 721. Twice, in 719 and 717, he sent troops north to the region near Lake Urmia to suppress local conflicts backed by Urartu troops. In 715 the Urartu became more aggressive, seizing twenty-two fortified cities from Ullusunu, an Assyrian vassal in Armenia. Sargon responded by quickly retaking the cities, then laying waste to Urartu's southern provinces. But Sargon realized that small punitive expeditions would not solve his strategic problem for long. The Assyrian monarch would return the following year in strength and finish what he had begun in a campaign that showcased the Assyrian military machine at war. It would be the eighth military campaign of his seven-year reign.

When Sargon set out in 714 BCE for the rugged terrain of Armenia he understood the logistical burdens faced by his army.[83] The expedition would march east by north-east and travel over the Zagros Mountains to the land of the Manna, a region just south of Lake Urmia. Sargon needed to re-establish contact with his vassal Ullusunu and establish a forward operating base. But crossing the Zagros Mountains was no simple task. This high, snow-capped range separated Assyria from the region of modern Iran, and the road Sargon travelled snaked through numerous passes and valleys, ascending to snow-covered mountain passes and descending into dense forests. According to Sargon's own correspondence, this terrain was 'too rough for chariots to mount, bad for horses, and too steep to march foot soldiers', forcing his engineers to clear obstacles and lay stone to make a suitable road.[84] In between these steep mountains ran swift rivers that also proved an obstacle. Sargon noted that he forded one wandering stream no fewer than twenty-six times.

Although no records exist for the size of the Sargon's expeditionary force, it was certainly a combined-arms army of at least 50,000 men, the traditional size of an Assyrian field army. The army moved in column formation, with special scouts sent ahead to reconnoitre the route. While on flat terrain, the king personally led the column from the basket of his war chariot, surrounded by the chariots of his commanders. These machines were followed by cavalry, infantry, engineers, scribes, diviners, interpreters and intelligence officers, and a baggage train consisting of camels and asses. The rear of the column was guarded by light troops, most probably cavalry in open terrain and infantry in rough terrain.[85] Because of this difficult terrain and the unlikelihood of a large chariot engagement, it is possible that the Assyrian chariot arm was very small, serving only as personal transportation for the king and his senior commanders.[86]

When Sargon reached the land of the Manna, he ordered his vassal Ullusunu to provide him with large numbers of horses, sheep, cattle and material supplies. Using this forward base, Sargon first secured his eastern flank by marching east and south of Lake Urmia into Median territory. The Medes were a fierce Indo-European steppe warrior people who specialized in light cavalry and lived in the region of northern Iran. Cousins to the Persians (who would later conquer them), the Median governors submitted to Sargon, providing him with the unique tribute of steppe peoples, including 'prancing horses, swift mules, camels native to their land, cattle and sheep'. Steppe camels were of the two-humped Bactrian variety and were superior to their southern cousins for cold-weather operations because of their thick fur and underwool and large, snowshoe-like feet. With his eastern flank secure, Sargon backtracked west to Manna.

The direct route between Mannean country and Urartu was a straight shot north-west from Lake Urmia to Tuspar (modern Van) on Lake Van. This route not only went through extremely rough terrain, it also was guarded by a string of strong fortresses controlled by Urartu. Not wanting to march into the waiting mouth of his enemy, Sargon decided to take a more circuitous route around the northern shore of Lake Urmia near Tabriz and then straight west, by-passing the Urartu fortifications. But even this route brought the Assyrian expedition through difficult geography and hostile territory. Checking his siege train, Sargon pushed west and took twelve fortified cities and eighty-four villages. According to the Assyrian king's own pen: 'I destroyed their walls, I set fire to the houses inside them, I destroyed them like a flood, I battered them into heaps of ruins.' Sargon's strategy was to secure his line of communications and leave no threatening fortresses or garrisons at his back as he marched further into enemy territory.

Meanwhile, Prince Rusa was rallying support from local princes to stop the Assyrian advance well short of its intended target, the Urartu capital on the shores of Lake Van. Rusa knew the direction of the Assyrian advance and he decided to intercept Sargon on a flat valley in the mountains south-west of Tabriz. Rusa's strategy was to draw the Assyrians through the defile and into the valley and then smash them before they could deploy from column into a line of battle. But unknown to the Urartu pickets, Sargon's scouts saw the Urartu deployment in the valley.

Choosing not to move his army piecemeal through the defile, Sargon did the unexpected: he moved it directly over the snow- and ice-covered ridge, descended the other side and deployed in the valley. But the forced march over the ridge took its toll on the Assyrians, who were exhausted and running on light rations. Prince Rusa's troops, on the other hand, were fully deployed and well rested, having arrived several days before. Sargon understood his precarious tactical situation, realizing that the fresh Urartu troops, defending their homeland, might massacre his invading army. With no line of retreat, no reinforcements and an enemy preparing to strike at any moment, Sargon chose to act quickly to gain the initiative.[87] Again the Assyrian king writes of the condition of his troops and his tactical predicament: 'I could not relieve their fatigue, nor strengthen the wall of the camp ... what was right or left could not be brought to my side, I could not watch the rear ... I plunged into [the enemy's] midst like a swift javelin.'[88]

Personally leading a combined chariot and cavalry charge into the Urartu ranks, Sargon rode his war chariot at the head of his bodyguard, a contingent of 1,000 heavy cavalry, straight into one wing of the Urartu deployment (history does not tell us which wing), shattering it on impact. The rest of the Assyrian army, seeing its monarch plunge into battle, quickly followed.

But Rusa's lines did not immediately rout, and at some point during the battle the Urartu launched a counter-attack. Sargon tells us that Rusa's warriors:

> the mainstay of his army, bearers of bow and lance, I slaughtered about his feet like lambs, I cut off their heads. His noblemen, counselors who stand before him, I shattered their arms in battle; them and their horses I captured, 260 of his royal kin, who were his officers, governors and cavalry.[89]

In the ensuing chaos, Rusa retreated to his fortified encampment. Sargon pursued and surrounded the king's camp, showering it with arrow and javelin from his light troops. Rusa eventually abandoned his chariot and escaped on horseback, leaving his routing army to be slaughtered by the Assyrians. In typical Assyrian fashion, Sargon ordered a ruthless pursuit which 'filled the gullies and gorges with horses while they, like ants in distress, made their way over most difficult terrain. In the heat of my terrible weapons, I went after them, filling the ascents and descents with the corpses of their warriors.'[90]

His enemy crushed, Sargon set off for the Urartu capital at Tuspar. The Assyrian monarch's strategy was now to punish the region that had supported his enemy. He systematically destroyed every fortress, city and town in the path of his march, leaving thousands dead in his wake. When Sargon reached Tuspar, Rusa fled into the mountains, eventually dying the king of a defeated state. Sargon entered the city triumphant, then razed it to the ground like 'a smashed pot'. During this phase of the campaign, Sargon had conducted military operations in all seven of Urartu's provinces and captured or destroyed no fewer than 430 fortified cities, towns and villages.[91]

With the Urartu field army defeated and its king hiding in the mountains, Sargon swung his army around the northern shore of Lake Van and headed south toward the ancient city of Khupushkia (modern Sairt). It was here that Sargon ordered his main army home to the new Assyrian fortress of Dur-Sharrukin (Fort Sargon, later Khorsabad), north of the old capital of Nineveh. Sargon stayed behind with 1,000 cavalry and struck out for the fortress city of Muzazira, the religious centre of the Urartu culture. It was here in the temple dedicated to Haldia, the Urartu war god, that monarchs were crowned and the national treasury kept. Sargon led his elite striking force east over a seemingly impenetrable mountain pass and sacked the city, returning home with 6,000 captives and Urartu's treasures to add to his imperial coffers.[92]

Sargon II, remembered as Sargon 'the Great', made the best of a difficult strategic situation when he attacked the Urartu in 714 BCE. His campaign was a textbook example of how to conduct a punitive expedition in hostile territory. He shored up his relationship with Ullusunu and made alliances with the Medes, gaining much-needed supplies and protecting his flank. He then built up his siege train and reduced every walled city and fortification in his path. By securing his lines of communication throughout his march, Sargon was able to operate in hostile territory more than 300 miles from his home base. Tactically, Sargon used his combined army to great effect, changing the balance of his army by reducing the number of chariots and increasing his cavalry and infantry to meet the needs of a campaign in rough terrain. Finally, by leading the assault against the Urartu, Sargon demonstrated to his men his own personal courage and sacrifice. Like Ramesses before him and Alexander, Caesar and William the Conqueror after, Sargon led by example and endeared himself to his troops.

Despite the effectiveness of their military machine, the Assyrians were unable to hold on to their imperial possessions. During the seventh century, Assyria faced rebellions by Babylon, the loss of the rich province of Egypt, and the rise of the Medes in northern Iran. Babylon finally won its independence in 626 and, with the help of the Medes, took Ashur in 614 and Nineveh in 612. By 605, the Assyrian Empire had ceased to exist, finally defeated by the next builders of imperium, the short-lived Chaldean dynasty (625–539 BCE) of Babylon, a Semitic kingdom that would itself fall to the rise of Persia in the sixth century BCE.

Cyrus the Great and the Persian Art of War

Traditionally, ancient Mesopotamian armies were infantry based, and this tactical bias would continue throughout the classical period. What changed in the early Iron Age was the general composition of Mesopotamian armies, evolving from the chariot and unarticulated infantry-based armies of Sumer, Akkadia and Egypt to the more balanced, but still incomplete, combined-arms armies under the Assyrians and Persians. These early Iron Age states utilized numerous forms of light infantry and heavy and light cavalry in support of heavy infantry, carving out successively larger empires.

The founder of the Achaemenid Persian Empire, Cyrus the Great (r. 559–529), and his successors conquered the largest empire the world had yet seen, including not only the old centres of power in the Near East and Egypt, but also extending into Thrace and Asia Minor in the west, and north-west India in the east. At its height in the early fifth century BCE, the Persian Empire consisted of 1 million square miles of territory, with nearly 70 million inhabitants.[93] With each successful conquest came additional troops for the Persian war machine. This remarkable military achievement exposed the Persians to regional martial specialization, and the Persians proved very willing to include foreign soldiers, technologies and tactics in their army.[94]

Cyrus organized his armies using a decimal system in which regiments of 1,000 men were called *hazaraba*, divided into ten *sataba* of 100, and ten *dathaba* of 10. Ten 1,000-strong *hazaraba* formed a *myriad*.[95] Herodotus tells us in his account of the Persian Wars of the most famous myriad, the Great King's division of 10,000 'Immortals' (*Amrtaka* in Persian), so named because when a member of this elite group fell, he was immediately replaced by a previously selected man.[96] One of the primary duties of the Immortals was to act as the Great King's bodyguard, and he was never without them on the battlefield. These handpicked troops were taught horsemanship and Persian martial arts (skills with sword, lance and bow) between the ages of five and twenty. For the next four years, they were on active duty with the elite myriad, and were liable to serve until the age of fifty.[97]

The primary tactical system employed by the Persians would be a modification of an Assyrian invention, a combination of unarticulated shield-bearing heavy infantry spearmen operating with archers. Together, Persian spearmen and archers were known as *sparabara* or archer-pairs. The Assyrian *sparabara* were composed of two different units of troops of equal strength, operating together in a tactical formation consisting of only a single line of archers behind a single line of shield-bearers. However, when historians find *sparabara* operating in the Persian army, both types of troops are operating in the same ten-man file or *dathabam* at a ratio of one shield-bearer for every nine archers. Furthermore, Persian shield-bearers, unlike their Assyrian counterparts, were now armed with short, 6 foot thrusting spears to better protect the file of nine archers behind. This new arrangement enabled the ratio of archers to shield men to be significantly altered in order to give a heavier concentration of arrow fire.[98]

Until the rise of Cyrus, the Persian army remained primarily an infantry force. But Cyrus recognized the necessity for a contingent of Persian cavalry if he were to deal successfully with the cavalry-using Lydians, Medes and eastern Iranian tribes. He organized and financed the first Persian cavalry himself using war treasure and land gained in campaigns in the west. Cyrus gave land to Persian nobles known as 'equals', and then required them to use this land to support the cost of cavalry from then on, creating one of the first mounted aristocracies in western civilization. The honorary title of *Huvaka* or 'Kinsmen' was given to 15,000 Persian noblemen. Cyrus went so far as to require the *Huvaka* to ride everywhere and made it disgraceful for these noblemen to be seen on foot.[99]

Like the Assyrians before them, the first Persian cavalry was most probably modelled after the light cavalry of the neighbouring Medians or Scythians, Indo-European horse peoples with extraordinary skills as mounted archers. Unable to match their nomadic neighbours' proficiency with bow from horseback, the Persians would instead equip cavalrymen with better armour. Consequently, the Persians became very proficient as heavy cavalry (*cataphractoi* in Greek) and shock combat.[100]

Assyrian and Persian Logistics

Larger, better-equipped armies constituted the prime component of empire building in the early Iron Age. But with empire came increased administrative burdens, chief among them the policing of newly acquired territory against rebellion. The need to support armies in the field for months, sometimes years, at a time was a function of the rise of imperium in any period. But as the size of Iron Age armies increased, the burden of logistically supporting these armies in the field also increased.

Changes in the composition of armies in the Iron Age added to the logistical burden. The Assyrian invention of large cavalry squadrons brought into existence a special branch of the logistical train to ensure that the army could secure, breed and train large numbers of horses to be deployed with these new forces. Up to 3,000 horses a month were obtained and processed for the Assyrian army.[101] The integration of cavalry with chariots and the introduction of siege-craft required the Assyrian army to become the first army to learn how to sustain three kinds of transport: chariots, cavalry and a siege train.[102] Assyria also instituted a well-supplied depot system throughout the empire for the manufacture, issue and repair of iron weapons. Archaeologists have found a single weapons room in Sargon II's palace at Dur-Sharrukin (Khorsabad) housing some 200 tons of iron weapons.[103]

The Persian Empire, linked together by a series of roads, facilitated military control and communications with the provinces on the empire's periphery and allowed the Great King to move forces quickly to any point in the empire to suppress rebellion or meet a threat from outside (Map 1.5). These broad, unpaved, packed-dirt roads could handle the movement of mobile Persian siege towers drawn by teams of oxen. A system of regular bridges over streams and other obstacles assisted in the rapid movement of men and material. The most famous of these roads was the Royal Road running from the Persian capital of Persepolis to Sardis in western Anatolia, a distance of over 1,600 miles. A messenger could travel this distance in fifteen days using a series of horse relay stations. Without roads this journey would have taken three months.[104] In addition to using a network of roads to project force throughout the empire, the Persians would use their subject Phoenician, Egypt and Ionian Greek navies to support ground operations whenever possible. In 490 and again in 480 BCE, maritime logistical support proved indispensable in the punitive expeditions against Greece during the Persian Wars.

The Persian army represented the most sophisticated military force yet seen in western civilization, a force responsible for conquering an empire stretching from the Balkans to the Indus River valley. The Persians, like the Assyrians before them, continued to have an infatuation with the war chariot, but this machine's role in shock and missile combat was increasingly replaced by more agile and less expensive horse archers and lancers. Persian heavy infantry remained unarticulated because it usually consisted of poorly trained and

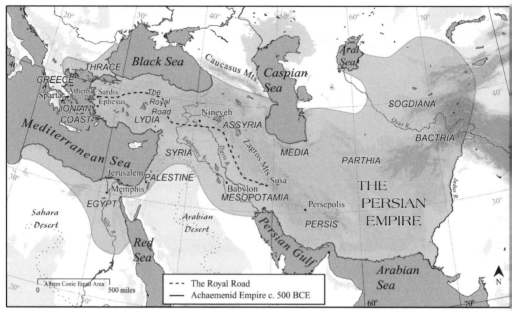

Map 1.5. The Persian Empire, c.500 BCE.

poorly motivated conscripts incapable of performing intricate offensive manoeuvres on the battlefield.

Articulated heavy infantry would not become a dominant feature of classical warfare until its wide-scale use by the Greeks in the seventh century BCE. And though unarticulated heavy infantry still remained the core of the Persian army, Cyrus' adoption and modification of the archer-pair from the Assyrians and addition of both light and heavy cavalry to the mix created a very capable combined-arms tactical system. This capable Persian army would face the Greeks and their articulated battle square in the beginning of the fifth century BCE, initiating a martial exchange of tactics and technologies that would transform classical warfare.

Chapter 2
Archaic and Hellenic Warfare: The Greek Phalanx at War

The Invention of the Greek Phalanx and the 'Cult of Symmetry'

By the middle of the seventh century BCE, a new style of warfare appeared in Greece requiring a warrior to fight in close order, standing shoulder to shoulder with his comrades in a battle square and forbidding individual acts of bravery. This battle square, called a *phalanx*, distinguished itself from other heavy infantry formations in the ancient and classical world in that it would evolve into a comparatively articulated weapon system capable of some offensive tactical mobility.

How and when this change in emphasis from individual to collective action on the Greek battlefield took place is still a matter of debate. In all likelihood, the revival of trade routes and the beginning of Greek colonization in the early archaic period (*c*.750–*c*.500 BCE) led to economic prosperity in the Greek mother-cities, prosperity which allowed an increasing number of farmers to equip themselves with helmets, armour, greaves and shields, and take their place in the battle line.[1] No one knows where in Greece the phalanx first appeared, but archaeological and textual evidence points to either Corinth or Pylos as the probable source of the phalangeal formation.[2] The increasing number of armoured heavy infantry was probably a major factor in the decline of individual warfare, and the Greek art of war began to change to accommodate larger numbers of soldiers.

In mountainous Greece the opposing phalanxes each sought level ground for their battles. It was control of the plains, not the mountains, which mattered in classical Greece because the plains contained most of the wealth of the ancient world. No Greek army could be satisfied with control of the mountains or the passes while the enemy pillaged the territory from which it took its living. Normally, the defenders could hope to enjoy a significant advantage by securing a position on a slight slope so that the attackers would have to march and fight uphill. But the uphill position was so great an advantage that attackers usually declined to engage in battle. Instead, attackers avoided the defending army and destroyed their crops until the defenders were compelled to give up their advantageous position. Defenders rarely enjoyed their advantage for long, and battles were fought by mutual consent on open level ground.[3]

For well over a century historians have debated how Greek armies actually joined battle. The old school of thought advocated an orderly advance into battle where front rank fought front rank, with the second rank waiting to fill the places of the fallen or fatigued. But a new generation of classicists and military historians has taken another look at the primary sources and concluded that infantry battle in classical Greece was much different than previously believed. The new interpretation describes phalanx battle as the collision of two battle squares, which, in the words of the Greek battle captain Xenophon, was a style of warfare where 'crashing their shields together, [soldiers] shoved, fought, slew and died'.[4] The typical Greek formation was to deploy the phalanx in a closely packed rank and file, usually, but not always, eight ranks deep. The organization of the phalanx was based more on files than on ranks, with the soldier belonging to his file rather than his rank. The basic idea was to maintain a solid front rank after collision to prevent gaps for the enemy to penetrate.[5]

The key to the Greek phalanx's success was in its innovative organization and technologies. The phalangeal formation consisted of heavy infantrymen or *hoplites*, so named because of the panoply (*hopla*) the Greek soldier wore into battle. This gear included a thrusting spear and short sword (*kopis*), and a heavy metal helmet and cuirass (breastplate and back), greaves and a wooden round shield (*aspis*) to protect the hoplite, though the precise panoply depended on the hoplite's wealth. Plutarch described the importance of the *aspis* to the Greek way of war when he said: 'Men wear their helmets and breastplates for their own needs, but they carry their shields for the men of their entire line.'[6]

The *aspis* itself was a round wooden concave shield nearly 3 feet in diameter and weighing over 15 pounds.[7] The essential difference between the new *aspis* and the old shield was that the old shield could hang by its strap from time to time, resting the arm, and was utilized in combat by holding a central grip behind the central boss. The round shield remained locked on the forearm with its weight being borne by the left shoulder, resulting in more effective and prolonged use. But this new carrying position also had a disadvantage. Since the shield was now gripped with the left hand near its rim, it effectively protected only the left side of the body, with half the shield projecting to the infantryman's left.[8] To correct the deficiencies of this new defensive technology, Greek soldiers began to stand side by side, utilizing the overlap of the shield on their right to protect the right side of their bodies. Thucydides explains the tendency of hoplites to edge to their right as the result of 'each man, in their anxiety, getting his unprotected side as close as possible to the shield of the man standing on his right, and thinking that the more closely the shields were locked, the better the protection.'[9]

Another consequence of this new defensive formation was the abandonment of the Bronze Age Homeric throwing spear for a thrusting spear, necessarily creating a weapon system that relied exclusively on shock. The thrusting spear had become so important that the sword was utilized only in emergencies.[10] Scholars are not certain whether the use of this new equipment spawned a radical change in battlefield tactics, or vice versa. It is believed, though, that the adoption of the *aspis* and the abandonment of the throwing spear reinforced the hoplites' dependence on collective warfare. Unlike the large rectangular shield of the later Roman legionary or the lighter round shield of the early medieval warrior, the *aspis* afforded the Greek heavy infantryman little protection from attack on his side and rear.[11] In fact, the entire hoplite panoply would evolve to satisfy the offensive and defensive role of the collective frontal attack.[12]

Hoplite battle consisted of the following phases: preparation, charge, collision, push, rout and aftermath.[13] As two Greek armies prepared for battle, each phalanx formed up on either end of the battlefield in ranks, generally eight files deep. Unlike other armies before or since, the general or *strategos* lined up with the common soldiers, usually in the first rank. This predilection to fight shoulder to shoulder with the veterans in the front of the formation usually cost the defeated commander his life. In fact, in a surprising number of engagements, the victorious general was killed as well, despite the success of his troops.[14] Elements of preparation included a pre-battle speech, usually by the commander, and the imbibing of wine. Because of the weight of the *aspis* and body armour, the Greek hoplite waited until just prior to the actual charge to don his armour, assisted by personal attendants who left the field to become spectators before battle was joined.

At the moment the battle commenced, the opposing phalanxes were between several hundred and a few thousand yards apart, depending on the battle in question. Arrayed in rank and file, the armies began to lumber forward at a trot of 4 to 6 miles per hour.[15] At perhaps 200 yards (the exact distance is difficult to know for certain), the hoplites began to charge at the enemy formation. In this kind of battle, timing was everything. Start the run too early and soldiers would be too exhausted for combat. Start the run too late, and the enemy had the advantage of momentum in the collision to come.[16] Trying not to drift to the right, the two phalanxes closed and then collided violently.

In hoplite warfare, victory on the battlefield came as a result of breaking through the enemy's ranks, pushing, and finally forcing a rout from the rear of the phalanx.[17] As the phalanxes collided, spear shafts shattered and live men tumbled over wounded and dead as the files compressed under the weight of the pressing rear ranks. Once the two armies joined, each side's files attempted to break through the opposing enemy ranks by literally pushing forward from the rear and tearing a hole or gap in the opposing line. In this push, the hoplite used close-quarters weapons such as the sword or remnants of the spear to inflict injury on his enemy. In addition, the sheer weight and pressure of the push from the rear ranks sometimes resulted in injury or death from suffocation. Once a phalanx began to tear and then finally disintegrate under the momentum of an enemy push, the hoplites in the rear ranks began to lose heart in the battle. Many of the casualties of engagement came in this phase. Routing infantrymen usually dropped their heavy round shields (*aspides*) and ran from the field. Without the protection of their characteristic round shields, many who fled were killed by pursuing hoplites. Throwing aside the *aspis* in retreat (*rhipsaspia*) was considered an act of cowardice. As one Spartan mother advised her son before a battle, 'You will either come home with your shield, or on it.'[18]

After the battle was decided, the final phase involved recovery of the dead and wounded. As in most conflicts, the wounded usually outnumbered the dead on the field of battle. However, wounds that prohibited a man from leaving the field under his own power generally proved fatal in the Greek world. Battlefield dressing and medicine could not save the soldier who suffered from severe bleeding or organ damage. Even a 'flesh wound' treated on the field often resulted in eventual death from infection.[19]

Hoplite battle represented a logical approach for the Greeks. Wars, especially in the archaic period, ended quickly, usually after just one battle. The impact on society was limited (though the destruction of file in battle could wipe out all the men of a particular village), and actual casualties usually did not exceed 20 per cent of a losing army. The victor suffered far fewer casualties, perhaps as little as 2 per cent.[20] Such figures pale in comparison to casualties inflicted on the Romans by the Carthaginians at Lake Trasimene and Cannae during the Second Punic War, where perhaps 60 per cent of the Roman forces may have been killed.[21]

Whether invented in Corinth or Pylos, this decisive heavy infantry weapon system could not be monopolized for long with the phalanx quickly spreading to other *poleis*. This diffusion instigated an arms race between Greek city-states, one that forced the evolution of the phalanx and in turn introduced phalangeal warfare as a cultural institution in archaic and Hellenic Greece. Because of tactical diffusion, heavy infantry all over Greece wore the same type of armour and fought according to identical tactical principles. Tactical specialization dictated a panoply effective only in a frontal attack. Therefore, efforts were made to increase the tactical mobility of the phalanx. And while there was a tendency over time to reduce the body armour in order to gain mobility, the phalanx never approached anything approximating genuine light infantry.[22]

Overall, greater battlefield articulation remained difficult to achieve because most hoplites were not professional soldiers, but militiamen. For the most part, members of the militia had full-time occupations as farmers, artisans and tradesmen. Though they engaged in some training and tried to keep in good physical condition, participation in group exercises constituted the extent of their preparation for war. One city-state, Sparta, solved this problem by creating a truly professional army, one that drilled for years, while other city-states experimented with the organization of the phalanx itself.

When tactical experimentation did take place, it usually involved an increase in the depth of the file of the phalanx rather than a broadening of the rank or frontage of the formation.[23] Common belief held that by increasing the depth of the phalanx, greater momentum could be gained in the initial collision, but the philosophy that more was better was not universally held. The soldier and historian Xenophon once asked, 'When a phalanx is too deep for the men to reach the enemy with their weapons, what harm do you think they do to the enemy or good to their friends?'[24]

With the widespread adoption of identical tactical principles, a cult of symmetry arose in Hellenic hoplite warfare. The idea of tactical symmetry on the battlefield goes back to Bronze Age chariot-based aristocratic warfare, but the ethos was reinforced with Homer's portrayal of Achilles battling man-to-man with Hector outside the walls of Troy. This infatuation with individual shock combat was projected onto collective warfare in the archaic and Hellenic periods. Inasmuch as light infantry was not an acceptable battlefield weapon system for the Greek citizen-soldier (except to screen hoplites as they formed from column to square), phalanx-versus-phalanx combat became the preferred mode of warfare in Greece at the exclusion of other means of killing.

The Homeric model of combat did not sanction the use of the bow. Its use was considered cowardly. While archery was recognized in early Iron Age Near Eastern warfare as the great battlefield equalizer, allowing death to be dealt out at a distance, it simply did not fit the confrontational image that was the essence of heroic warfare as defined by Homer in the eighth century BCE. Consequently, archery was relegated to a subordinate status in the Greek world, usually hunting.[25] This bias against light infantry would eventually change after contact with the Persians in the fifth century BCE. Cavalry was present on Greek battlefields, but in limited numbers. There is evidence that the Thebans used cavalry to screen their infantry in the Persian Wars, but combined-arms co-operation between Greek infantry and cavalry was a rare thing in most engagements during the archaic period.[26]

Archaic and Hellenic warfare tended to be very localized in its scope, with city-state battling city-state for territorial gain. But the relatively short distances between the various Greek city-states were not as forgiving to the hoplite army on the march as might be suspected. The mountainous nature of Greece, with its steep slopes, deep gorges, dry washes and narrow passes, dictated the utilization of regular routes to move armies. This alone often compromised strategic surprise while simultaneously reinforcing the ritualized character of phalangeal warfare.

Furthermore, hoplite arms and armour were much too heavy to wear in the summer while crossing difficult terrain.[27] This meant that even for a short campaign against a neighbouring city-state, arms and armour had to be transported along with several weeks' rations for the hoplite and his attendants. If pack animals or ox-drawn carts were used, the size of the marching column grew exponentially since as least some of the fodder for the pack or draft animals was carried as well. Even a small hoplite army of only a few hundred soldiers required a substantial baggage train.[28]

The Persian Wars: A Collision of Two Tactical Systems

In the fifth century BCE the Greek hoplite armies fought two of the most famous wars in all of western military history. The first, the Persian Wars (499–c.469) at the beginning of the century, was a defensive action against a combined land and naval invasion launched against Greece by the Persians, and the other, the Great Peloponnesian War (431–404) at the end of the century, was an epochal struggle between the Athenians and the Spartans and their allies for Greek hegemony.

The Persian Wars between the Greek city-states and the Persian Empire represent the collision of two different tactical systems, a collision that would radically change the way each civilization made war. As already noted, Persian warfare consisted of unarticulated heavy infantry spearmen protecting light infantry archers, chariots and cavalry, while Greek warfare from c.675 to 490 BCE consisted mainly of combat between articulated heavy infantry phalanxes. The absence of heavy infantry capable of close-order offensive action from the Persian art of war did not appear very consequential because chariots performed the role of shock combat, with the bowmen used to destroy the opponent's ranks, and spearmen performing the defensive role of protecting the archers. Moreover, chariots, a battlefield anachronism, were only truly effective against poorly trained and poorly motivated infantry.

On the other hand, the absence of a combined-arms tactical system in classical Greece did not seem to be a major weakness. Though the articulated Greek phalanx was very effective against an identical weapon system, it remained extremely vulnerable in its flank and rear to attack by cavalry, light infantry or skirmishers, but those weapon systems remained relatively unknown to the Greeks of this period. Therefore, the integration of other weapon systems into the Greek way of war would have a revolutionary effect. The Persian Wars would introduce to both systems more efficient means to kill, though both Persia and the Greek city-states remained resistant to change.

The occasion where Greek and Persian tactical systems met en masse for the first time was at the battle of Marathon in 490 BCE. The Persian Great King Darius I (r. 521–486 BCE), in response to Athenian support of a Greek rebellion on the western coast of Asia Minor, sent a punitive expedition directly towards the city-states of Eretria and Athens. In the previous year the Persian king had dispatched representatives to the Greek city-states demanding submission to Persia, but Athens executed them. In response, Darius ordered a Persian army, numbering about 25,000 fighting men and including perhaps 800 to 1,000 cavalry and 600 ships, to assemble in Cilicia in south-eastern Anatolia.[29] From Cilicia, the armada sailed across the Aegean and took Eretria in Euboea after a siege of seven days. From there the Persians proceeded to Attica, where they landed in the Bay of Marathon (Map 2.1).

The Athenians, under the leadership of Miltiades (*c*.550–*c*.489 BCE), debated whether to take refuge behind their walls or meet the Persians in the field. This decision was further complicated by the fact that the Athenians would have to face the Persian menace without the aid of the greatest hoplite army in the Greek world, Sparta. But Spartan assistance would be delayed until after the full moon because of a religious observance. The Athenians decided to strike at the Persian army at Marathon without the assistance of Sparta, a decision that probably surprised the Persians. The Athenian army numbered approximately 10,000 men, including a small force from neighbouring Plataea.[30] The Greek force took up position on the edge of the hills overlooking the Persian army encamped on the coast.

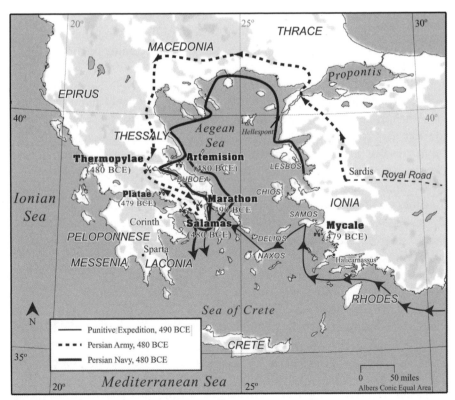

Map 2.1. The Persian Expeditions, 490 and 480 BCE.

After days of watching the Persian host on the plain below, the Athenians decided to act. There is speculation concerning what prompted the Athenian attack. Some historians believe that after a few days the Persians decided to split their army, leaving a holding force at Marathon, while embarking most of the host for a landing closer to Athens. Perhaps Miltiades saw an opportunity to attack the reduced force or some confusion in the Persian ranks when embarking and ordered the attack.[31] Whatever the reason, around 21 September, the Athenians prepared to strike the larger Persian army, deploying their hoplites in a thinner formation along the centre than the usual eight ranks deep in order to match the frontage of the enemy force (Map 2.2(a)).[32] To reduce the time the army would be within range of Persian arrows, Miltiades ordered the phalanx advance at the double to engage the Persians, about one mile away.

It is doubtful that the Athenians could have run for a mile wearing heavy armour and in formation. It is more likely that the Greeks marched until they came within range of the Persian archers (perhaps 180 yards), and then rushed.[33] Still, Herodotus clearly states that they achieved tactical surprise:

> The Persians, therefore, when they saw the Greeks coming on at speed, made ready to receive them, though it seemed to them that the Athenians were bereft of their senses, and bent upon their own destruction; for they saw a mere handful of men coming on at a run without either horsemen or archers.[34]

The Persians had little time to deploy, yet managed to repel and nearly break the Athenian centre (Map 2.2(b)). On the wings, though, the Athenians were stronger and eventually broke the Persian line and wheeled around to hit the Persian centre in the rear, executing a partial double envelopment. Those Persians who had not been enveloped, including perhaps some light cavalry, fled to the ships, while the Greeks pursued the Persian centre, inflicting heavy casualties with little loss. By the end of the battle, the Persians lost 6,400 men and seven ships. Greek casualties were 192 killed.[35] In the first major test between a mainland Greek heavy infantry phalanx and Persian unarticulated heavy infantry, the phalanx prevailed. This overwhelming victory created the myth among the Greeks that their way of war was superior to the Persian way. This myth was reinforced a decade later at the battles of Thermopylae and Plataea.

Darius' first punitive expedition in 490 BCE failed to bring the Greek city-states under Persian hegemony. Wounded but still wanting victory, the Persians sailed around to Athens, only to find that the Athenians had performed a forced march all night. When the Persians saw the hoplites waiting for them on the beach, they decided against landing and sailed home.

Darius' successor, Xerxes (r. 486–465 BCE), launched a second expedition against Greece in 480 BCE (see Map 2.1). Anticipating the Persian invasion, the

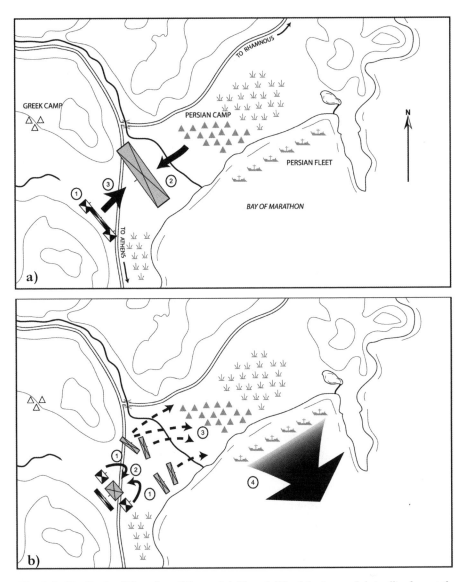

Map 2.2. *The Battle of Marathon, 490 BCE. (a) Phase I: The Athenians and their allies form at the edge of a hill (1). In order to prevent being outflanked by the larger Persian force (2), the centre of the Greek formation was thinner than the normal eight-rank depth. Miltiades orders a headlong charge (3) against the Persians in an effort to minimize casualties from enemy archery. (b) Phase II: As the Greek wings press the Persian flanks causing them to rout (1), the Persian centre gains ground against the thinned Athenian centre. Just as collapse seems imminent, the wing formations both wheel inward, striking the Persian formation in the rear (2). The dazed Persian survivors attempt to elude pursuit, some fleeing to the ships offshore, others to the marshland behind their camp (3). The fleet embarks the remnants of the army and retreats to Persia (4).*

Greek world joined together in 481 in a Panhellenic defence, with Sparta holding the chief command and Athens taking an important role because of the strength of its navy.[36] Abandoning the Thessalian frontier, the Greeks decided to make their initial stand against the Persian army and navy at the pass of Thermopylae and in the straits near Artemisium.

The Persians crossed the Hellespont and marched southward, where, at Thermopylae, 7,000 Spartans under the command of their king Leonidas held fast for three days against the Great King's troops, led by his elite Immortals.[37] The Greek hoplites again and again showed their prowess, although ultimately they were outmanoeuvred. In spite of standing strategically on the defensive, their tactics seem to have been offensive. Herodotus writes that the Spartans feigned a series of retreats, which induced the enemy to close with them. The less-protected Immortals were sucked in and slaughtered by better-armoured Greek heavy infantry.[38] Below is a thought-provoking reconstruction of Herodotus' assessment of Persian tactical capabilities in the narrow pass:

> 'Their shorter spears' and wider files in offense and their 'small round or irregularly shaped shields' in defense could make no headway against the longer spears of the closely arrayed Greeks, 'their entire bodies protected by shields.' The Persians could have had the 'advantage in open fields, since they were ... enabled to move more easily,' but not 'in narrow space' against enemies 'formed in close ranks.'[39]

Eventually the Persians were shown a mountain path by which the Greek flank could be turned. When Leonidas heard the Persian flanking force was at their rear, he decided to send back the majority of his allies while he and 300 Spartans retreated to the hill that was their final position. When Xerxes asked the Spartan king to lay down his arms, Leonidas' reply was only two Greek words, *Molon labe*: 'Come and get them.' Surrounded and outnumbered, the Spartans died to a man, probably from Persian missile fire.[40] Though the Spartans were eventually overrun at Thermopylae, their defeat resulted from overwhelming numbers and could not be attributed to a defective tactical system. This heroic action is known to western military annals as 'the Stand of the Three Hundred', an event which has immortalized Spartan courage ever since.

If the defeat at Thermopylae was not bad enough, the Greeks experienced another setback at the naval battle near Artemisium taking place at the same time as the holding action in the pass. Here, the Persian and Greek navies sparred for three days. On the second day, the Persian fleet was badly damaged by a storm while the Greek flotilla, sheltered by the lee of Euboea, was unscathed. On the third day the remaining Persian ships attempted to encircle the Greek fleet, but poor execution by the Persians led to a botched manoeuvre, with both sides badly mauled. When news of the Greek loss at Thermopylae reached the Greek fleet, it withdrew southward toward Athens.[41]

Protected by the Persian fleet, the Persian army overran most of Greece north of the Isthmus of Corinth, forcing the citizens of Athens to evacuate to nearby islands. With the Persians threatening Athens, the Greek world was split on how to meet the Persian advance. The Spartans wanted to seal off the Peloponnese with a stand at the Isthmus, while the Athenians favoured an aggressive naval strategy. As the Greek commanders argued, the situation for the Greeks worsened when the Persians sacked and burned Athens and the Greek coalition began to unravel. With the intent of forcing a battle before his alliance disintegrated, the Athenian commander Themistocles sent word to Xerxes that he was defecting to the Persians and that the Persian fleet, now reduced to some 350 ships could trap the Greek fleet of perhaps 300 vessels in the Straits of Salamis if it acted quickly. The Persian king ordered his fleet in, trapping the Greeks, or so he thought.[42] Themistocles' ruse pulled the numerically superior Persian fleet into the narrow waters, mitigating its strength. Pressed between the advancing Greek triremes and rocky cliffs, the Persian fleet was decisively defeated, losing 200 galleys to the Greek's 40 ships.[43]

After the battle of Salamis, Xerxes ordered the bulk of his punitive expedition back to Anatolia, leaving a formidable army of 50,000 men (including 10,000 cavalry) to harass the Greeks.[44] Commanding the Persian army was Mardonius, an able general who wished to accomplish what his Great King had failed to do – conquer Greece. The existence of such a large foreign presence north of the Peloponnese did have an effect. The Thebans had already gone to the side of the Persians, and the Athenians, their city burned and their hinterland occupied by a large Persian host, threatened an alliance with Mardonius if the Spartans did not abandon their position at the Isthmus and join the northern *poleis* in their defence of Boeotia and Attica. Fearing the defection or 'Medizing' of the largest navy in the Greek world, the Spartans joined the allied army, swelling it to perhaps 40,000 men (mostly heavy infantry) and marched to meet the Persians at Plataea.[45]

When the Greek army arrived at Plataea, it took up position across from the Persian camp along the foothills of Mount Cithaeron, above a broad field bisected by the Asopus River.[46] The Greek commander was Pausanias, the regent for an infant Spartan king. Both commanders thought defensively, selecting ground which best suited his dominant tactical system. Pausanias recognized that Mardonius had chosen to defend the level ground beneath the ridge with the intention of using his superiority in cavalry against the Greek heavy infantry, while the Persian commander could not afford to commit a full-scale attack against the Greek hoplites as they held the high ground. What followed was a confusing engagement, illustrating the strengths and weaknesses of Greek heavy infantry and the lighter, more agile Persian tactical systems.

For nearly two weeks the Persians and Greeks played a game of tactical chess, with neither army compelling the other to commit to decisive action. Meanwhile, the Greeks harassed Mardonius' supply lines, particularly vulnerable because of a lack of naval supplies. Mardonius attempted the same strategy, and on the eighth night a Persian cavalry raid successfully captured and slaughtered 500 Greek supply animals and their handlers.[47]

On the eleventh day Mardonius called for a council of war, vowing to attack the Greeks on the next day. Perhaps learning of this plan, Pausanias attempted to change his deployment, switching the Spartans from their position of honour on the right wing with the Athenians on the left wing.[48] Mardonius counter-moved, keeping his best Persian troops across from the Spartans. Inexplicably, though, the Spartan regent then ordered his wings to switch back, and once again, the Persians responded with a corresponding move. To make matters worse, the Persians had successfully poisoned two nearby springs, forcing Greek foragers to get fresh water from the Asopus. But each time the Greeks approached the riverbank, Persian light infantry and cavalry archers rained shafts down on their heads, denying them much-needed water.

On the evening of the twelfth day, Pausanias' supply problems forced him to withdraw in column under cover of darkness to a position closer to the city of

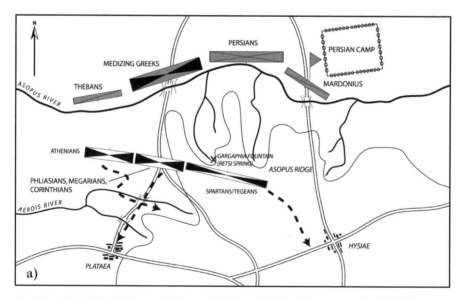

Map 2.3. The Battle of Plataea, 479 BCE. (a) Phase I: After almost two weeks of shuffling troops from one flank to another and a series of small-scale raids on both Persian and Greek supply lines, Pausanias withdraws the Greek army from the Asopus Ridge to positions closer to Plataea. The withdrawal is undertaken at night and results in much confusion and disorganization. The Greek centre either panics or becomes lost in the darkness, and camps under the walls of Plataea. A large gap now exists between the Athenians and the Spartan/Tegean element. (b) Phase II: Mardonius orders the Persian left-flank cavalry forward against the Spartans and Tegeans (1). The Persian infantry is ordered to assist in reducing the pinned Greek right (2). The Spartans close ranks, and the deploying Persian sparabara is met by Tegean light infantry (3). The piecemeal Persian advance continues as the Medizing Greek infantry and the Theban cavalry advance against the isolated Athenians (4). The

Plataea (Map 2.3(a)). But the nocturnal withdrawal became disorganized, and many Greek units lost contact with one another. Believing the chaotic withdrawal to be a retreat, Mardonius ordered a full-scale assault at sunrise

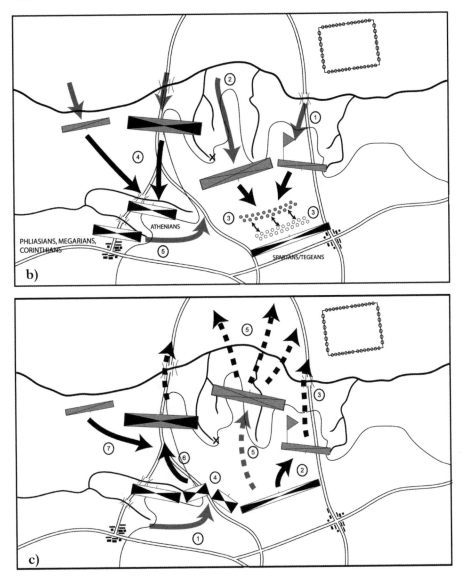

errant Greek centre moves to its former position between the Athenians and the Spartans (5). (c) Phase III: As the Greek centre moves to fill the gap (1), the Spartan phalanx moves to confront the Persian horse under Mardonius (2), causing the Persian left to collapse (3). Mardonius is killed during this part of the action. The Greek centre splits (4), the Corinthians moving to assist the Spartans, and the Megarians and Phliasians the Athenians. The Persian centre collapses when they see the left crumble (5). The Athenians press back the Theban infantry, who retire in good order (6). The Megarians and Phliasians attempt to pursue, but are checked by the Theban cavalry operating as a screen for the retreating hoplites (7). The death of Mardonius causes a complete Persian collapse, and the victorious Greeks sack the Persian camp, slaughtering the survivors seeking shelter therein.

before Pausanias could reorder his battle line. The ensuing attack was a rushed affair, and both sides seemed unprepared for the clash. On the Greek side, the withdrawing column was in disarray. The centre position, held by the Corinthians, Megarians and Phliasians, either panicked and fled or lost its way in the darkness and was not present at the beginning of the engagement. Their absence left the Greeks extremely vulnerable, with the Spartans and Tegeans on the right wing, the Athenians on the left wing, and a precarious gap in between the two contingents.

Seeing the broken Greek formation, Mardonius must have assumed that his enemy was in retreat. He quickly commanded the Persian left to advance at top speed toward the Spartans and Tegeans, followed by his Theban allies (Map 2.3(b)). Herodotus tells us that the attack was uncoordinated, 'no battalion having order in its ranks nor place assigned to the line'.[49] The Persian cavalry crossed the Asopus and charged toward the Spartans, pinning them down as they waited for the Persian infantry to arrive. As the Spartans closed ranks, the Persian *sparabara* ran to within bowshot of the enemy and set up their defences, the shield-bearers linking their reed shields as the archers unleashed arrows into the Greek phalanx. The Tegean light infantry were not as lucky. Unable to form up in a protective position, they surged forward against the Persian infantry, with the Spartan phalanx hard on their heels. The *sparabara* met the attack valiantly, but, poorly armed and armoured compared to the hoplites bearing down on them, the invaders were stabbed and crushed by the advancing phalanx.

Meanwhile, the Corinthians, Megarians and Phliasians had reformed and returned to the battlefield, taking their place in the centre opposite the Persian centre (Map 2.3(c)). But when the Persian left collapsed, the Persian centre abandoned the field and headed for the Hellespont. Splitting to reinforce their beleaguered colleagues, the Corinthians marched toward the Spartan lines and the Megarians moved toward the Athenians. The Athenians on the right were caught in the open, but fought well and pushed back the Thebans, who withdrew in good order. Perhaps wanting a chance to recover some honour, the Megarians and Phliasians pursued the Theban hoplites, only to be run down by Theban cavalry screening the retreating heavy infantry. Six hundred Megarians and Phliasians were killed.

The role of the Persian cavalry at this point in the engagement is difficult to establish. Perhaps it pulled back when the *sparabara* arrived, or screened the infantry as it fled?[50] But we do know that Mardonius personally led his cavalry against the counter-attacking Spartans, and it was in this action that he was struck down and killed, perhaps by a thrown rock. When news of the general's death reached the rank and file, the Persian effort disintegrated. Spartan and Athenian soldiers attacked the enemy camp and slaughtered the Persians seeking refuge there. Persian casualties were very high. With the exception of the retreating Persian centre, only 3,000 troops survived. Greek casualties were modest, varying from around 750 to 1,360 men.[51]

The Greek victories on land at Plataea and at sea at Mycale in 479 pushed the Persians out of Europe and gave the Greeks mastery of the Aegean. The Greeks' final victory at the Eurymedon River in Anatolia in the early 460s ushered in a new self-confidence in Greece, with the string of military successes against Persia reinforcing the perceived dominance of the heavy infantry phalanx and the cult of symmetry. These actions intensified Greek prejudices against the utility of other weapon systems, most specifically Persian-styled light infantry archers and javelin throwers.

Victory in the Persian Wars also launched Athens into a position of ascendancy in the Greek world. By using tribute from other city-states to fund its Delian League, the Athenians rebuilt their city and created a formidable navy that they used to enforce political and economic hegemony over the city-states north of the Peloponnese. But Athens' overwhelming self-confidence would turn to hubris, plunging the Greek world into a second conflagration in the same century. This second conflict, known as the Great Peloponnesian War (431–404 BCE), pitted the new sea power Athens against the traditional land power Sparta in a struggle that redefined the way Greeks fought each other, and later, under Macedonian leadership, fought the Persians.

The Peloponnesian War: The 'Cult of Symmetry' Challenged

Athens' rise to supremacy in the fifth century was accomplished by the sweat of its oarsmen. At its height the Athenian thalassocracy ruled directly or indirectly 179 states which included perhaps 2 million Greeks; the most remote of these were a mere eight-day voyage or 200–250 miles from Athens (Map 2.4).[52] Athenian power could be projected all over the Mediterranean, from Sicily to Egypt to the Black Sea, embracing perhaps 20 million people.[53] But Athenian hegemony did not go unchallenged. Sparta organized the Peloponnesian League and confronted Athenian supremacy in a series of land and, later, sea campaigns known to history as the Peloponnesian War. Athens' attempt to create both a land empire in Greece and a maritime empire in the Aegean led to the First Peloponnesian War (c.460–445 BCE), overextending the Athenians and involving them in a series of skirmishes with Sparta. After a series of defeats in 445 BCE the land empire of Athens disintegrated and Athens agreed to a Thirty Years Peace with the Spartans the following year. Tensions between the two leagues remained high, and the Second or Great Peloponnesian War broke out in 431 BCE.

The Great Peloponnesian War is divided into three phases: the Archidamian War (431–421 BCE), the Sicilian Expedition (415–413 BCE) and the Iono-Decelean War (413–404 BCE). The first phase was named after the Spartan king Archidamus and ended in a stalemate. Sparta attacked Attica with its army, but the Athenians stayed behind their city's fortifications, protected by long walls stretching down to the harbour at Piraeus. The strong Athenian navy protected the shipping lanes necessary to provide the city with supplies, while being large

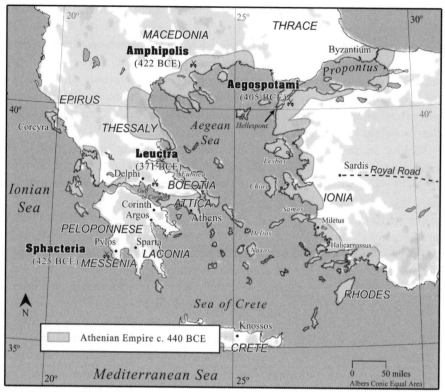

Map 2.4. The Athenian Empire, c.440 BCE.

enough to be used in offensive action against the coastline of the Peloponnese. Sparta, possessing the best-trained and most articulated hoplite army in the Greek world, ran roughshod over the Athenian-led armies in land campaigns.

Overall command of the Spartan army on campaign fell on one of Sparta's dual kings. This Spartan king in the field was assisted by his generals or *polemarchs*, who transmitted his commands to the troops through the officers in charge of units. The chief tactical unit of the Spartan army in the second half of the fifth century BCE was the *lochos*, essentially a battalion of 100 heavy infantry hoplites. The *lochos* was divided into two companies or *pentecostyes* of fifty men each, while each *pentecostys* was further divided into two platoons or *enomotiai* of twenty-five hoplites. The *enomotiai* each consisted of three files. The later Spartan army of the early fourth century BCE consisted of six divisions or *morai* of between 400 and 600 men and was commanded by a *polemarch*. Each *mora* comprised four battalions of between 100 and 150 men each.[54]

The Athenian army was not a professional force like the Spartan army: instead, the hoplites were a citizen-militia drawn from eligible men seventeen to fifty-nine years of age who fought in a phalanx eight men deep. This army was divided into ten divisions or *taxeis* representing the ten tribes of Athenian society. These *taxeis* were commanded by *taxiarchs*, and each of these *taxeis* was probably subdivided into battalions or *lochoi*. Ten generals or *strategoi* were elected annually, one from each tribe, with command of the entire army shifting between these commanders on a daily basis.[55]

Because of the difference in force composition, Athens improvised on land to compensate for its less articulated hoplite army. This improvisation took the form of adding light infantry archers and javelineers to assist their heavy infantry, giving the Athenians a limited combined-arms tactical system. The creation of an integrated army challenged the cult of symmetry that had dominated Greek warfare since the middle of the seventh century.

One of the first recorded instances of the Athenians using this limited combined-arms tactical system took place in 425 BCE on the island of Sphacteria, near the city of Pylos on the south-western coast of the Peloponnese. In 425 the Great Peloponnesian War had been in progress for six years. The war was in a stalemate, with neither side able to gain a decisive advantage. The Athenians were still relying on the strategy developed by their long-time leader Pericles, despite his death in 429. The Spartans, on the other hand, were still relying on their ground forces to wage war against the Athenians. This stalemate was broken at the battle of Sphacteria in 425.

That year an Athenian fleet sailing west to Sicily was forced by a storm into the bay at the Spartan port of Pylos. One of the Athenian commanders, Demosthenes, was allowed to stay with five vessels to capture and fortify the port, while the rest of the fleet continued to Sicily. The Spartans, realizing the danger, recalled their annual invasion army in Attica and sent to the area a fleet of sixty ships. The Spartan plan was to surround the Athenians by land and sea and force their capitulation. As part of this plan, a force of 420 Spartan hoplites was sent to fortify the small island located just south of Pylos.

The Spartans' first attempt to retake Pylos failed, and Demosthenes was able to send a request to Athens for help. Fifty ships responded to the commander's plea, sailing into the bay at Pylos. In the ensuing engagement the Athenians won control of the sea from the Spartans. They immediately placed a blockade on Sphacteria and its Spartan garrison. While this blockade was tight enough to prevent relief or reinforcement, it did not prevent the Spartans from using swimmers to resupply the garrison. As a result, attempts to starve the Spartans into submission failed.

Meanwhile, the Spartan leadership arrived to view the situation first-hand. After realizing there was no way to relieve the trapped garrison, the Spartans requested a truce with Demosthenes and sent a diplomatic mission to Athens to request peace. The Athenians were directed by one of their leaders, Cleon, to set terms so harsh that Sparta was forced to reject them. Cleon was then dispatched to Pylos to defeat the Spartans.

Arriving with a force mostly composed of light infantry archers, slingers and javelineers supporting heavy infantry hoplites, Cleon began planning with

Demosthenes for the assault on Sphacteria. Their initial attack took place on the south-eastern end of the island (Map 2.5(a)). Once on shore, Athenian hoplites easily overran the southern guard post and slaughtered the Spartan

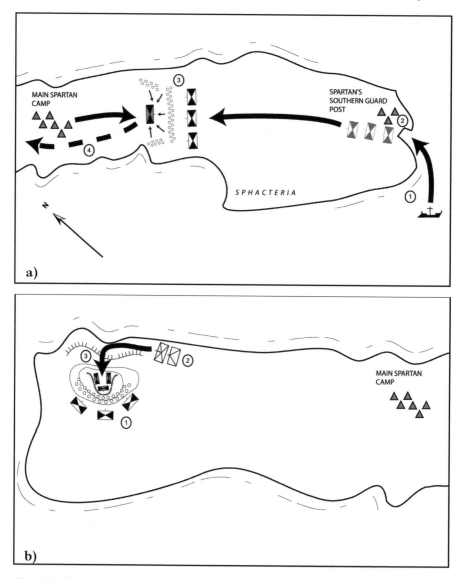

Map 2.5. The Battle of Sphacteria, 425 BCE. (a) Phase I: The Athenians land their assault force on the south-eastern end of the island (1), quickly killing the occupants of the Spartans' southern guard post (2). The Athenians advance and make contact with a Spartan force just south of the Spartans' main camp (3). The outnumbered Spartans, fearing encirclement by the Athenian peltasts and archers, retreat north, joined by the remaining Spartans in the camp (4). (b) Phase II: Having taken refuge on a hilltop ruin, the Spartans succeed in holding the Athenian hoplites and skirmishers at bay (1). While the Spartans' attention is focused on the threat directly to their front, a mixed Athenian force of peltasts and archers makes its way along the base of a cliff on the eastern shore of the island (2). Remaining undetected, the light infantrymen scale the cliff and launch a surprise assault on the Spartans' unprotected rear (3). Spartan resistance collapses, and the survivors surrender.

garrison still sleeping in their beds. Pushing north, Athenian heavy infantry (we do not know how many), accompanied by 800 archers and perhaps another 800 javelineers, met a small contingent of 420 Spartans and a similar number of allies just south of the Spartans' main camp.[56] Heavily outnumbered, the Spartan hoplites refused to close with the Athenian heavy infantry for fear of being overcome by the less encumbered Athenian light infantry, half of whom were javelin-wielding *peltasts*.

Originally, peltasts were Thracian tribesmen fighting in their native dress, but the term came to encompass all light troops of this type.[57] The peltast did not wear armour and carried a crescent-shaped wicker shield called the *pelta*. The peltasts' armament was composed of a bundle of javelins that gave them missile as well as limited mêlée capabilities. These troops proved very effective against heavy infantry, giving them the ability to manoeuvre around the slow-moving phalanxes and attack their vulnerable flank and rear.[58] On Sphacteria, the peltasts easily avoided the Spartans' charge while inflicting serious casualties, including killing the Spartan commander.

Constantly harried by arrows, javelins and sling bullets, and fearful of the peltasts reaching their rear, the remaining Spartans abandoned their main camp for a ruined hilltop position on the north end of the island.[59] Although a fire on the island destroyed all natural cover, the Spartans were able to temporarily hold off the attacking Athenians at the ruined fort (Map 2.5(b)). At this point, an enterprising allied officer led a force of peltasts and archers along a cliff top on the eastern edge of the island, reaching the Spartan rear. The Spartans, exhausted and demoralized by the appearance of Athenian light infantry to their rear, surrendered. Of the original 420 Spartans, the Athenians captured 292 hoplites, including 120 of the officer class, while suffering only fifty casualties themselves.[60]

The Athenians' successful use of combined arms shattered the myth of Thermopylae. Sparta was no longer invincible on land.[61] The battle of Sphacteria showed that a hoplite force could be defeated without a clash of phalanxes. The Athenians demonstrated that light troops could remain out of reach of enemy heavy infantry while inflicting heavy casualties. Moreover, Sphacteria illustrated the tactical agility of light troops. The manoeuvre along the cliff top into the Spartan rear could not have been accomplished by traditionally overburdened hoplites. Warfare was changing and the Greeks were beginning to see the importance of the tactical flexibility of a combined-arms army.

Three years after Sphacteria, at the battle of Amphipolis in 422 BCE, both the Spartan and Athenian generals were killed and the new Athenian leader, Nicias, negotiated the Peace of Nicias a year later. Although both parties agreed to keep the peace for fifty years, it took only six years for the truce to break down. The second phase of the Great Peloponnesian War was initiated by Alcibiades, a nephew of Pericles, elected to the generalship in 420 BCE. In 415 he convinced the Athenians to attack Syracuse, a Sicilian city-state friendly to the Peloponnesian League. Alcibiades argued that its conquest would give the Athenians a strong source of support to carry on a lengthy war against the Spartans. But the Sicilian Expedition was ill-fated. Alcibiades himself was removed from the leadership of the expedition on a charge of profaning the religious mysteries. Rather than return to Athens and stand trial, he fled to Sparta, where he gave advice on how to defeat the Athenian expeditionary force. To make matters worse, Alcibiades secured assistance from Persia, who gave both ships and men to the Spartan war effort.

In the mean time, the Athenians pursued their Sicilian policy. In the autumn of 415, the Athenian fleet occupied the harbour of Syracuse, landing 5,100 hoplites, 480 archers, 700 Rhodian slingers, 120 light infantry and 30 cavalry. With sailors and allies, the entire expeditionary force surpassed 27,000 men.[62] According to ancient custom, the attacking army began constructing a double encircling wall, the inner wall (*contravallation*) designed to hold in the besieged, the outer wall (*circumvallation*) to fend off any relief force, while the attackers held the ground between the two walls. More Athenian troops landed in the spring of 414 and it seemed Syracuse was doomed. But the commanding general pushed the construction of the walls so sluggishly that the Spartans were able to reinforce the garrison at Syracuse and build counter walls, squeezing the Athenians into the lower ground near the harbour. Additional reinforcements reached Syracuse from Corinth, Thebes and other Spartan allies.

Athens countered in the spring of 413 with the infusion of some 5,000 hoplites and skirmishers. But after a daring night attack failed to seize the high ground, the besiegers' momentum began to slow. Meanwhile, a substantial Athenian fleet of nearly 200 warships was gradually destroyed by the Syracusans and Spartans in a series of naval actions offshore. Unable to escape by sea, the Athenians attempted to escape by land into the interior of the island. Attacked while on the march, the last survivors of Athens' 40,000 troops were killed or captured. Six thousand Athenian prisoners were sold into slavery.[63] These heavy losses at Syracuse had immediate repercussions. The democracy was weakened and an aristocratic oligarchy was temporarily established between 411 and 410.

Despite the disaster, the Athenians refused to give up, raising new armies and sending out new fleets. But during this last phase of the conflict, the Iono–Decelean War (413–404), Sparta, now assisted by Persian coin, was able to compete with Athens for command of the sea. The final crushing blow to Athenian hegemony came in 405 when a Persian-backed Spartan fleet destroyed an Athenian fleet at Aegospotami on the Hellespont. Cut off from its Ukrainian wheat, Athens was besieged again by the Spartans and surrendered in 404. Athens' walls were torn down, the navy disbanded, and its empire destroyed.

The Great Peloponnesian War was finally over. The next seventy years of Greek history witnessed continuing warfare among the *poleis*, with the leading roles shifting between Sparta and Thebes. During this time, the Greek heavy infantry phalanx still ruled the battlefields of Hellas and the imaginations of Greek commanders. But the tactical lessons of the Persian and Peloponnesian wars, specifically the inclusion of light infantry in the tactical mix, were beginning to have an impact on how the Greeks waged war.

The hoplite heavy infantry formation was, in many ways, a tactical anomaly. Exclusive reliance upon heavy infantry, particularly in a country as mountainous as Greece, seems odd, especially considering the expense in both time and equipment. Heavy infantry by itself can make sense only in an environment where other armies were also utilizing heavy infantry. This proved to be the case in archaic Greece from *c*.750 to *c*.500 BCE. But the Greeks continued to emphasize the superiority of heavy infantry throughout the Hellenic period down into the fourth century BCE, even though their actual military experience of opposing hoplite forces supported by light infantry and cavalry proved how effective a limited combined-arms force was against an army employing a single weapon system.

So how does one explain the Greeks' preoccupation with the hoplite formation? The answer lies within the cultural character of classical Greek society. The phalanx was not simply a tactical formation – it represented a way of life, a code of moral conduct that was much more deeply ingrained in Greece than in most military societies. All free Greek men thought of themselves as warriors; it was a requisite as a citizen in Greek society. Moreover, the ritualized character of hoplite battle made change very difficult, even after the Greeks came into contact with the combined-arms tactical system of the ancient Near East. Resistance to these foreign institutions was, according to one authority on the period, 'moral and cultural and not based upon rational analysis or military science'.[64]

Greek victory in the Persian Wars contributed greatly to the perceived dominance of the heavy infantry phalanx. Although some Greeks realized that Persian errors also contributed to victory, the more common belief was that it 'represented the triumph of the spear over the bow or heavy infantry over light'.[65] The Athenian experience at Sphacteria during the Peloponnesian War augmented the Greek view of light infantry, but it was only one step toward a fully integrated army. The Greek city-states refused to adopt a complete combined-arms tactical system. This refusal cost them their freedom when King Philip of Macedon marched south and defeated *polis* after *polis* using a well-balanced tactical system.

As already noted, the Greeks learned a great deal from the Persians in the military art of logistics. The Greeks would begin learning these lessons in the decade directly following the close of the Peloponnesian War. Persia's support of Sparta during the war led to a greater respect for Greek heavy infantry by the Persians. After the Peloponnesian War, Greek mercenaries became a sought-after commodity in the armies of Near Eastern kings and nobles. In 401 Greek hoplites were employed by a pretender to the Persian throne, Cyrus the Younger, who challenged his older brother, the Great King Artaxerxes II (r. 404–359 BCE). In preparation for an armed *coup d'état*, Cyrus assembled a force of 40,000 to 80,000 men, including 13,000 Greek mercenary hoplites, in Anatolia. The Great King's force consisted of perhaps 60,000 to 100,000 men, including 6,000 cavalry, and 200 scythed chariots, designed to attack enemy infantry with their bladed wheels.[66] Cyrus marched his force from Asia Minor into Mesopotamia seeking battle with his older brother. The two armies came together on the field of Cunaxa, about 100 miles north of Babylon.[67]

The resulting battle of Cunaxa in 401 ended in a victory for Cyrus' forces and proved again the dominance of Greek heavy infantry hoplites over the lightly armed troops of the Persian Empire. But the pretender himself was killed in the battle and the army he led disintegrated in the aftermath, leaving over 10,000 Greek mercenaries roughly 1,500 miles from the Ionian coast. Choosing to make their way up the Tigris River toward the Black Sea, the Greek mercenaries were first pursued by regular Persian troops, then by guerrilla mountaineers, and finally by the forces of the northern Persian satrap (Map 2.6).

Known to history as the 'March of the Ten Thousand', the Greek mercenaries' return to friendly territory imparted and reinforced some valuable tactical lessons about the uses and limitations of Greek heavy infantry and the importance of utilizing light troops in rough terrain. Like the battle of Sphacteria in 425, the Greeks were obliged to fight under unfamiliar and mountainous conditions on their march, and consequently, the role of light infantry was enhanced. When attacked from above by enemy guerrillas, a contingent of Cretan light infantry peltasts was used to control the high ground until the hoplites marched past, then moved along the higher elevations to repeat the manoeuvre while an advance guard secured the next ridge. In the words of a commander present on the march upriver, the brilliant young Greek general Xenophon (*c*.428–354 BCE), writing about himself in the third person:

> Whenever the enemy got in the way of the vanguard, Xenophon led his men up the mountains from the rear and made the road-block in front of the vanguard ineffectual by trying to get on to higher ground than those who were manning it ... So they were continually coming to each other's help and giving each other valuable support.[68]

The role of light infantry in the retreat upriver was so important that the Rhodian contingent of heavy infantry were asked by Xenophon to put down their *aspides* and come forward and exercise their native skills as light infantry slingers.[69]

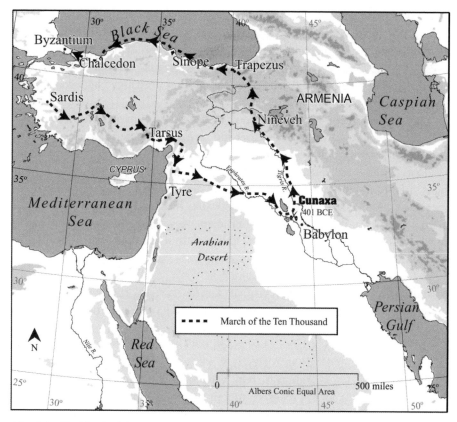

Map 2.6. The March of the 'Ten Thousand'.

The march to Cunaxa as a part of the Persian train showed the Greek leadership the effectiveness of the Persian supply system, while the 'March of the Ten Thousand' from Cunaxa upriver to the Black Sea imparted valuable lessons in combined arms and logistics to the Greeks.[70] The logistical problems suffered by the Greeks on their return journey convinced them of the necessity of organized supply. But perhaps most importantly, the lessons learned were shared with other Greek commanders, chiefly through the writings of Xenophon. He spent the next several decades analysing the lessons of military action against the Persians, and his accounts influenced the leading military figures of his age.

The Greek Military Revolution
The lessons of the Peloponnesian War and the Persian Expedition were not lost on Greek battle captains. In fact, such experiences led to the development of the first true military science in western civilization, a tacit recognition that warfare had become complicated in the classical world, and that the martial contacts between Greece and the Near East necessitated the implementation of

more systematic modes of warfare. The Greek military revolution in the first
half of the fourth century BCE was a response to this recognition. This military
revolution has been characterized as the co-ordination of 'the infantry of the
West with the cavalry of the East', a valuable appraisal, but one which fails to
appreciate the sophisticated nature of the martial exchanges between Greece
and the Near East.[71]

The military revolution of the fourth century BCE involved invention and
diffusion and adaptation of both ideas and technologies. Before the Greeks and
the Macedonians could penetrate the heart of Persia in 336 BCE, they needed
to create a well-articulated combined-arms tactical system including heavy and
light infantry, skirmishers, and heavy and light cavalry, as well as learn the
means of supporting such forces logistically. Besides creating an integrated
army, Alexander would require an efficient siege train to storm the highly
fortified strongholds of the Levant. Each of these elements was inherited by
the young Macedonian king from developments which took place all over the
Greek world in the previous two centuries.

With the increasing complexity of Greek warfare, the study of proper
generalship developed into a required science and gave rise to the emergence of
'professors' of tactics. Mercenary commanders such as Xenophon, Iphicrates
(*c*.412–353 BCE) and Chabrias (*c*.420–356 BCE) translated their experience on
the battlefield as generals into treatises on tactics. The appearance of these
professors indicates a change in how warfare was viewed by Greek society.
Warfare emerged from the realm of morality and honour to become something
more than a way of life to be conducted according to ancestral expectations.[72]
As the idea of combined arms gained acceptance in Greek society, there was a
switch in emphasis from the traditional to the innovative, with a necessary by-
product being an escalation in the diffusion of tactics and the invention of
improved weapons and armour.

As the Greeks began to experiment with light infantry, cavalry and
skirmishers, the age of hoplite-dominated warfare came to an end. But Greek
heavy infantry would experience a brief resurgence during the wars of shifting
hegemony in the 370s and 360s BCE with the wars between Thebes and the
Peloponnesian powers of Sparta and Mantinea. After thirty-three years of
sporadic warfare, Athens and Sparta agreed to peace terms in 371 BCE. The
third member of the truce talks, Thebes, insisted on signing on behalf of all of
Boeotia. This position by the Theban leader, Epaminondas (d. 362 BCE),
caused the negotiations to break down, forcing the Spartans to march into
Boeotia to punish the Thebans. The resulting battle of Leuctra in 371 pitted
the finest Greek heavy infantry armies against one another for regional
supremacy.[73]

The Spartans, commanded by their king Cleombrotus, camped to the south
of the flat plain of Leuctra on a ridge of hills facing the Thebans, who were
also on a ridge across the plain to the north (Map 2.7(a)). Epaminondas

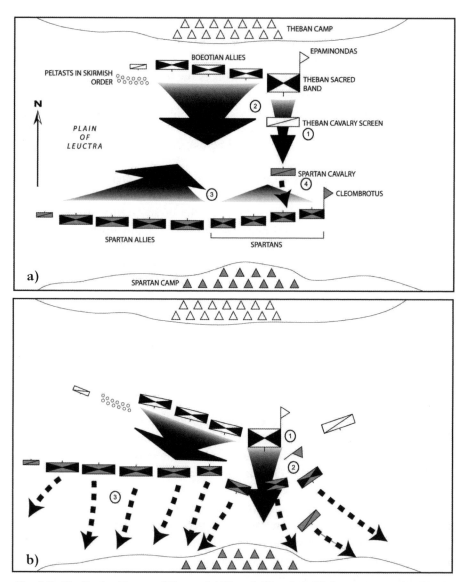

Map 2.7. The Battle of Leuctra, 371 BCE. (a) Phase I: Though the Thebans are outnumbered by the Spartan invaders and their allies, Epaminondas assumes the offensive. The Theban cavalry screening the Sacred Band advances against the Spartan cavalry (1). The Thebans begin a general advance, leading with their heavily weighted left flank (2). The Spartan force begins to advance to meet the Thebans (3) just as their cavalry is swept away by Epaminondas' horsemen (4). (b) Phase II: The Theban left wing, led by the Sacred Band, smashes into the Spartan right (1). King Cleombrotus is killed as the Spartan hoplites are driven from the field (2). Viewing the demise of the Spartans, the allies on the left and centre rout from the field (3).

arranged his 6,500 heavy infantry, 1,000 peltasts and 1,500 cavalry in an oblique formation, weighing his left wing with an extended phalanx at least 50 ranks deep (led by the elite group of homosexual hoplites known as the 'Sacred

Band'), while refusing his right wing.[74] Here the Theban general broke with tradition by placing his best hoplites across from the Spartans instead of on the right wing, the normal place of honour in Greek warfare. Epaminondas was seeking a decisive battle, one that would break the back of Spartan power in the region. The Spartans arranged their 10,000 heavy infantry, 1,000 cavalry and 1,100 light troops in a concave position, placing their hoplites in the traditional line twelve men deep.[75] Although they were heavily outnumbered, Epaminondas spurred his men forward across the plain, using his cavalry to screen his weighted left wing.

On the Theban left wing the cavalry drove back the Spartan horse. While the Theban cavalry prevented outflanking, the heavily reinforced Theban phalanx crashed into the Spartan right wing, driving the invaders back and killing the Spartan king Cleombrotus and perhaps 500 hoplites and light troops (Map 2.7(b)). The Spartan left wing routed before ever seeing action. As many as 300 Thebans were killed. The unorthodox use of a weighted wing gave the outnumbered Thebans a great victory over the best army in Greece. The battle of Leuctra shattered the military prestige of Sparta and ended its chance of establishing hegemony over Greece.

Nine years later, at the battle of Mantinea in 362 BCE, Epaminondas fought a confederation of Greek city-states challenging Theban hegemony in the region. Once again, Epaminondas defeated his enemies using an oblique formation and a left wing weighted with a deep hoplite formation. And once again, heavy infantry proved to be the decisive arm in the battle, crashing through the thin ranks of the enemy's line and precipitating a rout. But Epaminondas' untimely death on the battlefield disheartened the Thebans, who gave up their pursuit of the enemy and lost the initiative. After his death, Theban political fortunes declined, leaving a power vacuum for the rising hegemon of Macedon to exploit.

In the first half of the fourth century BCE, both the Greeks and the Persians made new attempts to apply the lessons learned from their previous battlefield encounters. The introduction of light infantry to Greece during the Peloponnesian War destroyed the dominance of the hoplite, while the diffusion of the articulated heavy infantry phalangeal formation to the Near East gave Persian battle captains another instrument for shock combat. The major difference between the two diffusions lay in how they were applied to warfare in each civilization. Consequently, the art of war in the classical world evolved with the Greeks' elevating it to a science through the introduction of professors of tactics, and later, under Macedonian leadership, the adoption of articulated heavy cavalry and the improvement of the hoplite equipment. The Persians also adopted heavy cavalry but failed to discard the anachronistic chariot. Hence, the Persians created a combined-arms tactical system consisting of heavy and light infantry, and heavy and light cavalry, but their reliance on chariots as a shock component on the battlefield proved to be both foolish and wasteful. When this old model Persian army met the new model army of Alexander the Great in the fourth century BCE, the battle for the largest empire the world had yet known would be won by a Greco-Macedonian force better trained, better motivated and better supplied than their Persian counterparts. The arms race in the Greek world would, ironically, be won by a state not officially within the traditional *polis* system. North of Greece, the kingdom of Macedon would adopt and adapt the Hellenic way of war, adding its own elements to the mix, and creating the most effective combined-arms tactical system ever fielded in the classical world.

Battle captains such as Xenophon and Epaminondas recognized the value of combined arms as a means of bringing a superior tactical system against an inferior one. The integration of light infantry archers and peltasts with heavy infantry hoplite soldiers profoundly affected Greek warfare, giving commanders additional tools to win the day. But the other elements of combined-arms warfare, heavy and light cavalry, had yet to be fully integrated into Greek warfare. With the addition of mounted shock and missile capabilities to the armies of Greece, classical warfare would reach its apogee. After the rise of Macedon, the era of phalanx-versus-phalanx warfare was never to return to the western way of war.

Chapter 3

Warfare in the Hellenistic Era: The Rise of the Macedonian Art of War

The Rise of Macedon and the Development of the Macedonian Art of War

The architect of the first balanced combined-arms tactical system in western civilization was King Philip II of Macedon (*c*.383–336 BCE). Born in the kingdom of Macedon, north of Thessaly, Philip spent three years of his childhood as a hostage in Thebes, where he learned the art of war under Epaminondas. After returning to Macedon, he became regent for his nephew, expanding Macedonian territory at the expense of his immediate neighbours. Made king of Macedon in 356 BCE, Philip used newly acquired gold and silver mines to finance a truly formidable army. He then turned his attention to the Greek city-states weakened by a half-century of internecine warfare.

King Philip's campaigns in Greece eventually gave him control of Thessaly, Thrace and the Bosphorus, and in 346 he gained control of the pass at Thermopylae. In 338 his army invaded Boeotia and defeated the Athenian–Theban forces at the battle of Chaeronea, a battle in which the eighteen-year-old Alexander successfully commanded the right wing of his father's army. Three months later, a congress of Greek states meeting at Corinth accepted Philip as captain-general of Greece and approved his plans for a Macedonian–Greek army to liberate Ionia from Persian rule. After Philip's assassination in 336, Alexander succeeded his father as King Alexander III of Macedon (356–323 BCE), reaffirming Philip's pledge to make war against Persia.

The refinement of the Macedonian art of war began with Philip II, and the army created by him represented a fusion of the best elements of Greek and classical Near Eastern warfare. To what extent Philip was influenced by Persia will probably never be known for certain, but we do have an excellent idea of how Greek tactics and technology affected the Macedonian way of warfare, specifically the use of light and heavy infantry in battle. Light infantry was adopted directly with few modifications in the Macedonian art of war, while heavy infantry would go through a metamorphosis. Under Philip, Macedon's most important original contribution to the Greek combined-arms tactical system, heavy cavalry, would be refined, creating an army utilizing shock and missile formations in effective concert.

Cavalry was always important to Macedon because the geography of the region acted as a crossroads between the horse peoples of the steppe and the more sedentary lifestyle of the Greek peninsula. In order to defend itself from both the steppe nomads of the north and the infantry-based city-states of the south, the kingdom of Macedon developed an aristocracy based on heavy cavalry as its primary means of defence. Heavy cavalry proved to be a happy medium because its mobility gave the Macedonians a means to repel the horse-borne nomads, while its defensive armour provided added protection against the light and heavy infantry from the south. This mounted aristocracy traditionally fought under the king's personal leadership and was called his 'Companions', fighting usually on the right wing, the place of honour in the Greek line of battle. Under Philip II, the Companions were expanded from feudal horsemen to a formidable cavalry arm of 3,300, including some Greeks attracted to the Macedonian court.[1]

The Companions were divided into fourteen squadrons or *ilai* of 200 to 225 men each, with an elite *ile*, the Royal Squadron, comprising 300 horse, which the king led personally.[2] Heavy cavalry units fought in a wedge formation as lancers, carrying long spears known as *sarissas* of cornel wood and a long, single-edged curved sword or *kopis*.[3] The *sarissa* was a lance measuring some 9 feet in length and was, like the Greek thrusting spear, double pointed.[4] Shock combat with lance was still very effective in the classical period, despite the absence of the stirrup and a saddle built up with pommel and cantle for longitudinal support. Given these conditions, the Macedonian heavy cavalryman employed his lance as a thrusting weapon, releasing the shaft immediately before or on impact, else the energy of the collision would unhorse the rider.[5] Still, when used collectively, heavy cavalry formations proved invaluable in breaking up unarticulated infantry units. Philip recognized this and gave the heavy cavalry weapon system a dominant role in the Macedonian art of war.

The primary functions of heavy cavalry remained to precipitate battle or act as a tactical reserve. Because of their tactical mobility, cavalry was often used to probe the enemy's line, searching for weakness that could be exploited. The Companions, organized in a wedge formation, proved particularly effective for riding through gaps in the enemy line. Alexander's biographer Arrian tells us that the Macedonians probably adopted the wedge formation from their contacts with the Scythians, the same fierce Indo-European horse people from the Ukraine who also influenced the development of Assyrian and Persian cavalry. Arrian explains the capabilities of the Macedonian heavy cavalry utilizing the wedge array: 'This formation seems especially useful in that the leaders are arranged in a circle and the front of the wedge converged to a point.

This makes it easy to cut through any enemy formation. It also allows the formation to wheel towards or away from an opponent quickly.'[6]

Sometimes, the Macedonians deployed heavy cavalry as shock troops in the centre of formations or on the wings.[7] A wing deployment was usually in response to an enemy deployment of heavy cavalry on the wings as well. This position in the line could prove to be very advantageous. If heavy cavalry was able to break through the enemy's position, it was then capable of running up the unprotected flank of the deployed infantry, causing a rout and killing many men. Philip, and later Alexander, would also use heavy cavalry as a tactical reserve, sending it into the battle when a tear was perceived in the enemy's line or in order to support a tear in his own.

In addition to heavy cavalry, the Macedonian combined-arms army utilized light cavalry as scouts and flank guards for larger and more valuable units. Light cavalry units were drawn from client kingdoms, so their weapon systems varied. Usually, these units consisted of lightly armoured javelin-throwers from Thessaly and Thrace, but later in the expedition Alexander added horse archers from the Eurasian steppes.[8] The addition of heavy and light cavalry to the Macedonian army gave Philip and Alexander new dimensions in tactical mobility and shock power, but these new dimensions remained contingent on a core infantry being capable of either holding its place in line or advancing in a well-disciplined manner against the enemy. The adoption and improvement of the Greek heavy infantry weapon system by Philip would provide this core.[9]

The Macedonian phalanx represents a syncretistic adoption of the Greek heavy infantry weapon system. Because of the nature of the combined-arms system, the role of Macedonian heavy infantry became highly specialized, creating *phalangites*. With its flank and rear protected by light infantry and heavy and light cavalry, the Macedonian phalanx was free to refine its role as an instrument of the frontal attack. This exclusive role required an evolution in both equipment and tactics, and the Macedonian phalangite's weapons and armour changed to fill this new role.

The major difference between the equipment of a Macedonian phalangite and his Greek predecessor was the length of his thrusting spear and the defensive value of his armour. The Macedonian's spear was, in effect, a longer variation of the cavalry's *sarissa*. The infantry *sarissa* was a pike between 15 and 18 feet in length and weighing 15 pounds. Because of the length and weight of the *sarissa*, the Macedonian heavy infantryman carried a smaller, rimless shield slung over the neck, permitting him to grip the heavy spear with both hands.

In the Macedonian phalanx, each man occupied a space less than 3 feet in width, but when receiving an enemy attack, it closed up still further into *synaspismos* or 'locked shield order', in which each heavy infantryman presented a front equal to the width of his shoulders.[10] The first five ranks extended their *sarissas* beyond the bodies of the men in the first rank, holding their pikes progressively higher in each rank, presenting an impenetrable hedge of *sarissas* to the enemy.[11]

Furthermore, the phalanx itself constituted a highly flexible unit, capable of assuming various formations. It could form a square, extend itself into a rectangular shape with broadside presented to the enemy, or it could become a solid column, capable of being directed either head-on or inclined at an angle against the enemy line. In addition, it could adopt either a wedge or an oblique formation.[12] Each of these formations is testimony to the extraordinary articulation of the Macedonian phalanx, as well as being characteristic of the integrated nature of the army as a whole.

The Macedonian phalanx consisted of two types of heavy infantry phalangites, the *Hypaspists* or 'Shield Bearers', the king's infantry guard 3,000 strong, and the *Pezetairoi* or 'Foot Companions', front-line troops recruited from Macedon.[13] Hypaspists were organized in three 1,000-man battalions, one of which was the elite *Agema*, similar to the Companions' 'Royal Squadron'. Because of their discipline and loyalty, the Hypaspists were often placed between the phalanx and the Companions, entrusted with filling the inevitable gap that appeared when heavy infantry and cavalry operated together in offensive action. The remainder of the phalanx consisted of the Pezetairoi, infantrymen who were organized in battle squares sixteen deep and sixteen wide. This 256-man square, called a *syntagma*, was organized six to a battalion or *taxis*, usually just over 1,500 men strong. The Macedonian army contained twelve *taxeis*.[14]

The Macedonian Logistical System

Philip II of Macedon greatly increased the range and flexibility of the Greek army by adopting features of the Persian model. The Macedonian king made wide use of the horse and camel as beasts of burden; five horses could carry the load of a single ox cart but could move the load at 4 miles an hour for eight hours.[15] Equally important was the ability of the horse to move over all kinds of terrain, and five horses required only half as much forage as a team of two oxen.[16] The ox cart team could move a 1,000 pound load only 10 miles per day, while a horse team could move the same load 32 miles per day at twice the speed and on half the forage. The adoption of the horse as the primary beast of burden greatly enhanced the strategic mobility of the Macedonian army.

Philip also contributed to the science of logistics in an original way. He discontinued the practice of allowing soldiers to take along attendants, wives, concubines and other service providers when they went to war. Under the old system, an army of 30,000 fighting men would have been dragging along behind perhaps 30,000 attendants and service personnel, as well as some 10,000 women. Philip allowed only one porter per four soldiers, and each soldier was required to carry his own arms, armour, personal possessions, and even some of his own food and water.[17] This change increased the combat efficiency and rate of march of the Macedonian army, so that Alexander's army could routinely move 13 miles per day, and separate cavalry units could cover 40 miles per day.[18] These rates of movement were impossible before Philip's reforms.

Efficient logistical trains are an absolute necessity when making war. Men and animals need to be fed and watered, and the hot and dusty climate of the Middle East made the physical maintenance of the soldier's body even more difficult on the march. It has been estimated that in this climate a soldier required 3,402 calories a day and 70 grams of protein to sustain him in minimal nutritional condition.[19] Alexander's army of 65,000 men required 195,000 pounds of grain and 325,000 pounds of water to sustain it for a single day. The army also required 375,000 pounds of forage per day to sustain the cavalry, baggage and transport animals.[20]

Philip's adoption of horses and camels as beasts of burden and exclusion of superfluous camp followers allowed his son to move the men and materiel necessary to conquer the Persian Empire. It should be remembered that Alexander's unprecedented strategic mobility was also made possible by the excellent highway system already in place in the Persian domains. Alexander made use of this highway system when it suited him. Even as far east as the Punjab, the lean Macedonian logistical train never failed to supply the Macedonian army.

The Macedonian Art of War in Practice: The Battles of Granicus, Issus and Gaugamela

In the spring of 334 BCE, Alexander crossed the Hellespont at the head of an army of perhaps 32,000 infantry (12,000 Macedonians), 5,100 cavalry, and 16,000 porters and siege train teamsters. When this army joined with an advance force operating in Anatolia, the entire complement was close to 50,000.[21] Architects, engineers, historians and scientists accompanied the Greco-Macedonian army, a clear indication of Alexander's grand vision and high expectations at the beginning of his campaign (Map 3.1).

Hearing of the invasion, the newly enthroned Persian ruler, Darius III (r. 336–330 BCE), ordered the governors or *satraps* of Anatolia to intercept the young Macedonian king with an army of 40,000 men, including a large contingent of Persian cavalry and some 20,000 Greek mercenary hoplites commanded by the renowned battle captain Memnon of Rhodes. Three days after Alexander's landing in Asia Minor, the two armies caught sight of one another near the shallow Granicus River in north-western Anatolia, near the mouth of the Propontis (Sea of Marmara). Both armies raced for the river, but the Persian cavalry arrived first (Map 3.2(a)). Under the command of Spithridates, the Persians held the opposite bank with perhaps 17,000 cavalry and waited for their allied Greek hoplites to catch up.

As the Greek mercenaries moved forward to buttress the Persian horse, Alexander deployed his army, arraying his Thessalian and Greek heavy cavalry

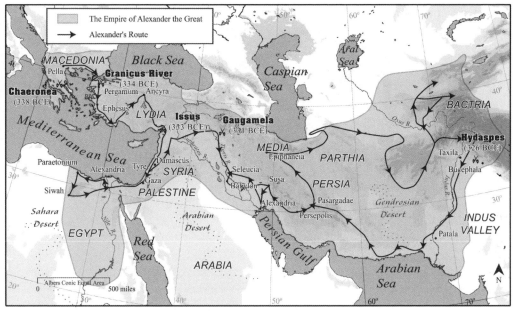

Map 3.1. The Conquests of Alexander the Great.

on the left wing and heavy infantry in the centre. On the right wing, the Macedonian king placed his Hypaspists and one squadron of his Companion heavy cavalry, along with light cavalry and light infantry.[22] Wanting to pre-empt the enemy heavy infantry from entering the battle, Alexander ordered an immediate attack along the entire length of his front. Personally leading his Companions formed in their famous wedge, Alexander charged across the river aiming obliquely at the Persian centre (Map 3.2(b)). As the Macedonian cavalry emerged from the opposite river bank in ever-increasing numbers, the Persian cavalry there broke and fled. A general rout ensued. A second Macedonian cavalry charge mowed down retreating Persian infantry, pinning half of the Greek hoplite mercenaries against a low hill until Macedonian infantry surrounded them (Map 3.2(c)). Deciding to make examples of the Greek traitors, Alexander sent the 2,000 surviving hoplites back to Greece in chains.[23] Alexander's total losses for the entire battle were 150 men.[24]

In heroic fashion, Alexander was wounded in the mêlée, his helmet shattered by an enemy's blow. Saved by the timely intervention of Cleitus the Black, the commander of the Royal Squadron, the young Macedonian king escaped without serious injury.[25] But his bravery endeared him to his troops as a king willing to share in the hardships of combat. Memnon eluded capture at Granicus, escaping to Halicarnassus and later to the island of Chios in the Aegean. Shortly after assuming command of the Great King's Anatolian forces, Memnon fell ill and died attempting to orchestrate a naval counter-offensive against the Greek mainland.

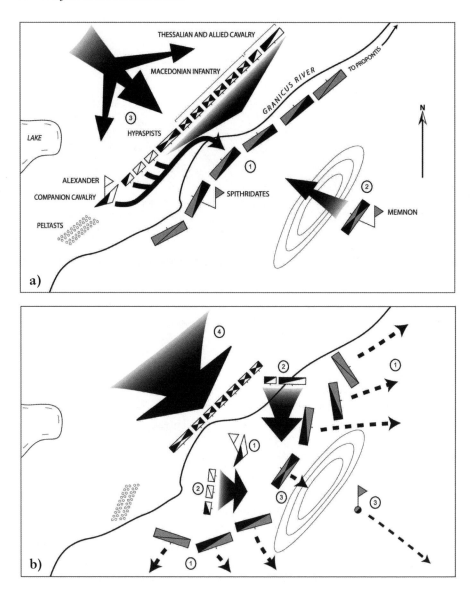

Alexander's use of heavy cavalry as the dominant arm illustrated the decisive nature of a combined-arms tactical system. Although the Persians enjoyed superiority in cavalry and higher ground, Alexander was not afraid to advance on the Persian horse with his entire force, utilizing his infantry in support of his Companion lancers. Here, Macedonian cavalry rebuffed the Persian cavalry on the right wing. The superiority of the heavy Macedonian *sarissa* over the light Persian spear proved decisive. After pushing through, Alexander's cavalry and infantry surrounded and annihilated the Greek mercenary infantry. Alexander won the day because he used an integrated army 'first against a line

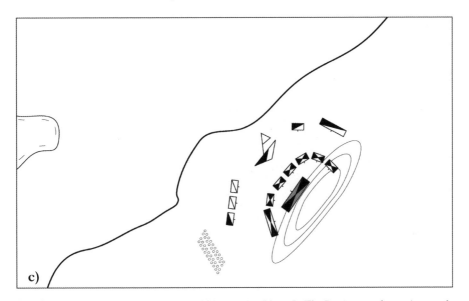

Map 3.2. The Battle of Granicus River, 334 BCE. (a) Phase I: The Persian cavalry arrives at the Granicus before the Macedonian army (1). As Memnon's Greek mercenary infantry attempt to close the gap between themselves and the cavalry (2), Alexander's army deploys (3). (b) Phase II: As the Macedonian cavalry splash across the Granicus, the Persian horse break and begin to rout from the field (1). A second Macedonian cavalry charge pins the Greek mercenary infantry against a rise (2) and their commander, Memnon, flees (3). (c) Phase III: The Macedonian heavy infantry phalanxes advance to surround and destroy Memnon's force. Two thousand of the mercenaries survive the action, only to be sent back to Greece in chains as an example to any other would-be traitors.

of Persian cavalry unsupported by infantry, and then against a line of infantry unsupported by cavalry'.[26]

After defeating the Persian army at Granicus River, Alexander marched south along the Ionian coast and freed the Greek city-states in western Asia Minor as promised by his father before his death. His lines of communication secure, Alexander led his army across Anatolia and through the Cilician Gates, starting down the Syrian coast. When he learned that the Great King and a Persian army of perhaps 100,000 troops and 20,000 cavalry were marching across his rear, he countermarched in order to deal with the threat to his communications.[27]

In November 333 Alexander encountered Darius' army standing firm behind the Pinarus River, next to the Gulf of Issus (Map 3.3(a)). The narrow distance between the gulf and the mountains favoured the Macedonians because it restricted the amount of troops Darius could array against Alexander. But even along this narrow front, the Persians placed 80,000 infantry (including perhaps 10,000 Greek hoplite mercenaries) and 20,000 cavalry and chariots against the Macedonian's 24,000 infantry and 5,000 cavalry.[28]

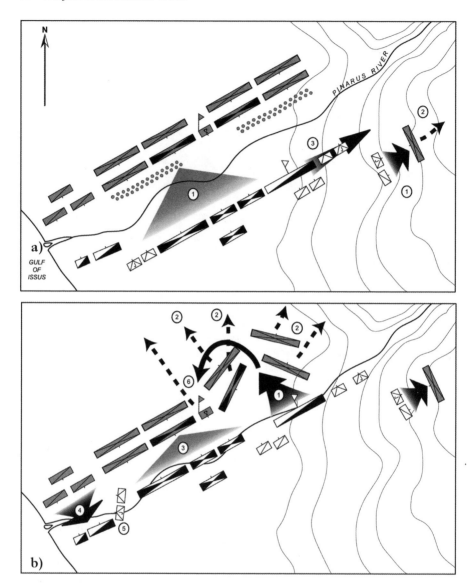

The battle of Issus conformed to the pattern of many ancient battles. Skirmishers protected both armies as the infantry and cavalry formed. On the north side of the river, the Great King's Greek mercenary hoplites and heavy troops were placed in the centre along the high bank. His cavalry held the wings, with the right wing more heavily weighted since the steep grade of the mountains provided little room for deployment on the left. Using his superiority in cavalry, Darius hoped to break through on his right wing and run Alexander's flank. Understanding his opponent's strategy, Alexander placed a small covering force of cavalry and light infantry on his right to defend against

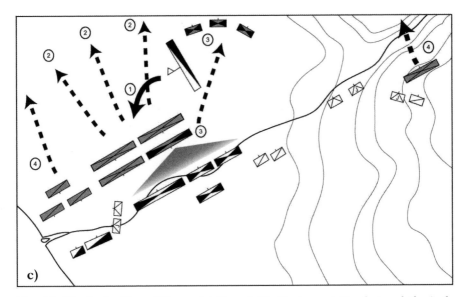

c)

Map 3.3. The Battle of Issus, 333 BCE. (a) Phase I: The Persians and Macedonians deploy in the narrow plain between the Gulf of Issus and an inland hill mass, their forces divided by the Pinarus River. Alexander takes the initiative, ordering a general advance against the Persians across the river as well as those on his right flank on the hill (1). The Persian contingent on the Macedonians' right is pushed back (2), forcing Alexander to shift slightly to cover the gap (3). (b) Phase II: Alexander secures his army's right flank and launches his Companion cavalry against the Persian left (1). Their flanks turned by the attack, the Persian infantry begin to rout (2). As the Macedonian phalanxes continue to press against the Persian and Greek mercenary infantry in the centre (3), Darius' cavalry attempts to turn Alexander's left flank (4). With the assistance of some light infantry, the Macedonian cavalry hold fast (5). Alexander and his Companions execute a turn into the rear of the Persian centre, engaging Darius and his chariot force. The Persian king and his chariot bodyguard flee the field (6). (c) Phase III: Having driven Darius from the field, Alexander wheels his Companion cavalry into the flank and rear of the Persians' main position (1). Trapped between the Macedonian phalanxes pressing forward from the Pinarus and Alexander's heavy cavalry, the Persian levies break and flee (2). The Greek mercenary infantry manage to extricate themselves, but suffer heavy losses (3). Seeing their king flee the field, and viewing the destruction visited on their comrades in the main line, the Persian flank units join the rout (4).

a mountainside attack, then shifted the majority of his cavalry to reinforce his left wing. With his heavy infantry holding the centre, Alexander took the initiative and marched forward toward the Persian line.

The order of battle pitted cavalry versus cavalry on the gulf side, infantry versus infantry in the centre and, because of the extended frontage of the Persian forces, Macedonian cavalry and light troops against Persian infantry near the slopes of the mountain. As the Macedonian phalanxes engaged the Persians at the river, Alexander's light troops pushed back the Persians on the hill, forcing the Macedonian king to edge right to protect the wing. With his right wing protected, Alexander and his Companion heavy cavalry pushed forward and outflanked the Persian infantry, causing a rout (Map 3.3(b)). While

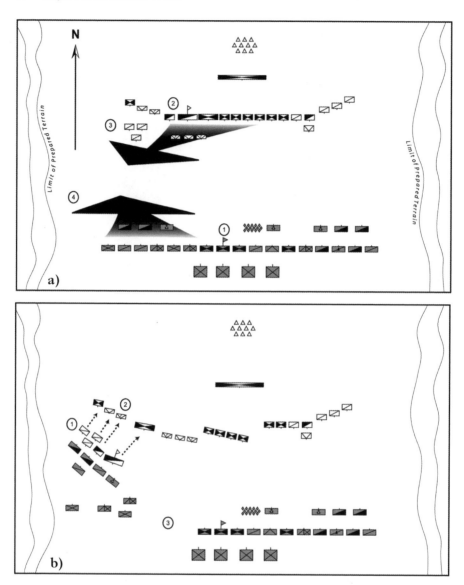

Map 3.4. The Battle of Gaugamela, 331 BCE. (a) Phase I: Darius (1) arrays his cavalry-heavy force on the carefully prepared battle plain. The Macedonian forces deploy in a roughly rhomboid-shaped formation, Alexander and his Companion cavalry taking up station at the hinge between the infantry in the centre and the right wing of the formation (2). Alexander approaches the Persian line obliquely, aiming for the enemy's left flank (3). Darius responds by shifting troops in the same direction (4). (b) Phase II: The weight of the Persians' cavalry and chariot attack on the Macedonian right presses Alexander's cavalry line back into a refused flank (1). This flank is buttressed by Macedonian infantry which stands fast against the Persian attack (2). Gaps begin to open in the Persian line as other units move to the assistance of the cavalry and chariots (3). (c) Phase III: Seizing advantage

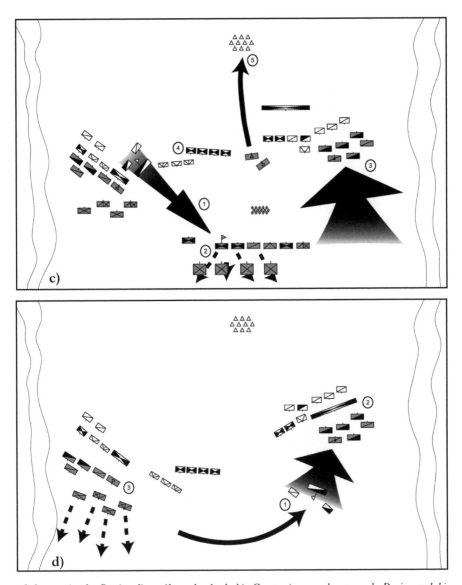

of the gap in the Persian line, Alexander leads his Companion cavalry towards Darius and his bodyguard (1). Darius panics and flees the field, and the now leaderless Persian centre begins to disintegrate (2). Heavily engaged with the Macedonian left, the Persians' right-flank units fail to realize their king has deserted them (3). As the Macedonian infantry moves to Alexander's assistance (4), Persian chariots attack through the gap into the baggage train (5), but are destroyed by the attendants. (d) Phase IV: Rather than pursue the fleeing Darius, Alexander sweeps across the battlefield to strike the rear of the Persian forces engaging the Macedonian left flank (1). The Persians, caught in a hammer-and-anvil manoeuvre, are crushed (2). The remainder of the Persian forces depart the field (3), leaving thousands of their comrades dead or dying behind them.

heavy infantry in the centre clashed, Darius' cavalry on the weighted right wing pushed the outnumbered Macedonian cavalry back, but the wing held when Macedonian light infantry reinforced the failing cavalry.

After routing the Persian infantry, Alexander swung left and engaged the Great King's chariots. A bitter battle ensued and Alexander was wounded in the thigh. Believing the Macedonians were gaining the upper hand, Darius fled the field. As the chariots left the battlefield, Alexander's Companions wheeled into the flank and rear of the enemy heavy infantry, pinning thousands of Persian infantry and mercenary Greek hoplites between phalanx and lancer in a classic 'hammer and anvil' manoeuvre (Map 3.3(c)).[29] With the Great King fleeing, the Persian right lost its will to fight, broke and ran. The Greek mercenaries managed to extricate themselves, but suffered heavy losses. In his haste to leave the battlefield and the area, Darius abandoned his mother, wife and children, as well as an extensive baggage train. Now Alexander had royal hostages for political leverage and a royal treasury to finance future campaigns.[30]

After the victory at Issus, Alexander marched south into Syria and Lebanon, liberating cities and capturing Persian naval bases along the way. When the city of Tyre refused to yield to Alexander in 332, the Macedonian king spent a year reducing the offshore fortress, constructing a mole half a mile long and conducting a tenacious siege until the city fell.[31] Alexander next freed Egypt from the Persian yoke. By the winter of 332 Syria, Palestine and Egypt were under Macedonian domination. Recognizing the threat Alexander posed to his reign, Darius offered to give the Macedonian king all of the territory west of the Euphrates River. Alexander refused the peace offering, then marched into Mesopotamia in search of a final battle with Darius.[32] As Alexander marched down the Tigris River, Darius moved to intercept his army of 47,000 men (40,000 infantry and 7,000 cavalry) with an army of between 75,000 and 250,000 men.[33] The two armies met on the plain of Gaugamela. On 1 October 331 Alexander faced the Great King in the largest battle of his military career.

Reconnaissance the night before revealed to Alexander Darius' order of battle and probable strategy (Map 3.4(a)). The Great King had formed up his cavalry-based army on the level plain of Gaugamela, removing all obstacles on the terrain so that his scythed chariots would have full use of the field.[34] In order to mitigate the threat of the war chariots and the manoeuvrability of Persian cavalry, Alexander arranged his troops in a rhomboid, placing his Hypaspists and heavy infantry in the centre, while positioning more heavy infantry on the right wing and cavalry on the left wing.[35] Alexander and his Companions held the hinge between the infantry centre and infantry right wing. Facing an enemy army that outnumbered his own perhaps three to one, Alexander massed his army against the Persian centre, planning to strike the enemy line where the banners of the Immortals suggested Darius was located and before the wings of the Persian army could engulf his own.

Personally leading a squadron of Companions at the hinge, Alexander and his army approached the enemy line obliquely left to right, compelling the more numerous and extensive Persian line to shift in the same direction in order to outreach the Macedonian flank. But the continuous shifting pulled the Persian army from the prearranged battlefield and away from level ground, forcing Darius to seize the initiative, sending his chariots and cavalry against the right of Alexander's line. The violence of the attack bent the line back into a refused flank (Map 3.4(b)). But Alexander's heavy infantry held, absorbing the Persian charge. When the majority of the Persian army advanced to the aid of the chariots, gaps appeared in the Persian line.

Seeing an opportunity to breach the Persian line and attack Darius, Alexander personally led his Companions through the gap and towards the Persian royal bodyguard (Map 3.4(c)). Once again, Darius panicked and fled the battlefield. But Alexander, instead of pursuing the Great King, swung his right wing into the flank of the advancing Persian line, crushing the enemy between the hammer of his wheeling cavalry squadrons and the anvil of his heavy infantry (Map 3.4(d)).[36] Although some of the chariots passed through the Macedonian phalanxes and attacked Alexander's baggage train, the damage was limited and the Persians were killed by armed attendants. By battle's end, thousands of Persians lay dead or dying, while Alexander's losses were only a few hundred men.[37]

The Great King lost more than a battle and an army at Gaugamela. Darius' inability to defeat a numerically inferior army at both Issus and Gaugamela eroded his prestige, and his own nobles assassinated him in 330.[38] Alexander encountered little resistance as he conquered Mesopotamia and western Iran. After entering the Persian capital at Persepolis in January 330, Alexander assumed the title of Great King, then set out to subdue the rebelling regions of his new Greco-Persian empire. Alexander's subsequent campaigns to extend Greek hegemony to Parthia, Bactria and Sogdiana were some of the most difficult of his career. Between 329 and 327 Alexander was engaged in almost constant warfare against mountain tribesmen in these remote areas, modifying his Macedonian troops to use lighter equipment or employing indigenous light infantry to deal with the guerrillas on their own terms.[39]

Alexander in India: The Battle of Hydaspes
Alexander subdued the rebelling eastern satrapies of his infant Greco-Persian empire between 329 and 327. By the spring of 326 he had crossed the Hindu Kush and entered the Punjab region of north-west India and seized the city of Taxila, the largest city between the Indus and Hydaspes rivers. Alexander's invading army was composed of over 20,000 infantry supported by 8,000 Greco–Macedonian cavalry and 1,000 Iranian horse archers. Opposing the Macedonian invasion was the Indian King Porus and his Indian army of perhaps as many as 30,000 infantry, 4,000 cavalry, 420 chariots and 200 war

elephants.[40] Having marched up to the banks of the Hydaspes, Alexander ordered his men to build an elaborate camp in an effort to convince his enemy that he was going to wait until the passing of the rainy season before crossing the river (Map 3.5(a)). As expected, Porus set up his main camp across the river opposite Alexander.

But the Macedonian king had no intention of waiting to cross the river. In preparation for his attack, Alexander ordered his ships brought to him in sections and reassembled, then commanded his soldiers to stuff water bags and tent skins with straw to make rafts. Next, for several consecutive nights, he ordered his cavalry to reconnoitre the riverbank as if searching for a suitable ford. Porus shadowed his movements from the opposite bank, then realized the invaders had no real intention of crossing the river. Maintaining a strong screening force all along his side of the river, Porus decided to remain in the main camp. Alexander would use his enemy's complacency against him in an audacious turning movement upriver.[41]

Organizing his army into three components, Alexander left a holding force of 8,000 infantry and 3,000 cavalry at his camp, then moved a turning force of 4,000 Macedonian heavy cavalry, 1,000 Iranian light cavalry horse archers, 10,000 infantry (including 3,000 *Hypaspists*, 3,100 phalangites, 2,000 foot archers and 1,000 javelineers). Supporting Alexander's turning force was a reserve of 1,000 cavalry and 5,000 infantry. Alexander chose a crossing point a full day's march upstream from his camp, a distance of 18 miles. River crossings are inherently dangerous in warfare. If Porus challenged the crossing and Alexander was caught in mid-stream, he risked being annihilated. After handpicking the crossing site himself, Alexander ordered his troops across the Hydaspes. Transporting 5,000 horses and 10,000 men took the entire night, with a violent rainstorm concealing the noise of the crossing. By morning, the army had successfully crossed to the east bank, but the endeavour did not go unnoticed. Porus' scouts sent word to their commander that the invaders were crossing the river and preparing to move toward the Indian king's camp.

Porus faced a difficult situation. Was the crossing a feint to draw his army away from his main camp so that the Macedonian holding force could ford the river and attack his rear? But if Alexander's crossing was in force, then Porus had to redeploy in the direction of the advance to meet the attack, thereby making himself vulnerable to an attack by the holding force opposite his main camp. Either way, the Indian prince faced a dangerous opponent who could now use exterior lines against him. Porus decided to remain in place, and ordered his son to lead a force of 2,000 cavalry and 120 chariots to challenge the crossing upriver.[42]

After fording the river unchallenged, Alexander commanded his phalanx to form up and follow in formation, then took the cavalry and advanced at speed. When the Indian reaction force came into view, Alexander ordered his Iranian light cavalry horse archers to attack and fix the enemy in position, then followed up with successive heavy cavalry charges, driving the Indians from the field (Map 3.5(b)). Four hundred enemy cavalrymen were killed, including Porus' son, and the Macedonians succeeded in capturing all of the Indian chariots. Recognizing the main body of the invading army was now on his side of the river, Porus redeployed his army to the north to meet the advancing forces. He then ordered his men to march upriver, leaving a strong rearguard facing the riverbank to protect his flank. Stopping on ground favourable to his cavalry, the Indian king waited for Alexander's approach.

Alexander's cavalry reached Porus' position well before his infantry who lagged some 2½ miles behind. Using his almost three-to-one advantage in cavalry as a screen, Alexander waited for his infantry to reach the battlefield and form up in phalanxes (Map 3.5(c)). Once his infantry deployed, Alexander shifted the majority of his cavalry squadrons (4,000 men) to his right wing, keeping a small detachment of horse (about 1,000 men) on the left to move against the Indian right cavalry.

Map 3.5. The Battle of Hydaspes, 326 BCE. (a) Phase I: From their camp, Alexander's cavalry reconnoitre the riverbank as though searching for a ford (1), eliciting corresponding reactive moves from Porus (2). Phase II: Under cover of darkness, Alexander leaves a holding force in camp, moves a smaller reserve to an intermediate crossing point (3), and crosses his main striking force during a violent storm (4). Porus sends his son with a mixed cavalry/chariot force to ascertain the extent of the threat (5), and the Macedonian cavalry press ahead to meet them (6). (b) Phase III: The Indian force is pinned by Alexander's Iranian horse archers (1) and subsequently destroyed by successive Macedonian heavy cavalry charges (2). The Indians lose heavily, the few survivors fleeing from the field (3). Porus' son is killed in the attack and all of the Indian chariots are captured. Porus' main force begins to move towards Alexander (off map, west of action). (c) Phase IV: Alexander's cavalry screen the slower-moving Macedonian infantry, allowing them to close with Porus' army (1). Once his infantry deploy, Alexander shifts the bulk of his cavalry to his right and leaves a smaller mounted contingent on the left (2). (d) Phase V: Alexander's mounted archers attack the Indians' left-flank

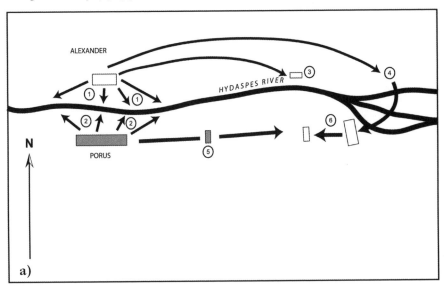

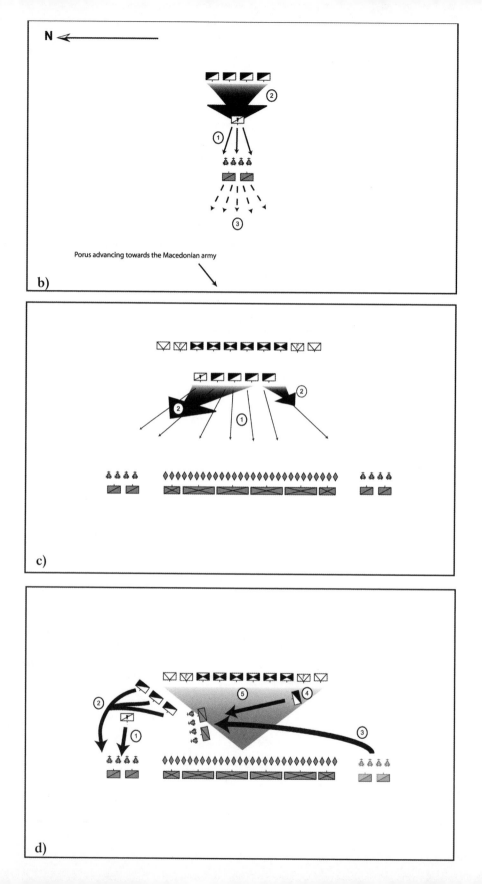

Porus advancing towards the Macedonian army

b)

c)

d)

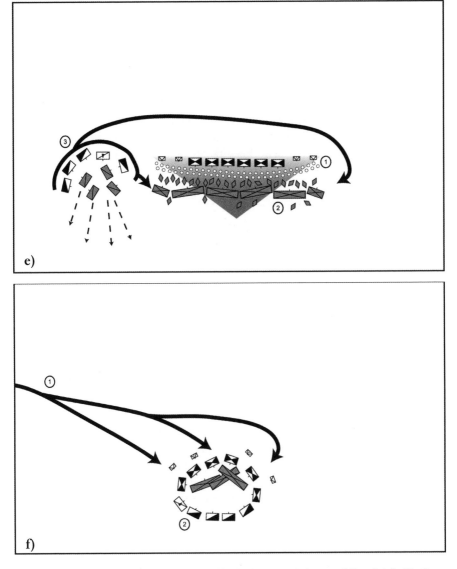

e)

f)

cavalry and chariots (1) while the heavy cavalry begins an encirclement of Porus' left (2). Porus reacts by ordering his right-flank mounted forces to reinforce the threatened flank (3). Alexander's left-flank cavalry squadrons attack these elements as they pass between the lines of opposing infantry (4). As the cavalry battle develops in the Macedonians' favour, Alexander orders his infantry forward in a general attack (5). (e) Phase VI: Porus' elephants are prevented from engaging the Macedonian cavalry as Alexander's infantry, preceded by a cloud of light infantry skirmishers, press the attack (1). As the Macedonian phalanx advances, the Indian formation loses cohesion as wounded elephants begin to seek avenues of escape (2). Having driven the Indian horse from the field, Alexander orders his cavalry to assist in the encirclement of the compressed mass of Indian survivors (3). (f) Phase VII: The slaughter continues for eight hours. Macedonian reinforcements arrive from their intermediate position on the far side of the river (1). Fugitives attempting to flee through the close-knit ranks of Macedonian foot soldiers are cut down by the cavalry cordon (2). Porus is wounded and later captured, and his army is destroyed.

Watching from atop an elephant on his own left flank, Porus surveyed the deployment of his army. Two hundred elephants were lined up some 50 feet apart in front of the 20,000 Indian infantry. On each wing, Porus placed 1,000 cavalry, screened by a chariot squadron 150 machines strong.[43] The Indian front would have extended slightly over 2 miles long, while Alexander's front would have been less than half that, with his infantry deployed eight men deep.[44]

Taking the offensive, Alexander first ordered his 1,000 mounted archers from his right to attack the chariots and cavalry on the Indian left, disrupting them with long-range missile fire (Map 3.5(d)). With 2,000 of his heavy cavalry in column formation, Alexander moved forward in an encircling and flanking manoeuvre against the Indian left in an attempt to draw the Indian cavalry away from its infantry support.[45] The feint worked. Porus reacted by shifting his right cavalry over, in front of his infantry line, to reinforce his left wing. But when the Indian cavalry crossed between the two opposing infantry formations, it was attacked in the rear by the cavalry squadrons on Alexander's left wing.[46]

Alexander now ordered a general attack. As the opposing cavalry engaged, the Macedonian infantry marched forward to prevent Porus from deploying his elephants against Alexander's cavalry (Map 3.5(e)). Here, according to Arrian, Macedonian light infantry was used to great effect against the pachyderms,

> shooting down the drivers and pouring in a hail of missiles from every side upon the elephants themselves. It was a bit of odd work – quite unlike any previous battle; the monster elephants plunged this way and that among the lines of infantry, dealing destruction in the solid mass of Macedonian phalanx, while the Indian horsemen, seeing the infantry at one another's throats, wheeled to the assault of the Macedonian cavalry.[47]

While the Macedonian phalanx held the elephants at bay with their long *sarissas*, special detachments of swordsmen waded into the Indian ranks to hamstring the pachyderms as archers and peltasts attacked the animals and their handlers from a distance. Slowly, the phalanx advanced, and Porus' elephants, cavalry and infantry were compressed by the Macedonian infantry into a tangled mass of bodies and beasts.

Alexander then ordered his cavalry to encircle the mass and his infantry to close ranks even further by locking shields, compressing the Indian units tighter. After a co-ordinated attack by heavy infantry, the immobile Indian cavalry were impaled on the shafts of the *sarissas*. Those who escaped the infantry cordon were run down by the ring of Macedonian cavalry. For eight hours the killing continued, with fresh Macedonian troops from the holding force entering the fray late in the battle (Map 3.5(f)). Porus was wounded and later captured. When the battle was over, the Indians had lost 12,000 killed, with 9,000 taken prisoner. Eighty elephants were captured, and all of the

Indian chariots were destroyed. Macedonian losses were 230 cavalry and 700 infantry.[48]

The battle of Hydaspes River was the last major campaign of Alexander's career. With the Punjab region a tributary state, Alexander turned his focus on India, only to be persuaded by his mutinous men to return to Persia. Taking his men down the Indus River to the Indian Ocean, Alexander split the army, sending half his men home by sea, then marched home with the remaining men overland back to Mesopotamia. In 323 Alexander fell sick with malaria and died in Babylon just short of his thirty-third birthday.[49] In his wake he left a new civilization, the Hellenistic, a fusion of eastern and western ideas and cultures. Fittingly, it was a civilization won on the battlefield with a tactical system derived from centuries of martial interaction between two of Macedon's vanquished foes, the Greeks and the Persians.

As revealed by his actions, Alexander's strategic plan called for defeating the Persian army in Anatolia, freeing the Greek city-states in Asia and neutralizing the superior Persian fleet by seizing its bases on the littoral of the eastern Mediterranean, and finally striking at the heart of the Great King's power in Mesopotamia and Persia. As part of his strategy, Alexander offered alliances to cities in his path that deserted the Persians, while taking extra time to reduce any city which remained loyal. His year-long siege of Tyre in 332 is testimony to his unwillingness to leave bastions of enemy support in his wake. He also pursued a policy of founding colonies to relieve Greek population pressures and ensure loyalty to the Macedonian king when his army left the region. His strategies worked. Between 334 and 323 Alexander the Great marched his army some 17,000 miles from Greece to north-west India, defeating one Indian and three Persian armies, and winning an empire.[50]

The Macedonian combined-arms tactical system at war represents the apex of organized violence in the classical world. As we have seen, light infantry skirmishers probed the enemy's lines seeking and often creating tears or gaps. The main instrument of exploiting this weakness was the Companion heavy cavalry, with the attack being made either against the centre or on the flanks. The phalanx barred the enemy's advance in the centre while the light cavalry guarded the phalanx itself from being outflanked. However, this general pattern left room for flexibility. The timing of the attack, which could easily convert a defensive action into an offensive action, was extremely important, and in this respect Alexander's judgement proved unerring.

Trends in Hellenistic Warfare

The reign of Alexander the Great ushered in the Hellenistic period (338–30 BCE), a period where Greek hegemony stretched from southern Italy to the Indus River valley. But an attempt to create a system of joint rule by Alexander's weak-minded half-brother and infant son under a regency of the most important Macedonian generals failed, and soon these military leaders were engaged in a struggle for power. After the battle of Ipsus in 301, any hope of unity was dead, and eventually four Hellenistic kingdoms emerged as the successors to Alexander: Macedon under the Antigonid dynasty, Syria and the Near East under the Seleucids, the Attalid kingdom of Pergamum, and Egypt under the Ptolemies (Map 3.6). During the next three centuries, no single Hellenistic kingdom was capable of dominating the others, leading to a pattern of shifting alliances and endemic warfare, one where mercenaries increasingly played a prominent role.

Except for a small cadre of Macedonians united with their leaders by a tie of common nationality, the armies of Alexander's successors depended mainly on mercenaries. These 'mixed' Hellenistic armies consisted of Macedonians, Greeks, natives and cash- or land-based mercenaries, changing the very character of Greek warfare. Hellenistic monarchies now had the ability to raise armies whose numbers would have been unthinkable during the Hellenic period.[51] For example, while Alexander normally fought with an army of about 40,000 infantry and 5,000–6,000 cavalry, by the late third century BCE the largest of the successor states, the Seleucids and the Ptolemies, could each put roughly between 70,000 and 80,000 men in the field. Hellenistic armies from Europe remained smaller, with the Macedonian kingdom typically fielding between 25,000 and 35,000 men.[52]

Loyal to individual Greek commanders and the war treasure their leadership could provide, mercenaries lived and fought together for years at a time, accumulating a life's work of looting in a 'soldier's laager' or personal wagon.

Map 3.6. The Hellenistic Successor States.

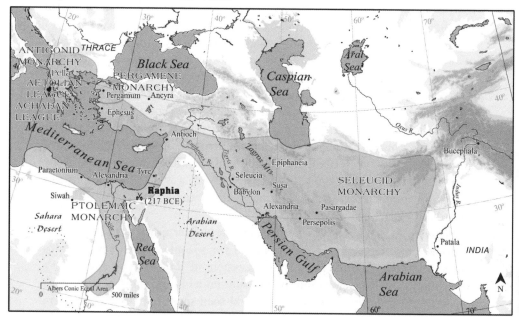

Gone were the days of Philip II's lean logistical train; now a mercenary soldier brought with him wives, children and retainers, and fought as much to add to his personal wagon as to protect it from the enemy.[53] And as a mercenary became attached to his baggage train, he lost all other allegiances. This preoccupation with plunder meant that the typical mercenary had little incentive to follow up a victory or pursue fugitives. In fact, it was not in the mercenary's interest to eliminate the opposing forces completely, for to do so would be to deprive himself of possible future employment, and therefore of a living.[54]

Moreover, under the Hellenistic successors it became a regular custom for a victorious general to enlist all of the soldiers taken prisoner and use them, even against their former employers. This practice and the frequency by which mercenaries could be persuaded to desert as a group made it prudent for a general to earn a reputation for being lenient to his prisoners and generous to his followers.[55] These facts help to explain why the wars fought between the Hellenistic monarchies were usually inconclusive.

Tactically, Hellenistic warfare benefited from advancements in organization and technology developed during the previous three centuries. The Hellenic period (*c*.500–336 BCE) began with the Greek *poleis* utilizing the heavy infantry phalanx as their primary weapon system.[56] At the battle of Marathon in 490 BCE, the Greek battle square attacked en masse in a solid line six to eight ranks deep, without the assistance of cavalry or light troops. Here, the extraordinary violence of the hoplites' shock attack was sufficient to push the enemy from the field. But in the late fifth century BCE, the addition of horsemen and light infantry granted an army more tactical flexibility. The cavalry, usually stationed on the heavy infantry's wings, protected the vulnerable flanks of the phalanx, while light infantry peltasts and archers employed their javelins and bows to screen the hoplites from enemy arrows, stones and javelins, then withdrew through their heavier counterparts' ranks when shock combat ensued. Sometimes, as at the battle of Sphacteria in 425 BCE, light troops alone could carry the day.

In the fourth century BCE, the Greeks developed a combined-arms tactical synthesis. The battles of Leuctra in 371 and Mantinea in 362 exemplified the tactical advances of the Theban army under the leadership of Epaminondas. Using an oblique attack, one wing of the Theban phalanx was 'weighted' to as much as fifty ranks and used to deliver the primary attack, while the other wing was refused and the enemy line pinned down by light troops and cavalry units.

Under Philip and Alexander of Macedon, Greek warfare reached its highest manifestation as a combined-arms tactical system. With light troops protecting their heavier counterparts and harassing the enemy line, the entire phalanx was doubled from eight to sixteen ranks deep, and now employed a lengthened pike or *sarissa*. But instead of using the phalanx as the main shock component, the Macedonians favoured using the deepened phalanx as an 'anvil' to their heavy cavalry's 'hammer', penetrating the enemy's line with a cavalry charge which swung into the enemy's rear while the phalanx engaged frontally either in a line, as at Issus in 333, or obliquely, as at Gaugamela in 331.

Warfare during the Hellenistic period (338–30 BCE) utilized all of the tactical developments of the time: the echeloned attack, heavy cavalry delivering the primary assault, light cavalry protecting heavy cavalry, and light troops screening and skirmishing.[57] But the Hellenistic empires added a new tactical element, the elephant. The pachyderm, first seen in combat by the Macedonians at Gaugamela in 331 and Hydaspes in 326, was later used by Alexander's successors to discourage enemy cavalry and disrupt enemy infantry lines.

War elephants provided Hellenistic generals with a new weapon system, one that fused shock and missile elements. The turret mounted on the animal's back was normally manned by a crew of three: a driver, a pikeman for shock combat, and an archer or javelineer for missile fire. Although it was slow and vulnerable to enemy missile attack, the war elephant's main advantages in combat were its size and the terror it inspired in troops and enemy horses unused to fighting it. Moreover, war elephants were sometimes used as living siege engines, forcing the entrance to cities.[58] Normally, Indian elephants were used for warfare, though in the late Hellenistic period smaller African forest elephants fought for the Ptolemies in Egypt and for Carthage.[59]

On the battlefield, war elephants were placed in the forward ranks of the formation and spaced 50 to 150 feet apart to discourage enemy cavalry charges, because horses that were not trained around elephants were frightened of their size and sound. But using elephants in a combat setting was also fraught with danger. If struck by too many arrows or javelins, an elephant might become uncontrollable and stampede through its own ranks. In order to protect the pachyderm cavalry, later successor generals added a permanent detachment of light troops (usually archers) and dressed the elephant in leather or metal barding to protect it from missiles and hamstringing.[60]

As war elephants became more common in warfare, special anti-elephant devices were adopted by their foes. The most common defence was planting the ground with sharpened spikes, thereby targeting the animal's soft foot tissue. Wounded in this manner, a war elephant was nearly impossible to control and often trampled its own troops. But perhaps the most effective means of defeating war elephants were other war elephants. This strategy can be seen at the battle of Raphia in 217 BCE, where Antiochus III's Indian war elephants did battle with Ptolemy IV's African elephants.

When Antiochus III took the throne of the Seleucid Empire in 233 BCE, he inherited little more than the capital of Antioch. The rise of the Kingdom of Parthia in the east robbed the Seleucid dynasty of most of its eastern possessions, while four decades of warfare with the Ptolemaic dynasty in Egypt gradually whittled away the western part of the empire. Determined to rebuild his inheritance, Antiochus marched south from his base in Syria, meeting Ptolemy IV at Raphia on the Palestine–Egyptian frontier.

Antiochus came to the battlefield with a massive mixed army of over 62,000 Syrian and mercenary infantry, 6,000 cavalry and 102 Indian war elephants, recruited in his remaining eastern province of Bactria (Map 3.7(a)).[61] He arrayed his 44,500 heavy infantry in the centre, then deployed his 6,000 heavy cavalry and nearly 19,000 light infantry on the wings. In front of his wings, Antiochus placed his war elephants protected by light infantry archers. Antiochus commanded the right cavalry wing himself.[62]

Ptolemy met Antiochus with a numerically inferior but still substantial army consisting of over 45,000 infantry, 4,000 cavalry and some 73 African war elephants. Ptolemy possessed superior numbers of heavy infantry and ordered his well-armoured troops to form up in the centre, then placed his Greek mercenary hoplites and heavy cavalry on the right wing. He then buttressed his left wing with 3,000 light infantry and his Royal Guard. Like Antiochus, Ptolemy personally commanded his Royal Guard cavalry on the left wing and, like the Seleucid monarch, ordered his own war elephants and their bowmen guards forward to protect his own wings from enemy cavalry and elephant charges.

The battle of Raphia began when Antiochus ordered his Indian war elephants on his right wing to charge, forcing the opposing African elephants back and disrupting Ptolemy's guard cavalry and infantry. Antiochus followed up with a Syrian cavalry and infantry charge behind his attacking elephants, defeating the Egyptian king's peltasts and royal troops, and pursuing the retreating Ptolemaic forces from the field. In the confusion, Ptolemy successfully escaped and took cover behind his phalanx in the centre.

On the Egyptian right, the smaller African war elephants refused to charge the opposing Indian pachyderms, but 8,000 of Ptolemy's Greek hoplite mercenaries counter-attacked the Seleucid left while his Greek heavy cavalry evaded the elephants and attacked the Seleucid left flank (Map 3.7(b)). Caught between the advancing Greek heavy infantry and flanking Greek heavy cavalry, the Syrian left broke. In the centre, the two heavy infantry phalanxes closed. But here, Ptolemy's slight advantage in numbers carried the day and the Syrians were pushed back. Antiochus returned to the battlefield to find his forces in full retreat. His losses were 10,000 infantry, 300 horse and 15 elephants. Ptolemy's casualties amounted to 1,500 infantry, 700 horse and 16 elephants.[63]

The battle of Raphia illustrates the virtues and vices of using elephants in combat. Antiochus' war elephants proved decisive on his right, pushing the opposing pachyderms back into their own troops and setting up the successful follow-on attack by Syrian cavalry and infantry. But on Ptolemy's right, the refusal of his smaller African forest elephants to charge forward against their larger Indian cousins proved how fickle war elephants could be in combat.

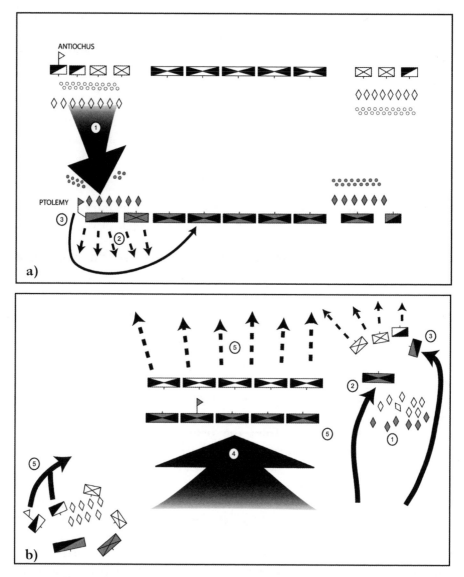

Map 3.7. The Battle of Raphia, 217 BCE. (a) Phase I: The two armies deploy in similar fashion with heavy-infantry centres flanked by combined army wings, screened by elephants and archers. Antiochus opens the battle, ordering his elephants forward against Ptolemy's left (1). The charge forces Ptolemy's elephants back, disrupting his guard cavalry and light infantry (2). Ptolemy escapes to lead his heavy infantry phalanx in the centre (3). (b) Phase II: The Egyptian army's smaller African elephants refuse to charge Antiochus' Indian pachyderms (1). Ptolemy's Greek mercenary infantry attack Antiochus' left (2) at the same time that the Egyptian right-flank cavalry evade the elephants to strike the flank (3), driving the left wing from the field. The Egyptian phalanx closes with its opposite number (4), and Antiochus returns from his pursuit of the Egyptian left wing to find his army in full retreat (5).

The Sumerian war chariot was the earliest example of chariot in western civilization. It was either of the two- or four-wheeled variety and was pulled by a team of onagers. It was heavy and unstable at speed, but was an excellent weapon against enemy infantry formations. As the chariot scattered enemy infantry, soldiers in the chariot's basket finished off the footmen with javelins and axes.

Sargon I ('the Great') was western civilization's first emperor. He created an empire in Mesopotamia that stretched from the Persian Gulf to the Mediterranean Sea. During his fifty-year rule the Akkadian ruler fought thirty-four military campaigns, inspiring generations of Near Eastern rulers to emulate his accomplishment. During the Sargonid period (c.2340-c.2100 BCE) the Akkadians contributed a major innovation in weaponry, the composite bow, which would transform the killing power of archery.

Warrior-pharaoh Ramesses II was one of New Kingdom Egypt's greatest rulers and military commanders. He ruled an empire that stretched from the Nile Delta into the Levant and threatened Hittite possessions in Syria. His victory at Qadesh in 1285 BCE against the Hatti is attributed to his ability to rally the troops and personally lead his chariots in a brilliant turning movement, shattering the enemy chariotry.

The centrepiece of Thutmose III's victory at Megiddo in 1458 BCE and Ramesses II's victory at Qadesh in 1258 BCE was the Egyptian war chariot. The Egyptians improved the control, manoeuvrability and speed of the chariot by moving the axle to the very rear of the carrying platform. Manned by a driver and a bowman, this machine differed from its Mesopotamian counterpart in that it was primarily a missile platform for the composite-bow-wielding archer, and not a shock weapon in itself.

Assyrian archers came from many regions within the empire, so bow types differed, with the simpler self-bow in use as much as the composite bow. The Assyrians invented a quiver that could hold as many as fifty arrows, with some arrows fitted with special heads capable of launching combustible materials. Notice the wheeled siegecraft on this bas-relief being pushed up a ramp toward the walls of the city. The Assyrians were masters at attacking fortifications.

Bronze Age Mycenaean warfare, like warfare in Egypt and Mesopotamia, was centred on the war chariot, with Mycenaean infantry in support. This detail taken from the *Warrior Vase* excavated at Mycenae shows the panoply of early Greek spearmen. The Mycenaean military inheritance was lost to the Greeks of the archaic and classical periods, who lagged behind their Near Eastern adversaries in many important military arts.

In the archaic period the Greeks perfected a way of fighting where men lined up in rank and file in a phalanx or battle square. This offensive formation was designed to obliterate enemy infantry formations through the collision and push of shock combat. It proved its worth against rival Persian formations at Marathon in 490 BCE and Plataea in 479 BCE, and was instrumental in the final Greek victory in the Persian Wars. This detail shows the moment of impact between two Greek phalanxes.

The Athenian general Miltiades was largely responsible for the Athenian victory over the Persians at the battle of Marathon in 490 BCE. He persuaded his troops to take the initiative and attack the Persian host assembling on the beachhead at Marathon, out-killing the invaders at an astonishing ratio of more than thirty to one. A fatal infection from a battle wound on Paros a year later ended his aspirations for an early Athenian naval expansion into the Aegean.

The Spartan king and general Leonidas is one of western civilization's most celebrated military leaders. He led an allied Greek force to Thermopylae in 480 BCE to hold the pass against an overwhelming invading Persian force. His courage became legendary through his stubborn refusal to abandon the pass once the Greek position had been compromised. The 'Stand of the Three Hundred' remaining Spartans has become an enduring symbol of unit *esprit de corps* and self-sacrifice.

During the Persian Wars the rough, mountainous terrain of Greece favoured the defenders. In 480 King Leonidas and his Spartan-led army made a valiant last stand against a huge Persian host at the pass of Thermopylae. Leonidas used the natural choke-point seen here to mitigate his foe's superior numbers and hold off the Persian king's 'Immortals' for three days before he and his army were overwhelmed. Their holding action gave the Greeks more time to prepare for the coming onslaught.

The battle of Plataea took place in this area in 479 BCE. For two weeks the Persians and Greeks played a tactical game of chess here, with neither side wanting to commit to decisive action. Taking advantage of a bungled Greek repositioning of troops, the Persian commander Mardonius ordered a full-scale assault. The resulting battle was mostly one of Greek heavy infantry versus Persian light infantry and cavalry, with the hoplites winning the day. The Greek victory of Plataea put the invaders on the defensive for the remainder of the Persian War.

The Great King's bodyguard was made up of elite warriors known as 'Immortals', so named because when a member of this elite group fell, he was immediately replaced by a previously selected man. These handpicked troops were taught horsemanship and Persian martial arts (skills with sword, lance and bow) between the ages of five and twenty. For the next four years, each Immortal was on active duty with his elite *myriad* or division of 10,000 men, and was liable to serve until the age of fifty.

No other politician is as closely associated with the 'Golden Age of Athens' as Pericles. A brilliant imperialist and statesman who ruled Athens for nearly thirty years, Pericles oversaw the rebuilding of the Acropolis in marble. He was also the architect of the disastrous Great Peloponnesian War, though he died as a result of plague only two years into the conflict. His strategy of standing behind the walls of Athens while his own troops ravished the coastline of the Peloponnese proved ineffective.

Alexander III, king of Macedon, inherited the army of his father, Philip II, and, through sheer military genius, conquered the Persian Empire in less than a decade. Alexander mastered how to co-ordinate cavalry and infantry on the battlefield, and his victories against superior numbers at Granicus River (334 BCE), Issus (333 BCE) and Gaugamela (331 BCE) won him an empire and cemented his reputation as one of western civilization's premier battle captains.

In 336 the Great King of Persia was assassinated, leaving the way open for a new ruler, Darius III, to ascend the throne. Darius spent the first years of his reign putting down rebellion, only to be faced with an invasion of his north-west frontiers by Alexander the Great. Darius met Alexander personally in two battles, Issus and Gaugamela. At Issus, Alexander fought his way nearly to the Great King's chariot, before Darius was pulled away by his bodyguard.

(Peter Newark's Military Pictures)

The brilliant Carthaginian general Hannibal Barca struck fear in the Roman Republic for two decades. His back-to-back victories at Trebia (218 BCE), Trasimene (217 BCE) and Cannae (216 BCE) robbed the Roman state of nearly one-third of its standing army. He held a multinational force together on enemy soil for over a decade and a half. His final defeat at Zama in 202 BCE had more to do with the overwhelming determination of his Roman foe than his own strategic or tactical failings.

Scipio 'Africanus' was the greatest Roman commander of the Second Punic War and a leading member of a powerful Roman dynasty. Having raised legions after the disaster at Cannae, Scipio defeated the Carthaginian forces in Spain and then took his veteran legions to north Africa, where he vanquished Hannibal at Zama in 202 BCE. After the war he fought in Gaul and became a leading statesman during the early second century BCE, steering Rome toward a more imperialistic stand in the Mediterranean basin.

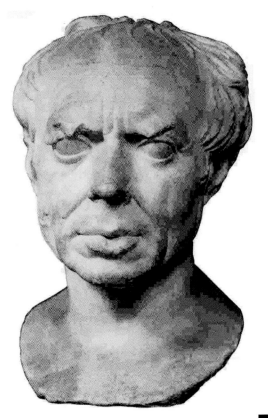

The first man in his family to be elected consul, Marius used this position to become the leading political figure of his age. He dominated Roman politics for decades and is traditionally believed to have remodelled the citizen militia into a professional army. Marius' reforms converted the cohort from an administrative to a tactical unit by making the arms and equipment of the legion's heavy infantry uniform, and by raising the number of legionaries in each legion to 5,200 men.

Crassus was both a skilled politician and an able military commander. His vanquishing of Spartacus in 71 BCE did not lead to the triumph (military parade and acclaim) he cherished. He later joined Pompey and Julius Caesar and formed the First Triumvirate. His position as governor of Syria brought him into proximity with one of Rome's greatest adversaries – Parthia. He picked a fight and lost both his legions and his life at Carrhae in 53 BCE.

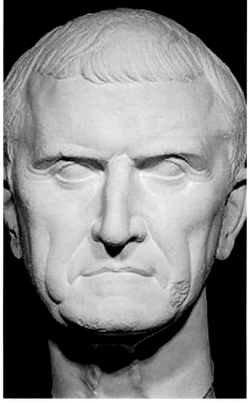

Rome's most successful general, Julius Caesar became part of the First Triumvirate in 61 BCE and looked to pacifying Gaul to make his military reputation. Between 58 and 50 BCE he conquered the Celts and Germanic tribes there (twice bridging the Rhine) and led expeditions to Britain, but was called back to Rome when his mentor Pompey sided with his political enemies. He defeated Pompey and his allies at Pharsalus and was appointed dictator for life just months before his assassination in 44 BCE.

The red-headed widow of an Iceni chieftain, Boudicca led a revolt against Roman occupying forces in Britain in 61 CE. The Celts first attacked the undefended town of Camulodunum (near modern Colchester), slaughtering the Roman settlers and those Britons collaborating with the enemy. Roman reprisals were swift, and a large Celtic force was destroyed by two Roman legions at Verulamium. After this catastrophic defeat, Boudicca took her own life with poison.

Nephew and adopted son of Julius Caesar, Octavian (later Caesar Augustus) became Rome's first emperor following the defeat of Marc Antony at Actium in 31 BCE. His forty-five-year rule witnessed the last intensive period of Roman expansion, though the setback in Germania at Teutoburg in 9 CE illustrated that Roman expansion was not infinite. Though not a formally trained soldier himself, Augustus was a brilliant administrator, creating many lasting imperial institutions.

To commemorate the pacification of Dacia, Emperor Trajan ordered the construction of a column that bears his name, one of the most intriguing war memorials and instruments of propaganda in history. This unusual monument consisted of a 131 feet tall marble column set atop a massive rectangular base. The column was made of seventeen hollow blocks of Carrera marble, and was topped by a gilded statue of the emperor himself, standing perhaps 20 feet in height.

This mannequin wears the typical panoply of a Roman heavy infantryman legionary from the late republican–early imperial period. The legionary is protected by an open-faced helmet and a chain mail *lorica hamata* probably copied from the Gauls, and is holding a heavy javelin or *pilum* and wearing a short Spanish sword or *gladius*. The *gladius* was the ideal close-quarters thrusting and cleaving sword, and was feared by Rome's opponents from Scotland to Parthia.

The first Christian emperor, Constantine spent nearly half his reign as a usurper, eventually reuniting the Roman Empire as sole ruler. He, along with Diocletian, brought stability to the land, and he was responsible for changing Roman grand strategy from defending the frontiers to a defence in depth, which some historians view as fatally weakening Roman defences.

This close-up of Trajan's Column shows a Roman legionary brutally escorting a Dacian prisoner. This bas-relief is emblematic of how Romans treated all captive peoples during their wars of conquest. Emperor Trajan fought two conflicts against Dacia at the beginning of the second century CE, eventually plundering and pacifying the region.

Fortunately for the Egyptians, the added mass was not needed to break through the Seleucid left wing.

Although Antiochus lost the battle of Raphia, he successfully rebuilt his army and reconquered most of his lost possessions, bringing Anatolia, Parthia and Bactria again under Seleucid hegemony and earning him the title of Antiochus 'the Great'. Yet despite the efforts of Antiochus and other Greek monarchs, the days of the Hellenistic empires were numbered. Caught between the rising regional powers of Rome in the west and Parthia in the east, the successor states would fail to adapt to the military challenges of their foes.

Cavalry, once the decisive offensive element of Hellenistic monarchs, became more difficult to recruit because their aristocratic horsemen required larger estates. In the third century BCE, as political conditions became more settled and local populations became loyal to their monarchs, it became more difficult for these same kings to seize vast tracts of enemy territory in lightning cavalry raids and distribute them to their nobles. Consequently, cavalry declined in both numbers and importance.[64] For example, where Alexander was able to field a cavalry force of 5,000 horse at the battle of Granicus River and some 9,000 horse at Hydaspes River, King Philip V of Macedon had only 2,000 Macedonian cavalry to put into the field against the Romans at Cynoscephalae in 197 BCE, and his successor, Perseus, fielded only 3,000 horse at Pydna in 168 BCE.[65]

Without an effective cavalry arm, Hellenistic commanders increasingly relied on infantry to decide engagements, but this switch in emphasis from the decisive cavalry battle to infantry-based warfare came too late in the conflict with Rome. In southern Italy and Sicily, and later in Greece and the eastern Mediterranean, Greek commanders could not cope with large Roman manpower reserves and the tactical flexibility of the Roman legion on the battlefield. In fact, Polybius calculated that in 225 BCE the Roman Commonwealth's military manpower stood at 700,000 infantry and 7,000 cavalry.[66] This huge reserve gave Roman commanders the luxury of rebounding from seemingly disastrous defeats against the Greeks and perfecting their generalship. In south-west Asia, the lack of a large and effective cavalry force severely hampered the successors in their wars against the Parthians, steppe nomads adept in the tactics of light and heavy cavalry. One by one, the Hellenistic states fell prey to the expansion of Parthia and Rome, with the last kingdom in Egypt, the Ptolemaic, ending with Roman occupation in 30 BCE.

Chapter 4

Republican Rome at War: The Rise and Evolution of the Legion

The Etruscan Inheritance

When Rome appeared as a city-state in the Tiber valley some time in the middle of the eighth century BCE, its first army differed little from those of other small communities in Latium. It is believed Rome's first military organization was based on the tribal system, reflecting the three original Roman tribes (the *Ramnes*, the *Tities*, and the *Luceres*).[1] Each tribe provided 1,000 infantry towards the army, made up of ten *centuries* consisting of 100 men. The tribal contingent was under the command of a *tribunus* or tribal officer. Together, these 3,000 men made up a *legio* or levy. This infantry force was supplemented by a small body of 300 *equites* or 'knights', aristocratic cavalry drawn equally from the three tribes.[2]

Initially, the organization of the early Roman army was heavily influenced by their powerful neighbours to the north, the Etruscans. Etruscan civilization emerged in Etruria around 900 BCE as a confederation of city-states. By 650 they had expanded in central Italy and become the dominant cultural and economic force in the region, trading widely with Greeks and Phoenicians on the peninsula. Under direct occupation by the Etruscans between *c.*625 and 509, Rome benefited greatly from this cultural exchange, with Roman villages transformed into a thriving city-state.[3] As in ancient Sumeria and archaic Greece, each Etruscan city raised its own army. And although these cities were united in a league of usually twelve cities, they seldom operated together unless faced with an outside threat. Like the Greek *poleis* to the east, the Etruscan city-states spent most of their energy fighting each other.

Some time in the sixth century BCE, the Etruscans adopted the Greek method of fighting and organized their militia-armies into phalanxes. After conquering the Roman city-state in the late sixth century BCE, the newly created Etrusco-Roman army was composed of two parts: the Etruscans and their subjects the Romans and Latins. The Etruscans fought in the centre as heavy infantry hoplites, while the Romans and Latins fought in their native style with spears, axes and javelins on either wing.[4] The army was divided into five classes depending on nationality.[5] The largest contingent, or first class, was composed of Etruscan heavy infantry armed in Greek fashion with heavy thrusting spear and long sword, and protected by breastplate, helmet, greaves and a heavy round shield. The second class contained spearmen conscripted from subject peoples and armed in Italian fashion with spear, sword, helmet, greaves and the oval Italic shield or *scutum*. The third class was lightly armoured heavy infantry spearmen with *scutum*, while the fourth and fifth classes were light infantry javelineers and slingers.[6]

The second of the Etruscan overlords in Rome, Servius Tullius, is credited in the middle of the sixth century BCE with attempting to integrate the population by reorganizing the army according to wealth and not nationality.[7] The Servian reforms reflected an old Indo-European custom where citizenship depended on property and the ability to maintain a panoply and serve in the militia. The reforms divided Etrusco-Roman society into seven groups.[8] The wealthiest group formed the cavalry or *equites*, made up of Etruscan nobles and members of the Roman patrician class. The *equites* did not act in the capacity of heavy or light cavalry, but served as mounted infantry and reconnaissance.[9]

The second wealthiest group acted as heavy infantry, fighting in the phalangeal formation and armed as before in the Greek manner. The third to sixth groups were armed in native Italian fashion identical to the pre-Servian period. The seventh class, or *capite censi*, were too poor to qualify for military service.[10] Tactically, the Servian army fought as before, with heavy infantry in the centre phalanx, protected by lightly armoured heavy infantry on the wings and light infantry skirmishers in the front until the phalanx engaged. There is no mention of archers in the Servian reforms. Like the Greeks, the Romans seemed to disdain the bow and arrow as a weapon of war, preferring it for hunting.[11]

The Early Roman Republican Army

In 509 BCE the Romans overthrew Etruscan rule. Newly independent Rome replaced the Etruscan monarchy with a republic governed by a council of elders drawn from the wealthy patrician class. This council, or Senate, annually elected two consuls as chief magistrates of the Roman state. From 362 *imperium*, or the authority to command the Roman army, was entrusted to the consuls, or to their junior colleagues, the praetors. Though the election of co-rulers ensured a balance of political power, it had serious military drawbacks. The two consuls shared responsibilities for military operations, alternating command privileges every other day. Recognizing the inefficiency of this system, Roman law provided for the appointment of a *dictator* in times of national crisis for the duration of six months.

The early republican army was a citizen army. In fact, the original meaning for the word *legion* (derived from *legere*, Latin for 'to gather together') was a draft or levy of heavy infantry drawn from the property-owning citizen-farmers living around Rome.[12] The army continued to adhere organizationally to the Servian reforms and consisted of three legions, each of 1,000 men, supplemented by light infantry provided by the poorer citizens and cavalry by the wealthy patrician class.[13] Divided into ten centuries of 100 men, each legion was commanded by a tribune appointed from the patrician class, while each century was commanded by a centurion promoted or elected from the ranks of the legionaries.[14] By the first century BCE, legions were organized around a battlefield standard bearing an eagle, below which was inscribed the legion's roman numeral and the letters 'SPQR' (*Senatus Populusque Romanus*), representing 'both the sovereign Roman people and the advisory Senate which guided its actions'.[15] And though the number of legions varied depending on the period, the importance of the legionary eagle as a visible sign of duty, honour and patriotism for generations of Roman soldiers remained constant for hundreds of years, even surviving Rome's transition from republic to empire.

Nothing brought more dishonour to a Roman commander and his legion than losing their eagle in combat, and emperors would go to great lengths to get them back if lost. Caesar tells us that when his legionaries hesitated while landing in Britain in 55 BCE, the *aquilifer* (eagle-standard-bearer) for the X Legion jumped into the waves and waded toward the half-naked, frenzied Britons. Fearing their eagle standard would be captured, the other legionaries flung themselves into the water and attacked the enemy.[16] Rome's first emperor, Octavian Augustus (r. 31 BCE–14 CE), spent large sums of money recovering the eagle standards lost by the Roman general Marcus Licinius Crassus to the Parthians fifty years earlier at the battle of Carrhae in 53 BCE. And when the elderly Augustus lost three legions and subsequently three eagles in the battle of Teutoburg in 9 CE, he is said to have wandered his palace muttering 'Quintili Vare, legiones redde' ('Quintilius Varus, give me back my legions').[17]

During the first century of republican rule, the Roman army continued to utilize the phalanx-based tactical system. But the battle square proved less effective against opponents unaccustomed to the stylized hoplite warfare favoured by the Mediterranean classical civilizations. When, in 390 BCE, 30,000 Gauls crossed the Apennines in search of plunder, the defending Roman legions were pushed against the Allia River.[18] The Gauls, or Celts as they were also called, were an Indo-European people who inhabited an area of western Europe including modern Britain, the southern Netherlands, Switzerland and Germany west of the Rhine. Most of the Gauls were semi-nomadic (influenced by contacts with Greeks and Romans), organized into tribes and capable of fielding very large armies. The Roman phalanxes, outnumbered two to one and overwhelmed by the ferocity and physical size of the Celtic marauders, were defeated, unable to cope with the barbarians' open formation and oblique attacks.[19] The sack of the 'Eternal City' in 390 left a lasting impression on the psyche of Roman civilization. The surviving Romans who witnessed the violation of their city from a nearby hill vowed never again to fight unprepared.

The Camillan Reforms and the Invention of the Maniple Legion

After the sack of Rome by the Gauls in 390, the pragmatism which is associated with Roman civilization as a whole was applied to warfare, with Roman commanders altering the panoply and tactical formation of the legions to meet the different fighting styles of their opponents, whether barbarian or civilized. The military reforms of the early fourth century are associated with the leader Marcus Furius Camillus, a man credited with saving the city from the Gauls and remembered as a second founder of Rome.[20] Although history cannot precisely answer if Camillus himself was responsible for the reforms, the changes that bear his name dramatically altered the character of the Roman legion in the fourth century.

As the Roman state grew at the expense of its neighbours in northern and central Italy, the Roman army expanded from three to four legions, and the number of legionaries per legion grew to perhaps 4,000 infantry.[21] By 350 the centuries had been reduced from 100 to between 60 and 80 men apiece, and the centuries in each legion were divided among 10 cohorts for administrative reasons.[22] The Roman army's experience against Gauls in the north and campaigns against the Samnites (343–290) in the rough, hilly terrain of central Italy forced a change in tactical organization, one which gave individual legionaries more responsibility and greater tactical freedom.

In order to achieve maximum tactical flexibility, the Roman army abandoned the phalanx altogether in favour of the most well-articulated tactical formation of the pre-modern world. This flexible linear formation consisted of four classes of soldiers defined not only by wealth, but also by age and experience.[23] The Greek-styled battle square was replaced by three lines of heavy infantry, the first two-thirds armed in an innovative manner with two weighted javelins, or *pila*, and a sword, and protected by helmet, breastplate, greaves and the traditional oval *scutum* favoured by the lower classes. The ranks of the forward of these two lines or *hastati* were filled with young adult males in their twenties, while the centre formation, or *principes*, comprised veterans in their thirties. The third and last line or *triarii* were armoured as above but for the old-style thrusting spear and *scutum*. The *triarii* consisted of the oldest veterans and acted as a reserve. The poorest and youngest men served as *velites* or light infantry skirmishers. Armed with light javelins and sword, and unprotected except for helmet and hide-covered wicker shield, the velites acted as a screen for their heavier armed and less mobile comrades. Each legionary was still responsible for supplying his own panoply, but in order to maintain uniformity within each century, the weapons were frequently purchased from the state.

Before battle, the *hastati*, *principes* and *triarii* formed up in homogeneous rectangular units or *maniples* of 120–160 men (two centuries probably deployed side by side), protected by the light infantry velites. Each maniple organized around a *signum* or standard kept by the *signifer*, who led the way on the march and in combat. Each maniple deployed as a small independent unit, typically with a twenty-man front and four-man depth, and may have been separated from its lateral neighbour by the width of its own frontage, though this is still a matter of some debate.[24] Livy tells us that the maniples were 'a small distance apart'.[25] Moreover, the maniples of *hastati*, *principes* and *triarii* were staggered, with the *principes* covering the gaps of the *hastati* in front, and the *triarii* covering the gaps of the *principes*. This chequerboard formation or *quincunx* provided maximum tactical flexibility for the maniple, allowing it to deliver or meet an attack from any direction.[26]

In battle the maniple legion presented a double threat to its adversaries. After the screening velites withdrew through the ranks of the heavy infantry, the *hastati* moved forward and threw their light *pila* at 35 yards, quickly followed by their heavy *pila*.[27] Drawing their short thrusting Spanish swords or *gladii*, the front ranks of the *hastati* charged their enemy, whose ranks were presumably broken up by the javelin discharge. As the Roman heavy infantry thrust into the enemy, the succeeding *hastati* threw their *pila* and engaged with swords. The battle became a series of furious combats with both sides periodically drawing apart to recover. When the two formations joined, the legionaries exploited the tears and stepped inside the spears of the first rank into the densely packed mass, and wielded their swords with much greater speed and control than the closely packed spearmen could defend against.[28]

During one of these pauses, the *hastati* retreated through the open ranks of the battle-tested and fresh *principes* and *triarii*. Meanwhile, the *principes* then closed ranks and moved forward, discharging their *pila* and engaging with swords in the manner of their younger comrades. If there was a breach in the Roman line, the veteran *triarii* acted as true heavy infantry and moved forward to fill the tear with their spears.

The new Roman system had many strengths. By merging heavy and light infantry into the *pilum*-carrying legionary, the Roman army gave its soldiers the ability to break up the enemy formation with missile fire just moments before weighing into them with sword and shield, in effect merging heavy and light infantry into one weapon system.[29] Once engaged, the maniple's relatively open formation emphasized individual prowess, and gave each legionary the responsibility of defending approximately 36 square feet between himself and his fellow legionaries, a fact which placed special emphasis on swordplay in training exercises.[30] But even if the maniple failed, it could be replaced by a fresh one in the rear. This ability to rotate fatigued legionaries with fresh soldiers gave the Romans a powerful advantage over their enemies.

The Tarentine and Punic Wars

The Camillan military reorganization would serve the republic well in its expansion against the Samnites, Etruscans and Gauls in northern and central Italy during the fourth century BCE. But Rome would face new challenges in the third century from the Greeks in southern Italy, the Carthaginians in Spain and north Africa, and Alexander's successor states in the Levant (Map 3.6). Rome's martial contacts with these other regional powers would test the effectiveness of the maniple legion against combined-arms tactical systems inspired by the success of the Macedonian art of war.

The first significant test of the maniple legion came against the Greeks in southern Italy in the Tarentine Wars (281–267 BCE). Rome's expansion into the lower peninsula forced the Greeks living there to forge an alliance with King Pyrrhus (319–272), a brilliant general from the Hellenized region of Epirus, north-west of Greece in what is now roughly modern Albania. Rome's struggle against Pyrrhus proved to be a difficult one, and over the course of the war Rome suffered two major defeats. But poor generalship, rather than an inferior fighting force, was the cause of the failures at Heraclae and Asculum in 279. But even while Pyrrhus' forces were victorious over the Romans, his battles, especially at Heraclae, cost him dearly, giving modern historians the term 'pyrrhic victory' to symbolize a costly victory. The Romans finally decisively defeated Pyrrhus' army at Beneventum in 275, and by 265 southern Italy was under Roman hegemony.[31]

Perhaps the greatest opponent faced by Rome during its republican period was Carthage, a former Phoenician colony on the coast of north Africa (modern Tunisia) that over time developed into a formidable military and naval power. As Rome was conquering southern Italy, Carthage (called *Punis* in Latin) was consolidating its power in the western Mediterranean, controlling north Africa and venturing into the Iberian peninsula, Corsica and, to Rome's dismay, the island of Sicily.

The Carthaginian presence in Sicily went back for centuries, with both Greek and Carthaginian colonists sharing the island. But after the Roman victory in the Tarentine Wars, Rome found itself at odds with Carthage over Sicily, an island Rome needed to feed its growing population. The resulting First Punic War (264–241 BCE) witnessed Rome taking to the sea in order to meet the Carthaginian threat.[32] Although the Romans did not have a history as mariners, they adapted well to naval warfare, building larger galleys than the Carthaginians and preferring grappling and boarding to traditional ramming. In fact, the Romans developed the *corvus*, or crow: an 18 foot gangway with a pointed spike under its outboard end.[33] Pivoted from a mast by a topping lift, the *corvus* was dropped into the adjacent ship, securing it in place as legionaries crossed the plank and engaged in hand-to-hand combat with enemy sailors. The application of the *corvus* in naval warfare allowed Rome to fight as a land power at sea, evening the odds against an accomplished naval power.

Although fierce storms destroyed large Roman fleets on two separate occasions, Rome eventually forced an unequal peace on Carthage. Under these terms, Carthage left Sicily under Roman hegemony and paid the Roman Republic a war indemnity. But the peace lasted less than a generation, with Rome and Carthage clashing over the fate of the city of Saguntum in eastern Spain. In the Second Punic War (219–201) the Carthaginian commander in Spain, Hannibal Barca (247–183), led an army of 40,000 troops and 37 elephants across southern Gaul, over the Alps and into northern Italy (Map 4.1).[34] In order to avoid a protracted war, Hannibal wanted to bring the conflict directly to Italy, defeat the legions on the field of battle and force Rome to sue for peace.

Despite heavy losses to the rigours of the long march, Hannibal defeated a Roman army at the battle of Trebia in 218.[35] Here, Hannibal's 19,000 infantry and 9,000 cavalry crushed a Roman army of 36,000 infantry and 4,000 cavalry.[36] His success convinced additional Gauls to join his army. The following spring he defeated a second Roman army on the banks of Lake Trasimene. Unwilling to risk another Roman army, the Senate elected Quintus Fabius Maximus as dictator. Fabius Maximus refused to meet the Carthaginian army in battle, preferring instead a strategy of delay and harassment. Rome's 'Fabian' strategy forced Hannibal to keep moving in order not to exhaust local food and forage.[37] Unable to besiege Rome because of the absence of a siege train, Hannibal crossed the Apennines and ravaged south-eastern Italy.

Unwilling to idly watch their country razed by an enemy army, the newly elected consuls Lucius Aemilius Paullus and Gaius Terentius Varro set out with an army consisting of sixteen legions to track down and defeat Hannibal's

Map 4.1. Roman Expansion in the Mediterranean, 3rd and 2nd Centuries BCE.

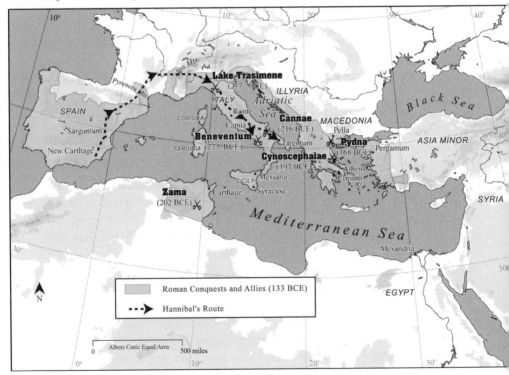

forces. In the summer of 216 the Romans caught up with Hannibal near the village of Cannae in Apulia. The resulting battle of Cannae pitted a Roman army of 80,000 infantry and 6,400 cavalry against Hannibal's allied army of 45,000 infantry and 10,000 cavalry.[38]

Hannibal camped west of the Aufidius River, while the Romans camped two-thirds of their army opposite the invading army, the remainder staying on the opposite side of the river to limit Carthaginian foraging. Varro, whose day it was to command the Roman army, lined up for battle on the east side of the river, placing his legionaries in the centre in an extra deep formation (in places, between thirty-five and fifty men deep) because of the narrowness of the plain. No more than 2,000 legionaries could engage the enemy at one time.[39] Moreover, many of the legionaries were fresh recruits recently added to make up for the horrendous losses suffered at Trebia and Trasimene.[40] Varro's strategy was simple: overwhelm the Carthaginian centre with the sheer weight of his legionaries. Betting on his heavy infantry to win the day, he then placed his inferior Roman cavalry on both wings to check the advance of the more numerous Carthaginian horse.

Understanding the threat to his centre, Hannibal arranged his troops south of the Romans, placing his infantry in the centre in a convex formation and making the centre deeper than the flanks in order to match the Roman frontage and delay the legions' advance. Hannibal kept his African infantry in reserve behind each flank of the crescent, and placed his cavalry on the flanks opposite the Roman horsemen. Outnumbered two to one in total numbers, the Carthaginian general placed his hope on his cavalry, which was superior to the Romans' in both numbers and quality.

As was typical of classical engagements, the battle opened with skirmishing, then Varro ordered the weighted Roman centre to close with the Carthaginians (Map 4.2(a)). At this moment Hannibal ordered the cavalry on his wings to strike the weaker Roman cavalry opposite. As the Romans engaged with the leading edge of the Carthaginian infantry, the centre yielded to the Roman advance, slowly transforming from a convex to a concave formation (Map 4.2(b)). On the wings the Carthaginian cavalry routed the Roman horse on both sides. As tens of thousands of legionaries were sucked into the centre of this rapidly developing killing field, Hannibal's African heavy cavalry ran the Roman flank and swung into the rear of the Roman army. Perhaps 60,000 Roman soldiers, including the consul Paullus, were killed, and another 10,000 soldiers were taken prisoner as a result of this classic double envelopment (Map 4.2(c)).[41] So thorough was the Roman defeat that never again did the Romans risk a large field army against Hannibal on Italian soil.

The defeat at Cannae underlined the weakness of the Roman heavy-infantry-based tactical system. At Trebia the legions managed to break through the Carthaginian centre, shattering the cohesion of the enemy army. At Cannae, the Romans massed their centre, determined to break through the

Spaniards and Celts forming the centre of Hannibal's line. But this was the tactic of a pike phalanx and a misuse of Roman swordsmen. By massing the centre, the Romans were so tightly packed that they could not manoeuvre or wield their short swords effectively, especially with rank upon rank pushing from behind. The situation was further aggravated as the Romans, pushed from behind, 'tumbled' over their own and enemy dead, further disrupting their ranks.[42] Hannibal's men had no such problem as they gave way into a concave formation.

In two years, Hannibal had killed or captured between 80,000 and 100,000 legionaries and their commanders, robbing Rome of a third of its standing military force.[43] Seemingly, the loss of three Roman armies in as many years should have satisfied Hannibal's plans for the defeat of Rome, but once again the Roman Republic survived the deprivations of an enemy army in its midst. Without a siege train, Hannibal could not capitalize on his battlefield successes. Moreover, the strength of the Roman federation soon became apparent when none of the key allied cities in Italy betrayed their capital on the Tiber. They acted instead as islands of refuge for Roman armies between disasters. Although able to march almost at will throughout the Italian peninsula, Hannibal was incapable of bringing the Second Punic War to a decisive conclusion, and time was on the Romans' side.

Hannibal's luck began to change in 207, when the relief army from Spain of his younger brother Hasdrubal was intercepted and annihilated at the Metaurus River. When news of the defeat and death of Hasdrubal reached the Carthaginian army in southern Italy, many of Hannibal's allies began to desert him. Unable to defeat Hannibal in Italy, the Romans focused on fighting other

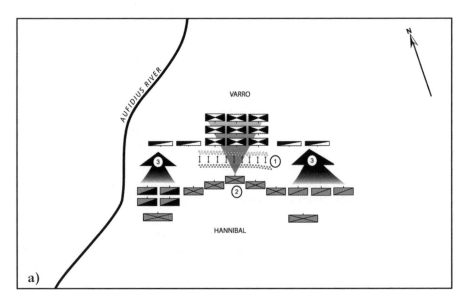

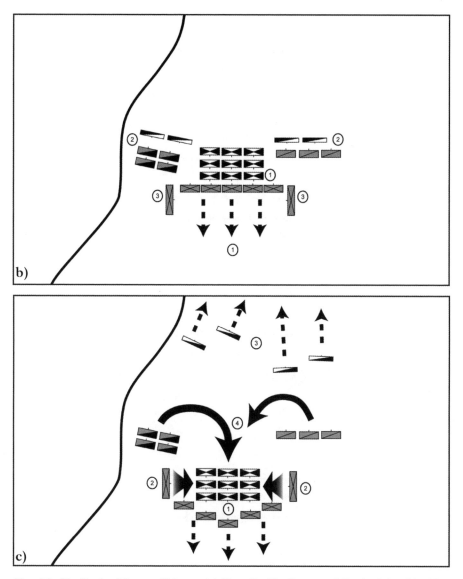

Map 4.2. The Battle of Cannae, 216 BCE. (a) Phase I: After Roman and Carthaginian skirmishers open the action (1), Varro orders his legions forward against Hannibal's infantry in the centre (2). Hannibal counters by ordering his cavalry forward on both wings against the inferior Roman horse (3). (b) Phase II: The previously convex Carthaginian formation begins to give way to the superior weight of the Roman infantry (1). As the Carthaginian horsemen begin to press the Roman cavalry (2), Hannibal's African infantry position themselves to flank the Roman breakthrough (3). (c) Phase III: The Carthaginian centre continues to give way, becoming a concave line (1). As Varro's legionaries press deeper into the trap, their flanks are suddenly assailed by Hannibal's African infantry reserves (2). Having routed the Roman cavalry (3), the Carthaginian cavalry close the trap by assaulting the rear of the infantry (4). Varro's legions are annihilated, losing 60,000 dead and another 10,000 taken prisoner.

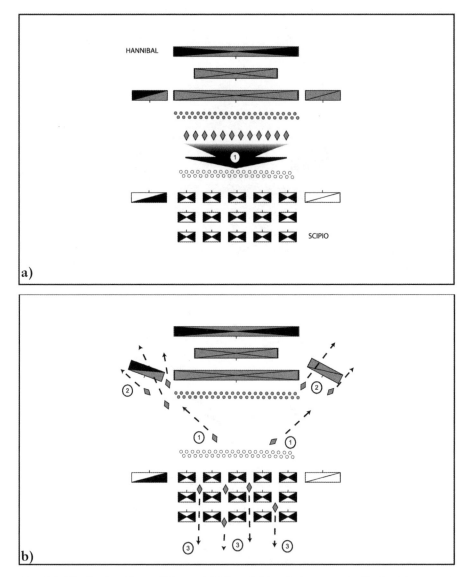

Map 4.3. The Battle of Zama, 202 BCE. (a) Phase I: Hannibal arranges the Carthaginian army in three lines, his veteran Italian army in the rear, the centre screened by light troops and elephants. Scipio adopts an unorthodox formation, aligning rather than staggering his maniples to form lanes. The Roman deployment is carefully screened by a line of velites. Hannibal initiates the battle by ordering an elephant charge against the Roman centre (1). (b) Phase II: The elephants pass through the Roman skirmish line without effect, and are stampeded by shouts and trumpet blasts from the front rank (1). Most of the Carthaginians' elephants stampede across their army's front and into the flanking cavalry formations (2). The few elephants successfully reaching the Roman lines are herded down the lanes Scipio had prepared in his initial deployment, passing harmlessly to the rear of the legions (3). (c) Phase III: Taking advantage of the confusion in Hannibal's cavalry ranks, Scipio orders his flanking horsemen to charge (1), driving the Carthaginian horse from the field (2). The legions close,

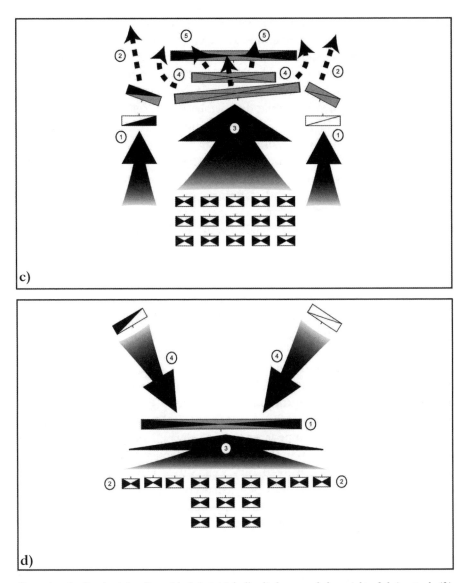

c)

d)

disrupting the Carthaginian line with their initial pila *discharge and the weight of their attack (3). The conscript infantry in the second line refuse to admit their fleeing comrades who subsequently force their own centre and stream around both flanks to safety (4). The second rank breaks under the pressure and the scenario is repeated between it and the veteran third rank (5). (d) Phase IV: Scipio orders his infantry to halt and reform. A lull occurs in which both sides redeploy, Hannibal bringing his veterans forward and extending their line (1) and Scipio responding by extending his flanks with his rested* principes *and* triarii, *his centre still manned by his now-weary* hastati *(2). Scipio hurls his infantry forward against Hannibal's veterans (3). As the infantry battle rages, the Roman and Numidian cavalry return from their pursuit and charge the Carthaginian rear (4). The Carthaginian army is destroyed, though Hannibal makes good his escape.*

Carthaginian generals in Carthage's sphere of influence. In 206 a Roman army under the command of Scipio the Younger (*c*.236–184 BCE) defeated the Carthaginians in Spain, and two years later he landed at the head of a Roman expeditionary force aimed at north Africa. In 203 Hannibal was recalled from Italy in order to assemble a defence force for Carthage.

Hannibal and Scipio met at the decisive battle of Zama in 202, some 100 miles south-west of Carthage.[44] For the first time, there was relative parity in numbers between the combatants, but the quality of Roman forces was superior to Hannibal's army, and Scipio proved to be an experienced general who understood the full tactical capabilities of the legion on the battlefield. Scipio's force was probably slightly inferior in infantry (he had 34,000 footmen against 36,000 Carthaginians), but was superior in cavalry after the defection of the Numidians to his side, with 6,000 cavalry against Hannibal's 4,000 horse and 80 elephants.[45]

Hannibal arranged his infantry in three lines (Map 4.3(a)).[46] He placed his light troops and dead brother's army in the front, hastily conscripted African levy in the middle, and his veteran army from Italy in the rear. In the very front of his infantry he placed his war elephants. Hannibal placed his cavalry on the wings, putting his heavy horse on the right and light horse on the left.

Scipio arrayed his infantry and cavalry with his legionaries in the centre and heavy cavalry on the left wing and light cavalry on the right wing. But instead of forming up his legions in the *quincunx* formation as was standard practice, Scipio arranged the maniples of *hastati*, *principes* and *triarii* directly behind and in front of one another, forming lanes through the ranks of soldiers. Scipio was careful to arrange his legions in this unorthodox manner under a screen of light infantry velites. The plan worked very well. When Hannibal initiated battle with a charge of elephants, most of them were confused by the yelling and trumpet blasts from the legions, and stampeded across the front of the armies and into their own cavalry (Map 4.3(b)). Those elephants that successfully reached the Roman line were goaded and herded down the lanes by velites, passing harmlessly to the rear of the legions.

Capitalizing on the confusion caused by rioting elephants pushing into the Carthaginian wings, Scipio ordered his cavalry to charge, pushing Hannibal's horsemen from the field (Map 4.3(c)). Meanwhile, as the infantry closed, Hannibal's first line was forced back by the *pilum* discharge and shock combat of the engaging *hastati*. But the African conscripts in the second line refused to admit the retreating first line, infuriating the allied Celts and Ligurians who forced their own centre or streamed around the flanks. The second line then cracked, pushing back into Hannibal's veteran third line who, like the second line, refused to let any of their retreating comrades pass through their ranks. Perhaps fearing an overextension or outflanking, Scipio ordered a recall of his legions.

The break in the battle allowed both sides to reform (Map 4.3(d)). Hannibal brought his fresh veteran infantry forward in a single line, then extended their frontage. Scipio ordered his *principes* and *triarii* to the wings to counter this move, keeping his tired *hastati* in the centre. But Scipio, faced with a corps of veterans who had served with Hannibal in Italy for a decade and a half, did not hesitate in sending his army again into the fray. As the infantry clashed, the Roman and Numidian cavalry returned to the battlefield and charged the Carthaginian rear. Though Hannibal escaped, the Carthaginian losses exceeded 20,000 dead and perhaps 20,000 prisoners. Scipio lost 1,500 legionaries and perhaps 3,000 allied cavalry.[47] Hannibal returned to Carthage and advised his government to sue for peace.

Carthage was never again a regional power after the Second Punic War, though Roman fears of a Carthaginian revival precipitated a Third Punic War (149–146 BCE). The result of the conflict was the razing of Carthage and the division of its territories between Numidia and the Roman province of 'Africa'. Scipio, dubbed 'Africanus' because of his victory at Zama, emerged as a leading statesman, while Hannibal found military appointments under various rulers in the Hellenistic East, committing suicide in 183 BCE in order to avoid being betrayed into Roman hands.

Legion versus Phalanx: The Macedonian Wars

Rome's war with Hannibal brought the Italian power into direct conflict with King Philip V of Macedon (238–179 BCE), one of Alexander's successors in the east, initiating a series of wars that eventually pulled Rome into the gravity of Hellenistic politics. The appeal of Rhodes and Pergamum for a Roman ally against the threat of an alliance between Philip V and Antiochus III of Syria piqued the Senate's interest in the region, initiating a series of conflicts in Greece known as the Four Macedonian Wars (216–146 BCE). Tactically, these wars demonstrated the superiority of the maniple legion over the fully evolved phalanx. Ever since the days of Camillus when the maniple formation was first introduced, the Roman legion, unlike the Macedonian-inspired phalanx, had developed consistently in the direction of flexibility. When these two tactical systems met on the battlefield, the result of the confrontation was usually catastrophic for the Greeks because of the vastly different capabilities of the weapon systems employed.

The historian Livy explained the psychological effects of Philip V's first encountered with Roman infantry. In 200 BCE, the Romans came to support their Athenian allies against the Macedonians. Philip's cavalry engaged the Romans the day before and, normal to Greek warfare, the fallen were to be buried with full honours as a sort of pep rally for the coming engagement. Philip soon wished he had not agreed to the ceremony, for his soldiers were not prepared for what they saw: 'When they had seen bodies chopped to pieces by the Spanish sword, arms torn away, shoulders and all, or heads separated from bodies ... or vitals laid open ... they realized in a general panic with what weapons and what men, they had to fight.'[48]

The Greeks, used to the neat puncture wounds inflicted by javelins and pikes, were visibly shaken by the wound signature of the short Spanish sword or *gladius*. The *gladius* was slightly less than 2 feet long with a double-edged blade 3 inches in width, adopted from the short thrusting sword used on the Iberian peninsula.[49] Slight modifications would transform this superior thrusting sword into a deadly cleaving instrument. The *gladius* was, according to one historian, 'the most deadly of all weapons produced by ancient armies, and it killed more soldiers than any other weapon in history until the invention of the gun'.[50] The *gladius* would be used to good effect by the Roman legionary against the *sarissa*-wielding phalanxes.

Three years later, at the battle of Cynoscephalae in 197 BCE, Philip V was defeated by the Roman commander Titus Quinctius Flaminius in a confrontation that illustrated the superior tactical flexibility of the maniple legion. The opposing armies were almost equal in number. The Roman army consisting of 26,000 footmen (18,000 legionaries and 8,000 allied phalangeal infantry from the Athenian-led Aetolian League), 2,000 cavalry and 20 elephants. The Macedonians fielded an army of 25,500 infantry and 2,000 cavalry.[51] The battle began as light infantry skirmishers met in the mists surrounding the Cynoscephalae hills in Thessaly (Map 4.4(a)).[52] Initially, the Roman light infantry enjoyed the upper hand until Philip's cavalry arrived, forcing the Romans to make an orderly retreat.

Seizing the high uneven ground along the ridge, the Macedonians deployed their heavy infantry phalanxes on the left wing and in the centre, then placed

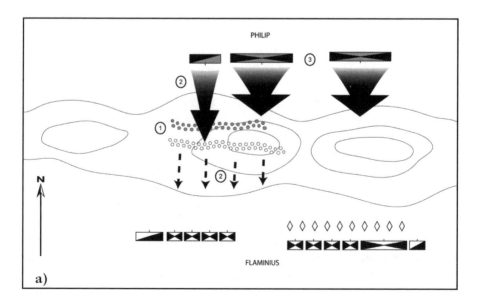

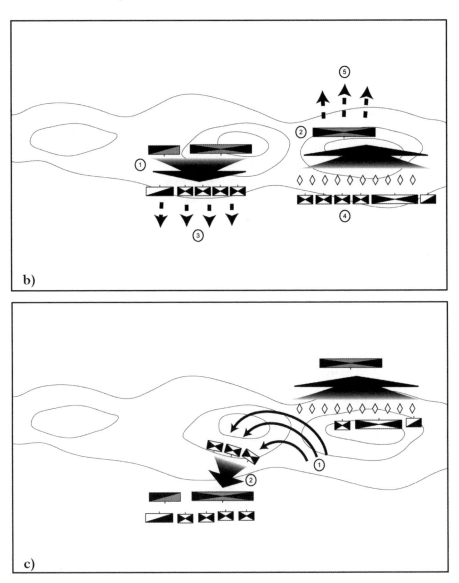

Map 4.4. The Battle of Cynoscephalae, 197 BCE. (a) Phase I: The battle opens as Roman and Macedonian skirmishers clash in the fog-enshrouded Cynoscephalae hills (1). After initially holding the upper hand, the Roman light infantry retreat in good order as the Macedonian cavalry advance against them (2). Philip orders his infantry forward, occupying the ridge line (3). (b) Phase II: The Macedonians launch a downhill charge against the Roman left (1), but the move occurs before their own left has fully deployed (2). The Romans' left is pressed back by Philip's charge (3), but Flaminius' right attacks the lagging Macedonian left (4) and pushes it back as well (5). (c) Phase III: As the Roman right pursues the Macedonian left, a Roman tribune orders his maniples to wheel to the left (1) and engage Philip's victorious right in the rear (2). The Macedonians, unable to protect themselves against this unanticipated onslaught, raise their sarissas in surrender. The Romans fail to understand the gesture and slaughter Philip's infantry.

their cavalry on the more even ground on the right. Flaminius split his two heavy infantry legions between the centre and the right wing, with the right wing further reinforced with the Greek phalanx and a detachment of heavy cavalry and all twenty elephants. On the left wing, Flaminius placed the remainder of his heavy cavalry across from the Macedonian horse.

Philip began the battle with a downhill infantry and cavalry charge, forcing the Roman centre and left wing back (Map 4.4(b)). But his attack was probably premature, because it took place before his own left wing was fully deployed. Seeing this opportunity, Flaminius ordered his right plus his elephants to attack the echeloned Macedonian left, easily pushing back the still-forming phalanxes. On both sides the right wing was victorious, but an unnamed tribune tipped the scales in Rome's favour when he peeled off twenty maniples from the Roman right and hit Philip's centre in the rear, slaughtering the exposed phalangites (Map 4.4(c)). The Macedonians, in retreat, raised their *sarissas* in surrender, but the uncomprehending Romans cut them down. In all, Philip lost 8,000 men, while Flaminius' losses were 700 dead.[53]

The last great stand of the traditional phalangite army against the Romans occurred at the battle of Pydna in 168 BCE against Philip V's son Perseus. In the battle, despite being outnumbered, a Roman army inflicted a crushing defeat on the Macedonian army. By 130 BCE, Rome had established hegemony over Greece, Macedon, and much of Asia Minor, and in the west, Rome conquered southern Gaul and most of north Africa before 100 BCE. The reputation of Rome's legions combined with adroit diplomacy was, at times, sufficient to win territory. Rome conquered the entire Hellenistic east virtually without fighting, relying instead on bluff and coercive diplomacy.[54] But when diplomacy did not work, the Roman army was capable of enforcing the will of the Senate through organized violence, creating a new Mediterranean empire in the process.

The Marian Reforms

At the end of the second century BCE a number of changes in the Roman army occurred that had great military, social and political implications, some of which are associated with the consulships of Gaius Marius (157–86 BCE). On the military side, two of Marius' reforms involved the conversion of the cohort from an administrative to a tactical unit by making the arms and equipment of the legion's heavy infantry uniform, and by raising the number of legionaries in each legion from around 4,000 to 5,000 men, including support staff.[55]

This modification in the legion's equipment and formation was due to the increasingly large tactical array of Rome's Germanic enemies during the second century BCE. Consistent with Indo-European tradition, Germanic infantry was organized into *hundreds*, a group of perhaps 100 warriors who swore allegiance to a local chieftain. These formations often fought in what the Romans called a *cuneus* ('wedge'), sometimes referred to as a 'boar's head' wedge.[56] This battle array placed the heaviest armoured and best-armed men in the front ranks, with lesser-armoured warriors filling in behind. This wedge formation had limited offensive articulation, but presented plenty of impact power on a small frontage. The boar's head array was launched at an enemy in order to break up opposing formations in a single movement. If the initial attack miscarried before determined resistance, then the barbarians retreated in disorder, but if the boar's head was successful in breaking up the opposing formation, then individual combat ensued, consistent with the Germanic fighting ethos and the reality of unarticulated heavy infantry.[57] Furthermore, barbarian command capabilities were not sophisticated enough to be able to control more than a single body of warriors. And though they sometimes used a second line of troops, there is little evidence supporting the use of reserves.[58]

Although the flexibility of the maniple proved adequate in battle against the civilized armies of the Mediterranean basin, its limited size of only two centuries did not allow it to meet the large Germanic battle square on equal footing. The cohortal legion would meet this need. Marrying the flexibility of the maniple to the mass of the phalanx, the cohortal legion could meet the large Germanic battle squares yet retain the tactical mobility that allowed it to deliver or meet an attack from any direction. Though it was probably used in battle before his consulships, Marius used his considerable political power to establish the cohortal legion as the standard legion.[59] It would remain virtually unchanged for the next 300 years. Marius is also credited with making the eagle (*aquila*) the standard for the Roman legion.[60]

The cohortal legion represented hundreds of years of tactical evolution. Over the course of the early and middle republic, the Roman legion was first provided with joints, then divided into echelons, then broken up into maniples only to be finally reorganized again into large, compact cohorts capable of great flexibility on the battlefield. This last evolution of the legion was attainable only by the extraordinary discipline of the Roman legionary, discipline that only increased as professionalism and length of enlistment increased. The cohort legion was organized as follows:

8 men to a *contubernium*	8 men
10 *contubernia* to a *century*	80 men
2 centuries to a *maniple*	160 men
3 maniples to a *cohort*	480 men
10 cohorts to a *legion*	4,800 men[61]

Under the Marian reforms the light infantry velites were abolished and became an allied responsibility fulfilled by *auxiliaries*. These were troops of non-Italian origin, recruited from local allied tribes and client kings. They employed the indigenous weapons of their nationality and served the Romans in the role of light infantry and light cavalry.[62] Julius Caesar made extensive use of Gallic and, later, Germanic cavalry in his conquest of Gaul, and these same troops proved effective against Pompeii during the Civil War. Auxiliary units raised in the provinces by treaty obligations were usually led by their own commanders, with successful battle captains rewarded with Roman citizenship and titles.[63] By the beginning of the Roman Empire (31 BCE–476 CE), auxiliaries were an indispensable complement to the legion.

With the covering forces now the responsibility of allies, the Romans concentrated solely on heavy infantry. Marius replaced the thrusting spear of the third line *triarii* with the *pilum* and *gladius* carried by the *hastati* and *principes*, creating a standardization of arms throughout the legion.[64] He also improved the *pilum* by replacing one of the two nails holding the metal head to the wooden shaft with a wooden dowel. The *pilum* would break on impact, ensuring that it could not be thrown back in combat.[65] Defensively, legionaries wore articulated banded armour known as *lorica segmentata*, which gave them excellent protection and unprecedented mobility. The familiar rectangular *scutum* also reached its final form about 100 BCE.[66]

Marius also improved the mobility of the Roman army by allowing only one pack animal for every fifty men, requiring every legionary to carry his own arms, armour, entrenching tools, personal items and several days' rations on the march.[67] Though his load might be 80 or 90 pounds, each of 'Marius' mules' was capable of travelling up to 20 miles a day over good roads and then fortifying the army camp as a precaution against nocturnal attack, a standard Roman practice when in hostile territory.[68] Furthermore, the Romans, like the Persians, developed a very sophisticated highway system to support their armies in the field. The Romans built 50,000 miles of paved roads and 200,000 miles of dirt roads linking the provinces, giving the legionaries unprecedented strategic mobility.[69]

The Jewish historian Flavius Josephus (b. 37 CE) tells us in his account of the Jewish revolt of 66–73 CE that when the Roman army was on the march, it usually conformed to a standard configuration, one which remained unchanged since the time of Polybius over 200 years before. Screening the column and acting as forward scouts were contingents of lightly armed infantry auxiliaries and cavalry, protecting the army from ambush. Next came the vanguard, comprising one legion plus a force of cavalry. Because the duty was dangerous, legions drew lots each day to determine which one should form the vanguard. Behind the vanguard came the camp surveyors, made of ten men from each century (or one man from each *contubernium* or tent). Their job was to quickly mark out the camp at the end of the day. Behind the surveyors marched the pioneer corps, engineers whose job it was to clear obstacles and bridge rivers. Next came the commanding general's personal baggage laagers, protected by a strong mounted escort. In the middle of the column rode the general himself, surrounded by a personal bodyguard drawn from the ranks of auxiliary infantry and cavalry. Following the general were those cavalry *alae* organic to each legion (made up of Roman cavalry regiments consisting of 120 horsemen per legion). Next came the Roman siege train, men and mules pulling the dismantled towers, rams and siege engines necessary to attack an enemy city. Senior officers – legates, tribunes and auxiliary prefects with an escort of handpicked troops – came next, followed by the legionaries themselves marching six abreast. Each legion was headed by the *aquilifer* and followed by its own baggage train controlled by each legion's servants. Behind the legions followed the rearguard, contingents of auxiliary heavy and light troops who fanned out to protect the column from rear attack. Finally, camp followers would have been found at the rear of the army, maintaining a close proximity for protection. These followers normally would have included common-law wives, children, prostitutes, merchants and slave dealers.[70]

Frequently outnumbered on the battlefield and attacked from many angles, the legion depended for its survival on following the direct orders of the army commander. Battlefield victory and consistent performance brought great opportunity for the legionary who, over time, could look forward to promotion through the various ranks of centurion, which by the time of Marius represented a whole class of officers.[71] Moreover, the senior centurion of a legion enjoyed considerable status, and the five senior centurions of each legion were included in councils of war held by commanders of field armies.[72] But if the orders of a centurion were not followed and a century was judged disobedient or cowardly in battle, the entire unit was subject to *decimation*. One soldier in ten was selected by lot and beaten to death by his comrades, enforcing an age–old adage that the key to battlefield success is the fear of one's own army over the fear of the enemy.[73]

Finally, Marius dropped the property-owning qualifications for military service, opening the ranks of the legion to the lowest social class, the *capite censi*.[74] Roman expansion in the third and second centuries BCE created a large slave class, and consolidation of small farms into vast plantations or *latifundia* worked by foreign slaves eroded the class of farmer which had always been the backbone of the Roman army. These displaced rural Romans moved to the cities and became urban poor. Seeking a better life, many of these young men enlisted for longer periods of service. Under Marius, length of service was increased to six years, replacing the citizen-militia army of the earlier republic with a professional army.[75] But, perhaps most significantly, in the unstable economic and political climate of the late republic, the allegiance of the legionaries shifted from the Roman state to individual generals, who provided their soldiers with status and booty during the territorial expansion and civil wars of the first century BCE (Map 4.5).[76]

The professionalization of the Roman army after the Marian reforms led directly to the use and abuse of power by generals seeking to usurp the power of the Senate. Lucius Cornelius Sulla (138–78 BCE), one of Marius' generals, marched on Rome with his legions and forced the Senate to name him dictator

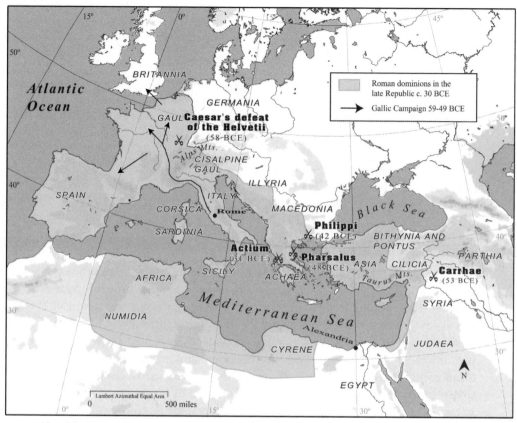

Map 4.5. Roman Possessions in the Late Republic, 31 BCE.

in 82 BCE. After conducting a reign of terror to wipe out all opposition, Sulla restored the constitution and retired in 79, but his use of military force against the government of Rome set a dangerous precedent.[77] His example of how an army could be used to seize power would prove most attractive to ambitious men.

For the next fifty years, Roman history was characterized by two important features: the jostling for power by a number of powerful individuals and the civil wars generated by their conflicts. Not long after Sulla retired, the Senate made two extraordinary military appointments that raised to prominence two very strong personalities – Cnaeus Pompeius Magnus (106–48 BCE) and Marcus Licinius Crassus (*c.*112–53 BCE). Pompey fought for Sulla and was given military commands in Spain and the eastern Mediterranean, returning to Rome as an accomplished military hero. Crassus had also fought for Sulla, but, despite putting down Spartacus' slave rebellion in 71 BCE, he was considered more of a statesman and businessman than military commander. In 61 BCE, Julius Caesar joined Pompey and Crassus in a power-sharing arrangement known as the First Triumvirate. Together, the combined wealth and political power of these three men enabled them to dominate the Roman political scene.[78]

The elder statesman Pompey had already proved his worth as a military commander (earning a triumph while he was too young to even be a senator), and Caesar and Crassus felt compelled to win an equally impressive reputation on the battlefield. Caesar chose Gaul as his area of influence and brought the Celts under direct Roman influence between 59 and 49 BCE. Crassus, hungry for military success to reinforce his political aspirations, set out for the east with plans to invade Parthia.

The Cohortal Legion at War: The Gallic Campaigns
The last major territorial expansion under the republic took place in Gaul between 59 and 49 BCE. As *proconsul* (governor with *imperium*) of Gaul, Gaius Julius Caesar (100–44 BCE) commanded at various times between six and eleven legions, and, counting auxiliaries (including Spanish, Gallic and German horse), the strength of his army varied between 40,000 and 70,000 men. Through many long and difficult military campaigns, Caesar used this army to bring Transalpine Gaul (the area of Gaul north of the Alps) under Roman hegemony.

Caesar's military reputation as a great commander was made against the semi-barbaric Gauls and the more aggressive Germanic tribes who periodically invaded Roman Gaul. In his Gallic commentaries, a mostly propagandistic work on his campaigns north of the Alps, Caesar tells us of an unnamed battle in 58 BCE in which perhaps 40,000 Roman soldiers and auxiliaries faced an invasion of Gaul by perhaps 150,000 Celtic Helvetii and their Germanic allies the Boii and Tulingi.[79] Caesar intercepted the barbarian tribes as they were attempting to migrate west from their homeland east of Lake Geneva across central France. After a few successful ambushes of barbarian camps and the slaughter of thousands of migrants on the spot, the Helvetii sent an ambassador to sue for peace with the Roman general. When Caesar's demand for damages and hostages was refused, a decisive engagement was all but assured. The two armies met at the southern edge of the rugged Morvan region in Burgundy.

According to Caesar's account, on the day of the battle he sent his cavalry to delay the enemy's approach and withdrew the remainder of his army to a nearby hill about 3 miles north-west of modern Toulon. He drew up the four veteran legions in his army in three lines of six ranks each halfway up the hill, and ordered his two recently levied legions and remaining auxiliaries troops to the summit, quickly converting the hilltop into an earthwork fortification and base camp. Caesar then ordered all of the officers' horses taken to the summit so that no one could entertain the idea of retreat.[80] The Helvetii were the first to arrive before the Roman position and, without waiting for reinforcements, attacked the Romans (Map 4.6(a)).[81] The Romans used their advantage in

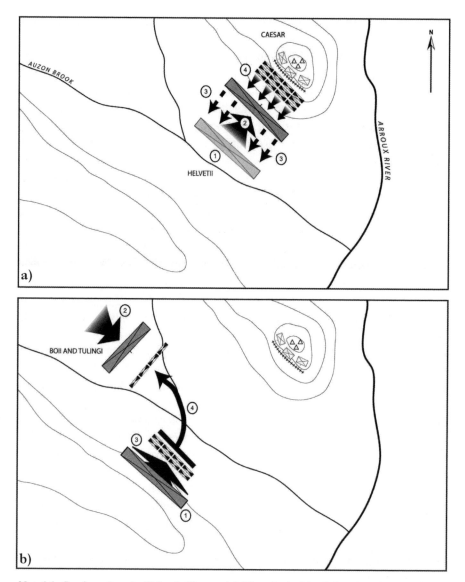

Map 4.6. Battle against the Helvetii, 58 BCE. (a) Phase I: Arriving before their Boii and Tulingi allies, the Helvetii (1) charge Caesar's veteran legions, which are deployed about halfway up the slope of a hill (2). The advantage of elevation increases the effectiveness of the Romans' pila attack and the Helvetii phalanx is driven back down the hill (3). The Romans draw their swords and advance after the retreating foe (4). (b) Phase II: The Helvetii make a fighting withdrawal to a neighbouring hill (1). As they establish a foothold on the hill, their Boii and Tulingi allies arrive on the Romans' right flank (2). Seeing this, the Helvetii press forward once again (3). Caesar responds to the crisis by ordering the third lines of his legions to shift to form a new front to counter the threat to his flank (4). The first two lines of the legions continue the fight against the Helvetii. The battle rages into the evening, the Helvetii and their allies finally giving way to the Roman infantry and escaping after nightfall.

elevation to rain *pila* down on the Germans, stopping the enemy advance in its tracks. Then the veteran legionaries drew their swords and advanced down the hill. Though the Helvetii resisted, they were finally forced to begin a slow fighting withdrawal toward a hill a mile away (Map 4.6(b)).[82] Just as the Helvetii gained the safety of the hill, warriors from the Boii and Tulingi appeared on the right flank of the advancing Roman legions and threatened their rear. Seeing the arrival of their allied tribes, the Helvetii once again pressed forward.[83]

Faced with a crisis, Caesar ordered his Romans to form a double front, the first and second lines to oppose the Helvetii counter-attack, and the third line to form a new front at an angle to the first in order to face the newly arrived enemy. The battle, fought in two directions, continued from early afternoon until evening, with Caesar recording in his commentaries that not a single Gaul was seen running away. But finally, after suffering perhaps 20,000 casualties, the Helvetii and their Germanic allies gave way before the Roman advance, abandoning their camp and baggage, and taking flight under the cover of night.[84] Though Caesar gives no figures on Roman casualties in this unnamed battle, he does state that the Roman army remained on the battlefield for three days in order to bury their dead, treat the wounded and rest before pursuing the Germans.[85] This victory forced most of the survivors back to their lands to act as a barrier against other barbarian tribes attempting to cross the Rhine.

Legion versus Cavalry: The Battle of Carrhae

In the second century BCE the Parthians carved out a south-west Asian empire at the expense of the Seleucid kingdom, one of Alexander's successor states. As horse nomads from the Eurasian steppe, the Parthians brought with them a strong equestrian tradition. The Parthian army was a cavalry force, consisting of light cavalry horse archers supplemented by noble lancers or *cataphracts* (from the Greek meaning 'covered over'), chain- or scale-mailed heavy cavalry whose ancestors reached back to the well-armoured Persian cavalry of Cyrus the Great.[86]

Parthian light cavalry wore little or no armour, instead relying on mobility and 'hit and run' tactics.[87] The standard Parthian horse archer practice was to canter in loose order toward the infantry enemy. At 100 yards the formation broke into a gallop and fired arrows. At about 50 yards (still out of range of most light infantry javelins), the formation wheeled right and, still firing, rode along the front of the enemy formation. Alternately, they reined in and skid-turned, then fired more arrows over their shoulders as they retreated out of enemy archer range. This last manoeuvre became known as the 'Parthian shot', although all Eurasian horse archers practised it. These charges and volleys continued all day, with swarms of horse archers darting in and out of dust clouds, and were designed to wear down defending infantry squares. Moreover, the Parthians were masters of the ruse and adept in the feigned retreat, pulling enemy cavalry into pursuit, then ambushing them far from their camp.[88]

Marcus Crassus was an experienced general, having served under Sulla in the 80s and gained notoriety as the commander who finally put down Spartacus' revolt in 71 BCE after it had defeated numerous Roman armies and pillaged the Italian countryside. But defeating a slave revolt did not earn him the most coveted reward in Rome – a triumphant parade. Instead, the Senate awarded Crassus the governorship of Syria, and he intended to use this position to push Roman hegemony east into Mesopotamia at the expense of the Parthians, despite a peace treaty between the two empires. At sixty years of age, he realized that this was his last chance to become the worthy heir of Pompey.

On his march toward the old Hellenistic capital at Seleucia in Mesopotamia, Crassus occupied numerous Parthian frontier towns, provoking an angry response from the Parthian king. The Roman army encountered the Parthian host near Carrhae. Although many of the Romans wanted to rest there, Crassus, urged by his son Publius, decided to march on. Publius was an aggressive commander in search of a military reputation of his own who had served with distinction under Julius Caesar in Gaul.

Unfortunately for the Romans, their slow moving, infantry-based army soon attracted a Parthian force consisting of 1,000 cataphracts and some 8,000 horse archers, led by the capable Parthian general Surena.[89] Crassus, recognizing the unfavourable strategic situation evolving around his army, formed up his troops into a battle square, placing his seven legions (28,000 men), 4,000 light troops and 4,000 allied cavalry around his baggage train as the Parthian horse archers surrounded and attacked the defending Romans (Map 4.7(a)).[90] According to Plutarch, the situation was dire:

> The Parthians stood off from the Romans and began to discharge their arrows at them from every direction, but they did not aim for accuracy since the Roman formation was so continuous and dense that it was impossible to miss. The impact of the arrows was tremendous since their bows were large and powerful and the stiffness of the bow in drawing sent the missiles with great force. At that point the Roman situation became grave, for if they remained in formation they suffered wounds, and if they attempted to advance they still were unable to accomplish anything, although they continued to suffer. For the Parthians would flee while continuing to shoot at them and they are second to this style of fighting only to the Scythians. It is the wisest of practices for it allows you to defend yourself by fighting and removes the disgrace of flight.[91]

The Parthians continued to harass the Romans with their 'hit and run' tactics, and were resupplied by camel with more arrows in order to keep the pressure on.[92]

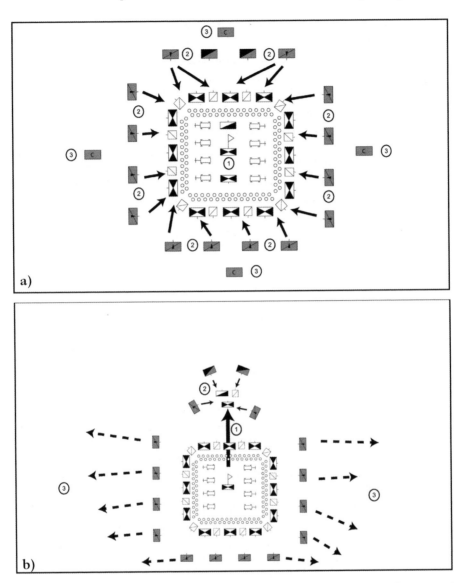

Map 4.7. The Battle of Carrhae, 53 BCE. (a) Phase I: Encountering a strong Parthian mounted army, Crassus forms a battle square (1), surrounding his baggage trains with his legionaries, light troops and auxiliary cavalry. The Parthians surround the square, their horse archers opening a galling fire against the Romans (2) as the camel trains provide a steady supply of arrows (3). (b) Phase II: Realizing that his forces are being steadily whittled away by the Parthian horse archers, Crassus orders his son Publius to sortie from the square with a mixed force (1) in an attempt to break the encirclement. Publius' force is cut off from the main body by the Parthian horsemen and annihilated (2). As night falls the Parthians withdraw (3). Crassus orders a retreat, abandoning many of his wounded. The Parthians deal with the retreating enemy piecemeal as Roman units lose their way in the dark. Two days later, Crassus and his officers are tricked by a Parthian ruse and killed.

Crassus tried to subdue the Parthian light cavalry with his allied auxiliaries, but their numbers were insufficient to deal with the mounted archers, and they were eventually forced back to the legionaries' lines. Understanding that his army was slowly losing the battle of attrition, Crassus sent forward his son Publius with eight cohorts, 500 archers and 1,300 cavalry, including a contingent of Gallic lancers (Map 4.7(b)).[93] The Parthians yielded to the Roman sally and Publius gave chase. But Publius' forces were surrounded by Parthian lancers and horse archers, and, separated from the Roman main body, annihilated. Publius' head was taken back to the Roman camp to taunt Crassus. Night fell and the Parthians withdrew. Under cover of darkness, the Romans retreated back to Carrhae, leaving behind an estimated 4,000 wounded, who were butchered by the enemy the following morning.[94] During the night, another four cohorts lost contact with the main force and were cut down by the Parthians.

Crassus and 500 of his cavalry made it back to Carrhae, while the remainder of Crassus' forces retreated to nearby mountains. But the Romans in the mountains abandoned their strong position to aid Crassus. Realizing that the Roman leader might escape, the Parthian commander, Surena, invited Crassus to a parley, where he and his officers were killed. Total Roman losses were 20,000 killed and perhaps 10,000 captured.[95] Ten thousand Roman troops did manage to escape to Roman territory. It was the worst Roman loss since Cannae.

Crassus' defeat at Carrhae illustrated the danger of bringing a poorly balanced combined-arms system into a hostile environment. The Roman army entered the flat plain of Mesopotamia with insufficient cavalry and light infantry. Unable to punish the Parthian light cavalry with their own archers, the Roman legionaries were forced into defensive battle squares and picked off by the enemy horse archers.[96] The Parthian victory clearly demonstrated the superiority of the light cavalry weapon system over heavy infantry when campaigning on terrain that favoured horses. Although heavy cavalry assisted the Parthian victory, the light cavalry horse archers could have won the battle against poorly supported Roman heavy infantry unaided.

Legion versus Legion: The Civil Wars

The death of Crassus at the battle of Carrhae in 53 BCE altered the balance of power between the surviving members of the triumvirate. Afraid of Caesar's growing popularity among the masses, Pompey forced the Senate to elect him as sole consul, and relieved Caesar of his proconsulship in Gaul. When the Senate ordered Caesar to relinquish his *imperium* in January 49 BCE, he reacted by crossing the Rubicon River in northern Italy and marching on the capital.[97] His action triggered the first of a series of bloody civil wars that would wrack the Roman Republic for the next twenty years. Pompey fled to the east where Roman legions rallied to him, and after suppressing resistance in Italy and

Spain, Caesar met Pompey's forces in Greece at the battle of Pharsalus in 48 BCE.

The armies of Pompey and Caesar first confronted each other at the battle of Dyrrhachium in 48 BCE in what is now modern Albania.[98] Caesar possessed the smaller army (25,000 legionaries and a few cavalry and auxiliaries), perhaps three-quarters the size of Pompey's (36,000 legionaries and a strong cavalry contingent), but Caesar's army was the better force, having campaigned in Gaul together over the past decade. Realizing this, Pompey wisely avoided a pitched battle against his opponent's seasoned veterans, and instead fortified an enclave on the Adriatic coast. Caesar enclosed the fortification with his own outer circumvallation and waited.[99] Pompey had access to seaborne supplies and reinforcements, while Caesar, without a navy, was cut off from Italy. As Pompey's forces rested and grew stronger, Caesar's army grew hungry. Eventually, Pompey's army broke out of the siege and a counter-attack by Caesar ended in disaster, killing 1,000 Romans.[100] Caesar marched east across the mountains of Epirus and into Thessaly, with Pompey following. The two armies would meet again at the battle of Pharsalus.

Julius Caesar camped south of the Enipeus River in Thessaly in the plains of Pharsalus, while Pompey camped a few miles away on a hill near Mount Dogandzis, close to the battlefield of Cynoscephalae, site of the Roman victory over the Greeks in 197 BCE.[101] For days, Caesar offered battle on the plains west of his enemy, but Pompey refused to leave his superior position. But with his supplies low, Caesar ordered his camp broken on 9 August, and on that same day, Pompey offered battle. Both armies used the river to the north and the rocky hills to the south to refuse flank. Pompey assembled elements of twelve legions in the centre (perhaps 50,000 men) with some of his auxiliaries (4,200) on the right wing next to the marsh, and the remainder with his allied cavalry (perhaps 7,000) on the left wing. Pompey's strategy was to outflank Caesar's right with his superior cavalry.

Caesar assembled elements of nine legions (23,000 men or 82 cohorts, many understrength) in the centre, then placed some of his auxiliaries on his left next to the rocky hills and his cavalry (1,000 allied heavy cavalry from Gaul and Germania) opposite Pompey's on the right wing. But Caesar, anticipating Pompey's strategy to outflank his cavalry, stiffened his right wing with light infantry and eight cohorts of legionaries.

Caesar seized the initiative and ordered his army to charge forward at 150 yards, but when Pompey did not march to meet him, Caesar ordered his army to stop and redress their lines (Map 4.8(a)). Both armies then closed and clashed. As both generals expected, Pompey's cavalry drove back Caesar's, and then, displaying superb discipline, turned back against Caesar's flank. To counter, Caesar ordered his eight reserve cohorts to attack Pompey's horse.[102] After driving off the cavalry, Caesar's heavy infantry cohorts easily defeated Pompey's light infantry archers and slingers. Supported again by Caesar's horse (which had returned to the battlefield), the cohorts attacked Pompey's flank (Map 4.8(b) and (c)). The Pompeian legions were unable to withstand the attack and broke. Potentially encircled, Pompey fled the battlefield. In two hours Pompey lost 6,000 soldiers. Caesar's losses were 1,200 dead.[103]

Caesar's victory over Pompey at Pharsalus is another occasion where the side possessing a preponderance in cavalry failed to ensure victory.[104] Caesar, recognizing his opponent's superior numbers in cavalry, reinforced his own horse with heavy and light infantry units. This combination proved too much for Pompey's cavalry, who fled the field. Like Alexander at the battle of Issus, Caesar understood the importance of mixing weapon systems when possessing inferior numbers in cavalry.

After Pharsalus, Pompey escaped to Egypt, where he was murdered in 48 BCE by the Ptolemaic king Ptolemy XII, who chose not to offer hospitality to the loser at Pharsalus. Ptolemy presented Pompey's head to Caesar, who, angered by the murder of his former mentor, intrigued with Ptolemy's sister Cleopatra VII, and removed the young Hellenistic king from his throne. Caesar continued the civil war against the supporters of Pompey in north Africa and Spain, returning triumphant to Rome in 45. Caesar was officially made dictator by the Senate in 47, and in 44 was proclaimed dictator for life. But on the Ides of March 44 BCE, a group of leading senators who resented his domination assassinated him, in the belief that they had championed the cause of republican liberty. In truth, they set the stage for another civil war that delivered the death blow to the republic.[105]

A new struggle for power ensued in 43 BCE. Caesar's heir, his nineteen-year old grand-nephew Octavian (63 BCE–14 CE), took command of some of

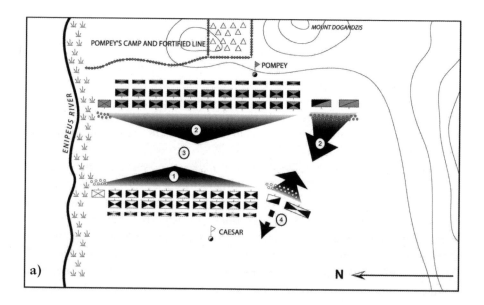

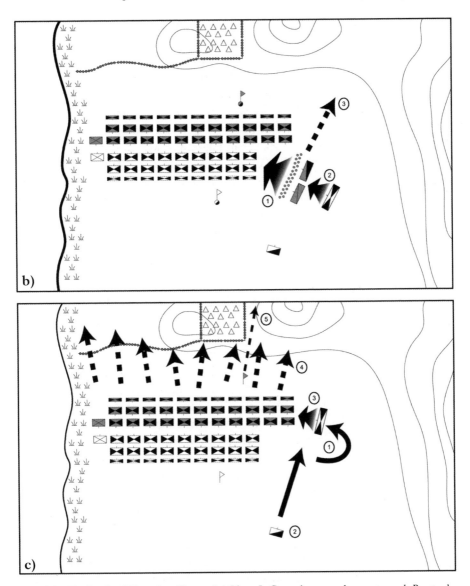

Map 4.8. The Battle of Pharsalus, 48 BCE. (a) Phase I: Caesar's army advances towards Pompey's, halting momentarily to dress its ranks (1). Pompey orders his troops forward in response to Caesar's opening move (2), and the main bodies of the two forces clash (3). Pompey's numerically superior cavalry drive back their opposite number, but the eight cohorts of legionaries on Caesar's right flank stand firm (4). (b) Phase II: As the main bodies of infantry remain locked in close combat, Pompey's cavalry turn from their pursuit of Caesar's horse and assail the enemy legion's flank (1). The eight unbroken cohorts advance and attack Pompey's mounted units in the rear (2), driving them and their supporting archers and slingers from the field (3). (c) Phase III: The eight cohorts of Caesarian legionaries manoeuvre against Pompey's left flank and are joined by Caesar's cavalry as they return to the fray (2). As the heavy infantry force strikes the left-most formations (3), panic sets in and Pompey's army begins to crumble from left to right (4). Pompey abandons his army to its fate and flees the field (5).

Caesar's legions and made himself into a political player of great importance. After forcing the Senate to name him consul, Octavian joined forces with Mark Antony, Caesar's ally and assistant, and Marcus Aemilius Lepidus, who had been commander of Caesar's cavalry. Together, the three formed the Second Triumvirate, which was legally empowered to rule Rome. The three commanders pursued Caesar's assassins and defeated them at the battle of Philippi in 42 BCE. Pushing Lepidus aside, Octavian and Antony divided the Roman world between them – Octavian taking the west and Antony the east. Antony allied himself with Julius Caesar's lover and ally, Cleopatra VII, and in response, Octavian accused Antony of catering to the Egyptian queen and giving away Roman territory. Octavian and Antony soon came into conflict, culminating in the battle of Actium in the autumn of 31 BCE.[106]

At the beginning of the conflict, Antony's forces were primarily located in Greece, where his base of power was located. He controlled 230 warships and a total of 23 legions (most of them understrength), with four being primarily regulated to the role of marines. Octavian's forces numbered approximately 24 legions and some 400 ships, sent east to engage Antony near Epirus. Octavian wanted to catch his opponent before his fleet was fully manned. Octavian's lieutenant Agrippa checked Antony's naval units in the summer of 31, cutting off Antony from his supply sources in the Peloponnese. Without supplies, Antony's navy suffered both plague and starvation, and even attempted to break the blockade, only to be pushed back into the Gulf of Ambracia. Octavian was able to land a portion of his force to the north of Actium, building a fortified camp. Antony favoured a land battle, but Octavian preferred to wait and starve his enemy into submission. Desperate, Antony moved some of his forces across the narrow strait in an attempt to surround and cut off Octavian's land contingent. Although his landing was successful, his attempt to move around the flank of Octavian's army was beaten back.

At midday on 2 September, the combined fleet of Antony and Cleopatra moved to finally break out of the blockade. Antony ordered his ships into three squadrons formed up in two lines, with merchant ships, payships and Cleopatra following behind. Octavian's navy, superior in numbers and quality of sailors, was also arrayed into two lines. Antony's strategy was to row forward, left wing advancing first in order to peel back Octavian's line and open an escape route south. But when Antony attempted this manoeuvre, Octavian ordered his second line to extend north and south to contain the attempted breakout. With Octavian's second line now thinned, Cleopatra took advantage of the sudden favourable wind, hoisted sail and broke through the centre. She deserted the battle, taking the payships with her. Following his Egyptian queen, Antony abandoned his legionaries and sailors to their fate. Cut off and surrounded, Antony's forces either surrendered or defected.

Octavian treated the defeated troops well, recognizing the end of a bloody era was at hand. And though most of the legions were dismissed, a few simply transferred back under his command. Antony and Cleopatra could not raise a new army, and soon their political support evaporated. Both fled to Egypt, where within a year they committed suicide. The Civil Wars were over and Octavian entered Alexandria triumphant. There, he viewed the embalmed body of Alexander the Great. At the age of thirty-two, Alexander had died just as he had won an empire. The same age, Octavian stood as supreme ruler of the Mediterranean world and prepared to forge an empire that would last another 500 years.

Chapter 5

The Roman Empire at War: The Augustan Reforms, *Pax Romana* and Decline of the Legion

The Augustan Reforms

Octavian's victory at the battle of Actium in 31 BCE ended nearly a century of turmoil and civil war. Taking the name Caesar Augustus (the 'exalted one'), he understood that nothing had contributed more directly to the failure of the republic than the growth of client armies and the inability of the Senate to control their commanders. Augustus was determined that the same fate would not befall his own regime. In order to stop this dangerous trend, he set about designing a system under which the Roman army would be clearly subordinate to him alone. To do this, he combined the title of *Imperator* (originally reserved for commanders of victorious Roman armies) with the consular powers of commander-in-chief, from which evolved the title 'emperor'.[1] As both head of state and commander-in-chief, Augustus enjoyed a double hold over provincial governors. He took further precautions by transferring these governors at least once every four years, reserving the more sensitive commands for his relatives, and personally controlling all important promotion, rewards and pay rises in the army.[2]

During Augustus' reign, the Roman army was reduced from the sixty legions left after Actium to 300,000 men in total, consisting of 150,000 Roman citizens in twenty-five legions and 150,000 non-citizens in auxiliary infantry cohorts and cavalry regiments.[3] For the next 200 years the number of legions varied between twenty-five and thirty, not a large army for an empire that contained nearly 60 million people (Map 5.1).[4] Under Augustus, the length of enlistment changed dramatically, increasing from six to twenty years, with a further five years required for veterans retained as officers.[5] The reason for this increased service was probably financial, because the pressure of providing grants of land or money to discharged soldiers was very taxing to the empire, so an extended enlistment was required to ease the economic burden.[6]

Augustus did not modify the tactical organization instituted by the Marian reforms. The Augustan legion still consisted of ten cohorts, but some time in the middle of the first century CE, the strength of the first cohort was doubled

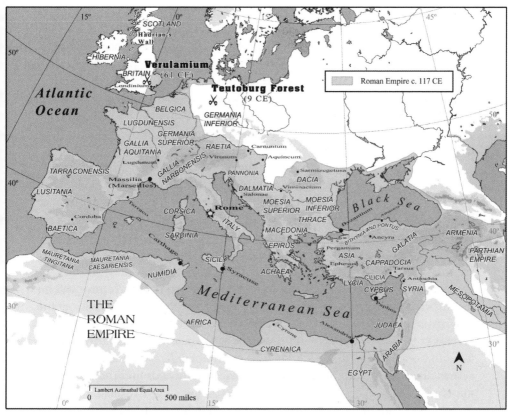

Map 5.1. The Roman Empire under the Pax Romana.

to five centuries of 160 men.[7] Perhaps this was done to provide the legion with a larger tactical formation when dealing with barbarians, or as a tactical reserve. Augustus did, however, make a regiment, or *ala*, of 120 cavalrymen organic to each legion.[8] These men were drawn from the ranks and mounted as scouts (*exploratores*) and messengers. The early Roman cavalry was lightly armoured and capable of limited shock and missile action. But the role of Roman cavalry on the battlefield increased because of prolonged contacts with cavalry-based tactical systems in the east, and in the early second century the Roman emperor Trajan raised an *ala* intended purely for shock combat. Using the two-handed lance or *kontos*, these heavy cavalrymen could not make effective use of a shield, so heavier armour was worn, modelled after the Persian cataphracts.[9] Called *clibanarii*, these lancers and mounts were protected by composite chain- and scale-mail armour.[10] As the empire wore on, *clibanarii* formed an increasingly higher proportion of Roman cavalry and would become the dominant tactical system of the later Byzantine Empire.[11]

The role of the auxiliary also increased in importance in the early imperial period, with the auxiliary's organization and number becoming standardized under Augustus. During the Civil Wars auxiliary units varied in size and there was no set total of units authorized. Under Augustus, the number of auxiliary troops rose to a number roughly equal to that of legionary troops. Auxiliary cohorts and *alae* contained about 480–500 men, and were called *quingenaria*, or '500 strong'. It was not until after the emperor Nero (r. 54–68) that this number rose to 800–1,000 men, called *cohortes milliariae* and *alae milliariae* ('thousand strong'). In addition, an auxiliary cohort made up of a mix of both infantry and cavalry units was created (*cohortes equitatae*), with the proportion of these mixed units probably close to four to one infantry to cavalry.[12]

As the empire wore on, auxiliary units gained significant influence within the Roman war machine's command structure. Initially commanded by their own chieftains, the Augustan reforms placed auxiliary troops under Roman commanders. Over time, the value of the auxiliary on the battlefield could be seen by the prestige associated with commanding these troops. The title of *tribunus* was granted to the commander of the auxiliary *cohors milliaria*, a title equal in seniority to that of a tribune of a legion.[13]

Augustus also created a new imperial grand strategy, placing Roman legions in a forward position on the frontiers, far away from Rome itself.[14] This grand strategy emphasized a fortified and guarded border or *Limes*, placing the legions in perpetual contact with the barbarians and ensuring that the Roman legionary was always in a high state of training and readiness.[15] The *Limes* system also helped keep the legions far from the Roman capital and away from imperial politics.

To protect himself and ensure domestic tranquillity in Rome, Augustus created a personal bodyguard called the Praetorian Guard consisting of nine double-strength cohorts. The guardsmen were organized, trained and armed like the regular legionaries, but were handpicked men of Italian origin who were paid three times as much as normal Roman soldiers, and received benefits after only sixteen years of service.[16] The Praetorian Guard was the only fighting force stationed in Italy. Augustus originally organized the guard so that only three cohorts would be in Rome; the other six were to police the hinterland, with rotation back to Rome each spring and autumn.[17] But after Caesar Augustus' death in 14 CE, this rotation fell apart and the majority of the guard stayed at home, where they often participated in the selection of future emperors. In fact, four of Rome's emperors were elevated to the purple from the ranks of the Praetorian Guard.[18]

Further Roman expansion was blocked in the Near East by Parthia, but Augustus used his legions to put down revolts in the Roman provinces of Iberia and Illyria, and launched expeditions into Dacia (modern Romania) and against German tribes east of the Rhine. Augustus' campaign across the Rhine ended in disaster when a Roman army consisting of three legions ventured into northern Germany in 9 CE and was ambushed by a large force of German tribesmen in the Teutoburg Forest. In this battle, the Roman heavy infantry legionary would face a capable and determined Germanic foe utilizing light infantry tactics.

Legion versus Light Infantry: The Battle of Teutoburg Forest

In 6 CE Augustus sent Publius Quintilius Varus to keep the peace in the newly occupied region of Germania, an area east of the Rhine River in what is now modern Westphalia. Though it was pacified after nearly twenty years of occupation, the Romans maintained a strong base at Aliso (modern Haltern) defended by three legions, XVII, XVIII and XIX (18,000 infantry and 900 cavalry), and allied auxiliaries (3,500–4,000 allied infantry and 600 cavalry), perhaps 23,500 troops all together.[19] The atmosphere in Germania was calm in the autumn of 9 CE, and the legions were used to Romanize the region, felling trees and building roads and bridges.

In September the calm was broken by a minor insurrection of Germanic tribesmen. Setting out for his winter quarters at Minden, Varus decided to pass through the troubled region. But unknown to him, the insurrection was orchestrated by one of his own military advisers, Arminius, a man of Germanic birth who had been granted Roman citizenship and held equestrian rank.[20] Arminius engineered this uprising in order to draw Varus through what appeared to be friendly but difficult terrain, with the intent of annihilating the Roman forces. Although tipped off about the possible plot by a subordinate officer, Varus disregarded the threat and marched south-west with his army in column, followed by a long baggage train and the soldiers' families (Map 5.2(a)).

On the second day out, Arminius and his Germanic contingent suddenly disappeared from the Roman column (Map 5.2(b)). Shortly thereafter, reports reached Varus that outlying detachments of soldiers, probably scouts and foragers, had been slaughtered. Fearing an ambush in hostile territory, Varus then turned his column and headed south toward the Roman fortress of Aliso. The march to Aliso would take the encumbered column through the Doren Pass in the Teutoburg Forest, between the Ems and Weser rivers. Here, the manoeuvrability of the column was severely limited by thick woods, marshes and gullies, exacerbated by seasonal rains and the presence of the heavy baggage train and camp followers.

The first attack on the Roman column took place as Roman engineers were cutting trees and building causeways in the difficult terrain. Despite the disappearance of Arminius and his men, Varus refused to take any special security precautions. Instead, the troops were thoroughly mixed in with the civilians. As the column slowed and piled up, the wind surged and the rain began (Map 5.2(c)).

In the midst of this confusion, Arminius suddenly struck the Roman column's rearguard as his Germanic allies emerged from the woods on the Romans' flanks, hurling javelins into the mass of the unformed Roman ranks.

Varus ordered his own auxiliary light infantry to engage the barbarians, but these troops were Germanic to a man and, either seeing the futility of the situation or in a prearranged plot, deserted the Romans to join Arminius' forces. Gradually, the legions formed, but not before taking significant casualties. As the Roman column's vanguard prepared for a counter-attack, the German attackers disappeared as quickly as they had appeared. Roman engineers sallied out and found some flat, dry terrain and began to construct a field camp. As the Roman column made its way to the safety of the camp, Varus ordered his supply wagons burned and nonessential supplies abandoned.

At dawn Varus set out again, this time with his army in field marching formation (Map 5.2(d)). His objective was Aliso, now less than 20 miles away through the Doren Pass. As the Roman column marched out of the forest and into open terrain, Arminius' troops shadowed the invaders, skirmishing with the Romans at every opportunity, but refusing to engage in force. The barbarians hurled their javelins into the Roman ranks to good effect, but without their own light infantry they could not return fire. The situation became worse when the column entered the woods. The barbarians attacked again as they had the day before, hurling javelins from the woods and engaging in small-unit attacks when the terrain and numbers favoured them.

At day's end, the Romans built a second field camp about a mile from the opening of the Doren Pass and tended their wounded. Unfortunately, Varus did not fully understand the magnitude of his strategic situation. Every major Roman outpost east of the Rhine had been attacked, and most were overrun. Aliso, his objective, was besieged by Germanic tribesmen and was barely holding on. Meanwhile, Arminius' forces were swelling, and soon he had enough troops to successfully overrun the Roman camp.

Arminius spent the night felling trees to obstruct the floor of the ravine, forcing the Romans to slow their march and fight for every foot of passage through the pass. The Germans then took up positions on the hillside and prepared for the Romans. The following morning, Varus pushed toward the Doren Pass. As the Romans pressed up the pathway, they began to meet heavy resistance from Germanic light infantry hailing down missiles from the hillside (Map 5.2(e)). The Romans gradually gained ground, but when a heavy rain began, the slick surface slowed the Romans' ascent.

Finally, unable to secure passage through the pass in the face of inclement weather and a determined foe, the Romans in the van began a controlled retreat down the ravine. At this moment, Arminius ordered a general attack, sending his infantry into the ravine to meet the Romans in hand-to-hand fighting. Germanic swords and javelins struck at Roman cavalry, forcing the horses back into the Roman infantry. In the midst of the mounting confusion, Varus ordered a retreat to the base camp (Map 5.2(f)). The Roman retreat, which began in good order, turned into a general rout. Some Roman cavalry broke away from the column and rode into open terrain, only to be run down by

Germanic cavalry. Back in the ravine, the barbarians cut the column in several places, isolating and then overwhelming the Roman units. A contemporary historian of the battle notes that the Roman army 'hemmed in by forests and marshes and ambuscades was annihilated by the very enemy that it had formerly butchered like cattle'.[21]

At Teutoburg Forest, three Roman legions and 10,000 camp followers were killed during two days of intensive fighting.[22] Like the battle of Carrhae half a century earlier, the Romans lost because they were unable to compel their enemy to meet them in close-quarter combat. The Germanic light infantry used terrain to good effect, ambushing the Romans and attacking at a distance with javelins, then disappearing back into the forest. This form of 'hit and run' tactic wore down the Romans, forcing the legions, in the words of recent authorities on the battle, to 'die a death of a thousand cuts'.[23] When close battle was finally offered, the Roman heavy infantry was in full retreat, discouraged,

Map 5.2. The Battle of Teutoburg Forest, 9 CE. (a) First day: Varus' three legions, a column of German auxiliaries under Arminius, and a large baggage train followed closely by the soldiers' families winds its way through the densely wooded terrain of the Teutoburg Forest. The troops are travelling in a marching formation and are disposed for mobility rather than combat. (b) Second day, Phase I: Arminius' German auxiliaries disappear from the Roman column (1). Varus begins to receive reports that his scout detachments are being ambushed and destroyed. Varus decides to turn the column south, towards the Roman fortress of Aliso. (c) Second day, Phase II: As the column moves south, the terrain becomes rougher, the route cut with gullies, streams and swamps. As Roman pioneers labour to construct causeways (1), the camp followers and families become intermingled with the military units (2). As storms roll into the area and contribute to the confusion, German skirmishers begin to attack the Roman rearguard (3). The German auxiliaries sent by Varus to deal with the attack desert and join their fellow tribesmen. By the time the legions form for a counter-attack, the Germans have faded away into the forest. (d) Third day: After burning the supply wagons and spending the night in a hastily built

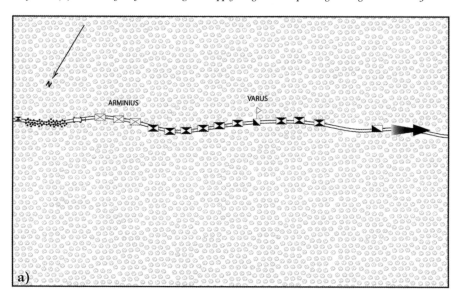

a)

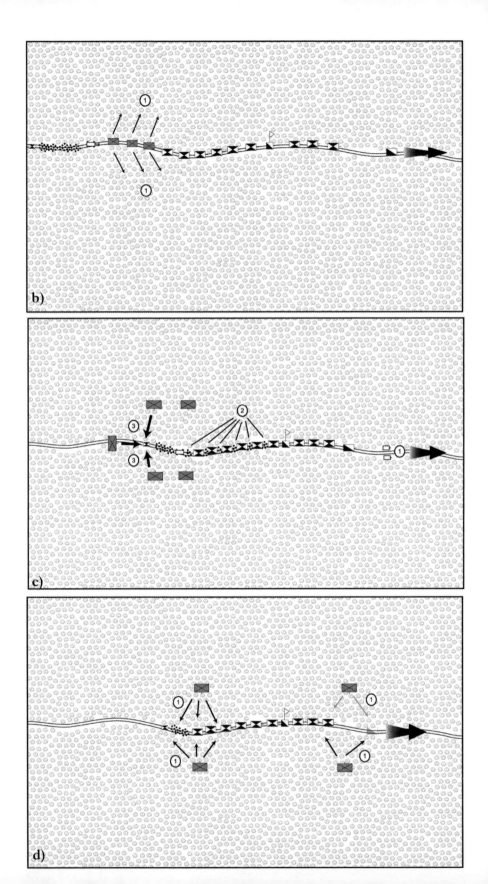

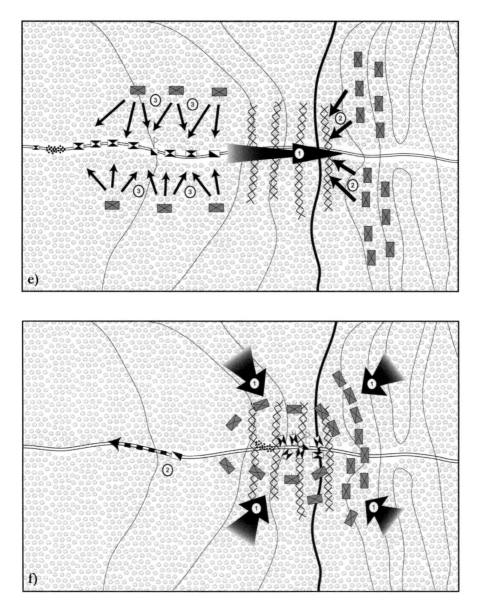

camp, Varus' legions set out again for Aliso, travelling in a field marching formation as they now expect trouble. Arminius' troops shadow the legions, engaging the Romans with javelins when the terrain favours such attacks (1). At the end of the day, Varus' column constructs a second field camp, approximately 1 mile from the opening of the Doren Pass. (e) Fourth day, Phase I: Varus' column pushes towards the pass, its progress in the ravine slowed by trees felled by Arminius' now-reinforced army during the night. As the Roman vanguard struggles to ascend the far slope (1), it is met by a hail of javelins from the foe (2). German hit-and-run attacks continue to plague the Roman column (3). (f) Fourth day, Phase II: The rain-slick slope, felled trees and German pressure force the Roman cavalry back into their advancing infantry formations, compressing the column in the ravine. Varus orders a retreat, which degenerates into a rout. The Germans attack (1), cutting the column up into small pieces and destroying them in the ravine. Some of the Roman cavalry manage to break free of the encirclement (2), only to be destroyed by German cavalry when they break into open terrain. Three Roman legions and 10,000 camp followers are slaughtered in the forest.

disorganized and overwhelmed by a numerically superior foe. But even under these dire circumstances, the Romans fought in small units for hours, meeting and beating wave after wave of barbarian attackers. One small troop of legionaries fought on throughout the day and into the next, being overcome by the barbarians the following morning and killed on the spot.[24]

As a consequence of this defeat, the Romans never occupied more than the fringe areas of Germania, instead relying on the Rhine and Danube rivers as a natural barrier demarcating the Roman Empire's northern border. Territorial expansion did take place under the successors of Augustus, but with the exception of the annexation of Britain by Claudius (r. 41–54 CE) in 43 CE, the expansion remained within the natural frontiers of the empire – the ocean to the west, the rivers to the north and the desert in the east and south. Still, three areas prompted special concern. In the east, the Romans used a system of client states to serve as a buffer against the Parthians. In the north, the Rhine–Danube frontier became the most heavily fortified frontier area because of the threat from Germanic and Asiatic tribes, while in the north-west, Britain served as a safe harbour for Celtic tribes, prompting the Romans to cross the English Channel and challenge the barbarians for mastery of the island.

Legion versus Chariots: The Roman Campaigns in Britain

Rome's first foray into Britain took place in August 55 BCE when Julius Caesar led two legions in a reconnaissance expedition against the Celtic tribes. By then three years into a very successful Gallic campaign, Caesar set his sights on the relatively unknown island on the edge of the known world, perhaps wishing to secure a piece of the tin trade or possibly to gain more political fame in Rome by subduing yet another foe. Caesar returned to Britain in the following summer with five legions, landing north-east of Dover in modern Kent. Pushing through weak resistance on the beachhead, Caesar marched inland and crossed the Thames River near Brentford. The British chief Cassivellaunus avoided a large battle against the Romans, instead harassing the invaders with war chariots and cavalry raids.

This meeting between Roman legion and Celtic chariots was in essence an encounter between the finest Iron Age army of the classical period and a battlefield anachronism whose origins dated back to the Bronze Age. Yet, despite never meeting the Britons in a pitched battle, Caesar was impressed with the barbarians' chariots, describing their harassing tactics in his *Gallic Wars*:

> They begin by driving all over the field, hurling javelins; and the terror inspired by the horses and the noise of the wheels is usually enough to throw the enemy ranks into disorder. Then they work their way between their own cavalry units, where the warriors jump down and fight on foot. Meanwhile the drivers retire a short distance

from the fighting and station the cars in such a way that their masters, if outnumbered, have an easy means of retreat to their own lines. In action therefore, they combine the mobility of cavalry with the staying power of foot soldiers. Their skill, which is derived from ceaseless training and practice, may be judged by the fact that they can control their horses at full gallop on the steepest incline, check and turn them in a moment, run along the pole, stand on the yoke, and get back again into the chariot as quick as lightning.[25]

Perhaps recognizing the capabilities of Caesar and his veteran legions, Cassivellaunus finally agreed to peace terms at Verulamium (modern St Albans, 20 miles north-west of London), surrendering hostages and agreeing to pay tribute to Rome. Satisfied, Caesar retraced his route to the coast and re-embarked for Gaul. The expedition achieved no permanent gain for Caesar (no tribute was paid or significant plunder gained) and Britain remained outside of Roman imperium for another ninety-seven years.

Emperor Claudius' invasion of Britain in 43 CE marked the beginning of a four-century period of occupation and Romanization. The British Celts, politically divided, offered only temporary resistance to the four legions sent by the emperor to pacify the island. In the years following the Roman invasion, these legions repeatedly breached the Celtic defences, storming hilltop fortresses and occupying first the south-eastern lowland zone and finally, after some difficulty, the highlands in northern England and westward through Wales to the Irish Sea. The greatest challenge to Roman occupation took place in 61 CE when several Celtic tribes rebelled against harsh and humiliating treatment by the Romans in East Anglia, initiating a killing spree of all foreigners in their wake.[26] Led by the red-headed Boudicca, the widowed warrior queen of the Iceni tribe, the Celts first attacked the undefended town of Camulodunum (near modern Colchester), slaughtering the Roman settlers and those Britons collaborating with the enemy.

Rushing from its barracks in Lindum (modern Lincoln) to put down the revolt, the IX Legion was overcome by the sheer numbers of the Celtic tribesmen and annihilated. At Glevum (modern Gloucester), the commander of the II Legion, Poenius Postumus, refused to leave the protection of his encampment, while the other two legions in Britain, the XIV and XX under provincial governor Suetonius Paulinus, were in Wales. Before the Welsh legions could intervene, Boudicca's rebels attacked Londinium (London), murdering its inhabitants and burning the small Roman city to the ground. The rebels then turned to the north-west and destroyed the city of Verulamium. As many as 70,000 people are estimated to have been killed in the three massacres.[27]

In a forced march from Wales, governor Paulinus' two legions arrived outside Verulamium and took up position in a strong defensive position in a large defile. With his flank and rear secured by heavily wooded hills, the Roman commander arrayed his infantry (6,000 legionaries and 4,000 auxiliaries) in the centre in a slightly concave formation, with cavalry *alae* (500 men each) on the wings, and light infantry on the flanks.[28] The Romans, drawn up in their defile, watched as masses of Celtic chariots, cavalry and infantry filled the plain before them, followed by wagons and carts filled with booty from the sacked towns. Assured of victory, the Britons also brought with them their women and children so that they might witness the destruction of their Roman overlords. A modern estimate places the total British force at between 40,000 and 60,000 men, with perhaps another 40,000 spectators. Tacitus tells us that on the British side, 'cavalry and infantry bands seethed over a wide area in unprecedented numbers'.[29] Whatever the actual figure, the Romans were outnumbered at least four to one, and probably by a larger ratio.

Classical writers tell us very little about the progress of the battle of Verulamium, leaving modern historians to speculate on its course and the veracity of casualty figures. According to custom, the Britons placed their war chariots in the front of their army, where they drove up and down their adversary's ranks, hurling insults and javelins into their enemy's lines in a hope of taunting their opponents into breaking their formation (Map 5.3(a)). Whether this was tried at Verulamium is unknown, but contemporary accounts tell us that the Romans did not break ranks, staying safe behind their own shield walls and returning fire with their own light and heavy *pila* as the huge barbarian host neared.

When the Romans finally counter-attacked, they adopted a series of wedge formations and, with auxiliary archers in support, pushed forward from the

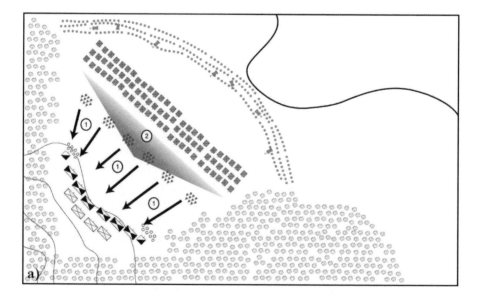

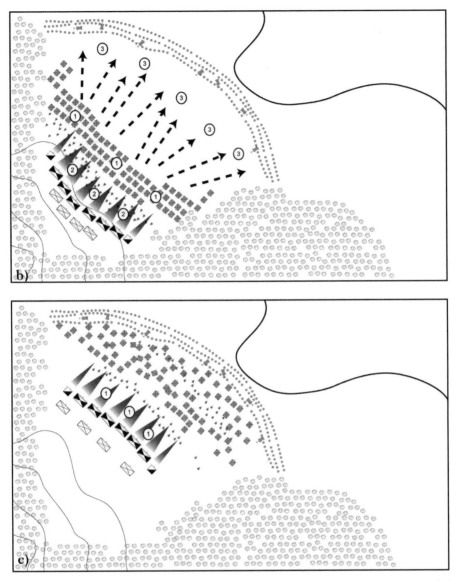

Map 5.3. *The Battle of Verulamium, 61* CE. *(a) Phase I: The Britons' chariots may have skirmished with the Roman formation, attempting to goad it into a premature attack (1). The main element of the barbarian force begins to advance towards the Roman force arrayed on a hillside flanked by woods (2). (b) Phase II: As the Britons press ahead, the flanking woods act as a funnel, making jumbled ranks even more mixed and compact (1). The legions counter-attack in edge formations, the downhill grade adding to the assault's momentum (2). The barbarian mass is further compressed and the Britons begin to rout (3). (c) Phase III: The Britons' army degenerates into a fleeing rabble, penned in by their wagons and their families. The Roman legions close in and slaughter the barbarians (1), giving no quarter to any, including non-combatants.*

defile (Map 5.3(b)). As the legionaries advanced, hacking and thrusting their way through the unarticulated masses of barbarians, their wedge formations quickly consumed the precious ground between them and their enemy, pressing the Celtic chariots, cavalry and infantry into one another. The British lines broke and a rout ensued. Any hope of retreat was thwarted by the enormous crowd gathered to watch the battle. Caught between the Roman killing machine and their own wagon laager, the Britons were slaughtered by the tens of thousands (Map 5.3(c)). No quarter was given to man, woman or child. Roman sources claim 80,000 Britons were killed, while Roman casualties were just over 400 dead and a similar number wounded.[30]

Having escaped the massacre at Verulamium, Boudicca took her own life with poison, while the Roman commander at Glevum, Poenius Postumus, fell on his sword in disgrace.[31] Over the next few centuries, Roman Britain would enjoy unbroken peace and prosperity, with Roman institutions gradually penetrating Celtic and pre-Celtic cultures. The Roman army pushed the frontiers northward to the borders of Scotland, building first Hadrian's Wall, a defensive structure 80 miles long across northern England, and later Antonine's Wall in the second century to keep the Picts in Scotland at bay. But the expense of keeping 10 per cent of the Roman army garrisoned in this far-off province proved too costly for the empire. After the barbarian penetrations of 410 CE, the British legions were recalled to the continent, leaving the heirs of four centuries of Romanization to fend for themselves. Attacked from the west and north by the Irish and Celts, and from the east by the Angles and Saxons, the Romano-British would finally succumb to the invaders. By the early medieval period, Roman Britain would be quickly transformed into Anglo-Saxon England.

The Roman *Limes* Threatened: The Return of Civil War and Invasion

At the beginning of the second century, Emperor Trajan (r. 98–117) broke with Augustus' policy of defensive imperialism by extending Roman rule into Dacia, Mesopotamia and the Sinai peninsula (see Map 5.1). Trajan's conquests represent the high-water mark of Roman expansion. His successors recognized that the empire was overextended and pursued a policy of retrenchment. Hadrian (r. 117–138) withdrew Roman forces from much of Mesopotamia and, though he retained Dacia and Arabia, went on the defensive in his frontier policy, reinforcing the *Limes* along the Rhine–Danube frontier and building the wall in England that bears his name. By the reign of Marcus Aurelius (r. 161–180), the vulnerability of the empire had become apparent. Frontiers were stabilized, and the Roman forces were established in permanent fortresses behind the frontiers.[32]

Although the *Limes* system was strengthened in the second century, the Roman army remained the primary instrument for the defence of the frontiers. In 14 CE it numbered twenty-five legions, but increased to thirty by the time of

Trajan at the beginning of the second century CE.[33] The auxiliaries were increased correspondingly, making the imperial army a force of about 400,000 soldiers in total (legionaries and auxiliaries) by the end of the second century. Since legionaries were required to be Roman citizens, most recruits in Augustus' time were from Italy. But in the course of the first century, the reluctance of Italians to enlist in the military led to the recruitment of citizens from the provinces. By the middle of the first century, 50 per cent of the legionaries were non-Italian, and by 100 CE, only one in five was Italian.[34] In the second and third centuries, more and more recruits came from the frontier provinces than from the more Romanized ones.

The death of Marcus Aurelius in 180 CE marked the end of the *Pax Romana* and the beginning of more than a century of militarism and civil war. Decline was temporarily halted under the reign of Publius Septimius Severus (r. 193–211) and his heirs. Severus created a military monarchy, viewing his legions as his ultimate source of authority. He abolished most of the remaining class distinctions in the army, raised its pay by a third and broke with tradition by stationing a legion in Italy in order to have a strategic reserve. Moreover, the army itself was expanded to thirty-three legions, and military officers were appointed to important government positions.[35]

Military monarchy was followed by military anarchy. For a period of almost fifty years (235–284), the Roman Empire was mired in almost continuous civil war. Adding to the effects of the growing chaos within the Roman government was the increasing threat of barbarian invasion into Roman territory. In 250 the Goths penetrated the Roman *Limes* and raided as far south as Greece, annihilating a Roman army in Thrace led by the emperor Decius.[36] The Franks advanced into Gaul and Spain, and the Alemanni even invaded Italy itself (the city of Rome was fortified for the first time since the Punic Wars). Moreover, military commanders took advantage of the chaotic conditions and seized areas in Gaul, Syria, Egypt and Anatolia. It was not until the reign of Emperor Aurelian (r. 270–275) that most of the boundaries were restored. Although he abandoned the Danubian province of Dacia, he reconquered Gaul and re-established order in the east and along the *Limes.*[37]

Invasions, civil wars and plague brought back from the east by legions led to a considerable loss of population and a shortage of military manpower in the third century. Also, financial strains made it difficult to enlist and pay the necessary soldiers. Whereas in the second century the Roman army was recruited from citizens in the provinces, by the mid-third century, the state was relying on hiring barbarians to fight under Roman commanders. These soldiers had no understanding of Roman traditions and no real attachment to either the empire or the emperors. The 'barbarization' of the Roman army had begun.

The Late Empire: The 'Barbarization' of the Roman Army

By Aurelian's reign, Roman units on the frontiers were undergoing a profound transformation, one that fundamentally changed the character and appearance of the Roman imperial army. Mobile elements of the army were increasingly mounted in order to meet and defeat the barbarian incursions. The increased presence of non-Romans within the ranks of the army led to the inclusion of eastern and Germanic arms, armour and fighting methods within the Roman army. In the eastern provinces, a new Roman heavy cavalry was introduced, modelled after the Persian cataphracts. By the late imperial period there is evidence that in the eastern provinces the Romans sometimes armed their shock cavalry with bows or used auxiliary light cavalry (*equites sagittarii*) armed with the Asian composite bow to supplement their tactical mix.[38]

In the course of the third century, the Roman Empire came close to collapse. At the end of the third and beginning of the fourth centuries, it gained a new lease of life through the efforts of two strong emperors, Diocletian (r. 284–305) and Constantine the Great (r. 324–337), who restored order and stability. The late empire's 'Indian summer' began when Diocletian split the state into eastern and western zones (Map 5.4) and appointed a fellow *augustus* (co-emperor) and two *caesars* (deputy emperors) to govern in a *tetrarchy* (rule by four). Diocletian also returned to a preclusive strategy that advocated stopping invasions along the frontiers. To do this, he divided the empire into military districts administered by a *vicar*. Each district was somewhat self-contained, with its own pay, supply and militia structure. Diocletian then increased the size of the army to between 400,000 and 500,000 men, and added specialized infantry units to the legion, including the *Ioviani* and *Herculiani* and heavy cavalry lancers (*lanciari*).[39] These arrangements made governing the empire easier, but they also set the stage for a permanent political and cultural split, one that would ultimately create the Byzantine Empire centred on Greece in the east, and a weakened Western Roman Empire centred on Italy in the west. Diocletian's abdication in 305 precipitated another civil war, and complete order was not restored until Constantine united east and west in 324.

Under Constantine a switch in emphasis in Roman grand strategy was finally completed, a change that compromised the integrity of the Roman tactical system and opened the door for a full-scale 'barbarization' of the Roman imperial army and the final demise of the legion. During this period, Roman grand strategy moved away from its traditional static frontier defence toward a defence-in-depth. Since the reign of Augustus, imperial grand strategy placed Roman legions in a forward position on the frontiers, far away from Rome itself.[40] Because of perpetual contact with the barbarians, the Roman legionary was always in a high state of training and readiness, a fact that helped ensure peace and prosperity in the empire for centuries. But plague and endemic political chaos in the third century eroded the Roman Empire's ability to defend itself against the barbarian tribes massing on its borders. In response

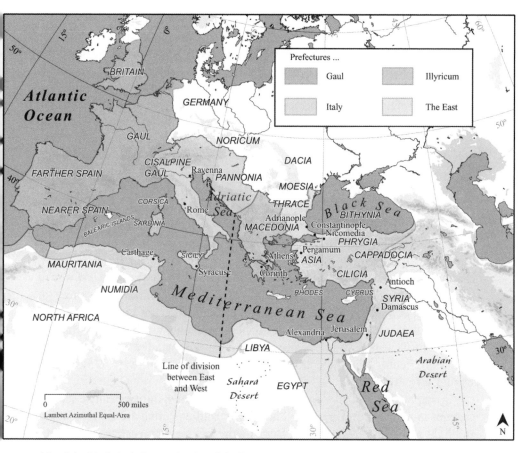

Map 5.4. Diocletian's Reorganization of the Empire.

to this increased threat, Constantine implemented a change in grand strategy when he unified the empire. His solution to barbarian penetrations was a change from a linear defence to a defence-in-depth posture.[41] This grand strategy favoured a central reserve of troops with great mobility, with cavalry preferred to infantry. Strong points on the border would serve as pockets of resistance to slow, pin and harass the enemy while the mobile reserve moved in and counter-attacked. The mobile army was a large force of perhaps 100,000 men commanded by two field marshals, a commander of the infantry (*magister peditum*) and the commander of the cavalry (*magister equitum*).[42]

Since the defence in depth required greater mobility to be effective, the cavalry's position in the Roman army was raised. Emperor Gallienus (r. 253–268) probably initiated the mobile field army in the mid-third century, raising the stature of cavalry in the Roman army and stationing the cavalry force in Milan. Gallienus also increased the legion's organic regiment from 120 horsemen to over 700, paving the way for the demise of the traditional infantry-based Roman army.[43] But this cavalry reserve was probably not a permanent force. It would be during the reign of Constantine (r. 324–337) that a permanent mobile army was formed. He went so far as to disband the Praetorian Guard, replacing it with elite cavalry *palatini* regiments, recruited mainly from the Germanic tribes.[44] With the emergence of cavalry the position of Roman infantry began to erode, and traditional Roman infantry tactics, driven by harsh discipline and constant training, simply disappeared.[45] The Romans even adopted the Germanic war cry, the *baritus*, when in battle.[46] The deterioration of the emperor's army would have ominous results when Roman infantry proved unable to beat barbarian infantry on the battlefield at Adrianople in 378, Pollentia in 402 and Rome in 410.[47]

By the beginning of the fourth century the legion completely disappeared, replaced by the *palatini, comitatenses* and *limitanei* in order of importance. The *palatini* were the emperor's guard, cavalry regiments chosen by merit and replacing the Praetorian Guard. The *comitatenses* made up the field army, comprising mixed regular and barbarian regiments, while the *limitanei* were a militia, retired legionaries mustered to defend their homeland. In times of emergency, *limitanei* could be promoted into the field army, receiving the title *pseudocomitatenses*. The complement of these new units was about one-third of a first-century legion. While Septimius Severus commanded 33 legions in the early third century, by the end of the fourth century there were 175 of these smaller formations.[48]

Further evidence of the 'barbarization' of the Roman military can be seen in changes in weapons and armour. The Roman soldier's offensive arms of heavy and light *pila* and *gladius* were replaced by the Germanic thrusting spear and a longer slashing sword or *spatha*, a straight two-edged sword used by both infantry and cavalry.[49] Though the *spatha* was pointed for thrusting, it was usually utilized for cut-and-slash strikes, emulating the favoured tactics of the Germanic tribes. 'Barbarization' also affected the defensive characteristics of the Roman soldier. By the early fourth century, body armour was almost completely abandoned by Roman infantry.[50] The Roman soldier's protection came from his shield, a Germanic-inspired round or oval shield that replaced the rectangular *scutum* of the early empire.[51] Consistent with Germanic practices, heavy cavalry continued to wear mail shirts and metal helmets.[52] By the end of the fourth century, both weapon quality and weapon training had deteriorated drastically from earlier standards.[53]

Constantine's conscious adoption of a defence-in-depth strategy in the early fourth century increased the importance of cavalry, giving Germanic equestrians greater leadership opportunities in the Roman army. With this increased influence came the natural adoption and adaptation of Germanic arms and armour at the expense of the traditional Roman panoply, leading to greater 'barbarization' of the Roman army. Two significant examples of the ramifications of this 'barbarization' of the Roman military machine came in the late imperial period with the battles of Adrianople in 378 and Châlons in 451.

Roman Infantry in Decline: The Battles of Adrianople and Châlons

After Constantine's reign the Roman Empire continued to be divided into western and eastern parts, with the Western Roman Empire coming under increasing pressure from invading barbarian forces, while the Eastern Roman Empire faced the emerging power of the Sassanid Persians. Emperor Julian the Apostate (r. 361–363), so named because of his refusal to adopt the rising religion of Christianity, faced a difficult strategic situation with Persia. Though Julian's army was tactically proficient, he misused its capabilities, losing his life in a battle a few miles from Maranga on the Tigris in 363. His successor, Jovian (r. 363–364), negotiated a humiliating peace with Persia, ceding northern Mesopotamia to the Sassanid rulers.[54] The loss of an emperor on the battlefield would have deep psychological effects, and unfortunately for the Romans, he would not be the last Roman ruler killed in action. Fifteen years later, the emperor Valens (r. 364–378) would face a similar fate at the battle of Adrianople.

At about the same time as the Romans were battling the Persians in Mesopotamia, another threat was emerging in the east. Nomads from the Eurasian steppe known as Huns moved into eastern Europe, putting pressure on the semi-nomadic Germanic tribes massing against the Roman *Limes* (Map 5.5). One of these tribes, the Visigoths (western Goths), sought Valens' permission to cross the Danube and settle in Roman territory. The emperor agreed to the migration if the Visigoths gave up their arms and settled in Thrace as farmers. In late 376 the Visigoths crossed the Danube (perhaps 200,000 strong, including men, women and children) but were exploited by Roman officials. By 378 impending starvation forced the Visigoths to ravage Thrace and besiege the city of Adrianople (modern Edirne, Turkey), where they had been resisted and denied food by local authorities.

To meet this threat, Emperor Valens assembled an army and marched north from Constantinople to meet the barbarians. At Adrianople, Valens waited for the arrival of the Western Roman emperor, Gratian. But, believing the Goths only had 10,000 men under arms, Valens decided to attack immediately and seize all of the glory for himself. On 9 August the Roman emperor left the city at the head of an army of between 15,000 and 20,000 troops.[55]

Eight miles out of Adrianople, Valens' column surprised a Gothic wagon laager formed in a defensive circle on a low hill, containing an army comparable in size to the Roman host (the proportion of infantry to cavalry is unknown for either army). Valens deployed his infantry behind a screen provided by his right wing cavalry and light infantry archers (Map 5.6(a)). As the Romans were deploying from column, the Visigothic leader Fridigern ordered the grasslands

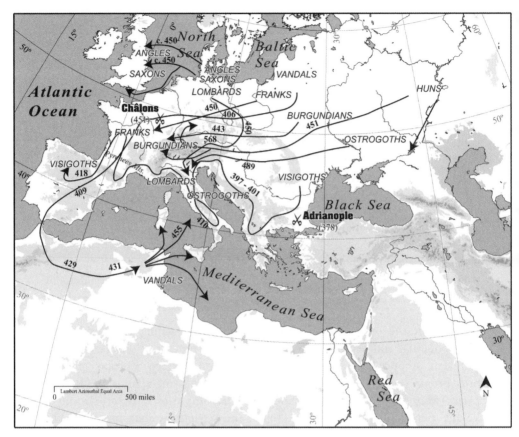

Map 5.5. The Barbarian Invasions.

set on fire. In response, Valens ordered his skirmishers to attack in order to buy time as his column deployed.

But the Roman skirmishers, light infantry archers (*sagittarii*) and elite cavalry (*scutarii*) from the emperor's bodyguard, committed themselves too strongly to the effort (Map 5.6(b)). Instead of performing the traditional role of light troops (harassing enemy formations, then retiring behind their own infantry), the Roman skirmishers engaged with the Visigoths. The Visigothic counter-attack threw the Roman skirmishers into their own infantry lines, disrupting the Roman centre (Map 5.6(c)). At that moment, the Gothic cavalry returned from foraging and attacked the Roman right flank and drove off the Roman cavalry. The Roman line finally gave way, but not without spirited fighting. Seeing the Roman centre in disarray, the Goths sallied out of their wagon circle and attacked the Roman centre as additional Gothic cavalry struck the Roman left, driving off the Roman cavalry. Outflanked by barbarian cavalry and encircled by enemy infantry, the Roman foot soldiers were pushed into a mass of bodies so compacted that they were unable to wield their swords properly (Map 5.6(d)).[56] Perhaps two-thirds of the trapped Roman army was killed, including Emperor Valens; his body was never recovered.[57] The contemporary historian Ammianus tells us that it was the worst Roman defeat since Cannae.[58]

Though cavalry was present on both sides, the Gothic victory over the Romans at Adrianople was essentially one of infantry over infantry.[59] This fact is significant in itself in that the Roman army was unable to defeat a barbarian army only slightly larger, when in centuries past it had regularly defeated enemy hosts many times its own size. No doubt the Roman army's abandonment of the close-order drill utilizing *gladius*, rectangular *scutum* and body protection which had served them so well during the *Pax Romana* contributed to this debacle, depriving the soldiers of a significant advantage over their enemies. And though Gothic infantry carried the day, the barbarians' use of cavalry as a part of a combined-arms attack also was a harbinger for the role cavalry would play in later Byzantine warfare in a way reminiscent of Alexander or Hannibal.[60] The superior Gothic horse, by defeating their Roman counterparts, turned the tide of the battle by hemming in the Roman foot soldiers, allowing for the massacre of over 10,000 Roman veterans.

After the battle of Adrianople, Rome agreed to allow the victorious Visigoths to settle in the Roman Empire. In return, the Visigoths promised to fight for the empire as allies or *foederati*.[61] As such they retained their Germanic commanders and were allowed to roam within the boundaries of the empire. But by virtue of their strength they soon capitalized on the weakness of their Roman hosts, and began marauding throughout the Balkan peninsula. The very same Visigothic tribe that crossed the Danube in 376 seeking refuge from the Huns sacked Rome in 410, something that had not been done since the Celts took the city some 800 years before. Even with the assistance of *foederati*, the Roman military was unable to hold back the invading Germanic and central Asian tribes. By the first decades of the fifth century, the barbarians were regularly crossing the frontiers into Roman territory.

Perhaps the most infamous of these tribes, the Huns, were united under a charismatic and brutal chieftain named Attila (d. 452), who regularly terrorized the Danubian frontier and the Eastern Roman Empire, exacting a large tribute from the emperor Theodosius II. When Theodosius' successor refused to pay tribute in 450, Attila suddenly shifted his attention to the west, leading his Hunnic confederation across the Rhine and into Roman Gaul. But the army of the Huns had changed since the nomads first appeared from the Eurasian steppes in the mid-fourth century. The Hunnic army then was predominately cavalry, relying on a mix of light cavalry horse archers and heavy cavalry lancers reminiscent of the Parthians.[62] When the Huns moved out of the Eurasian steppes and entered the Hungarian plain, they lost the ability to support their large mounted army logistically.[63]

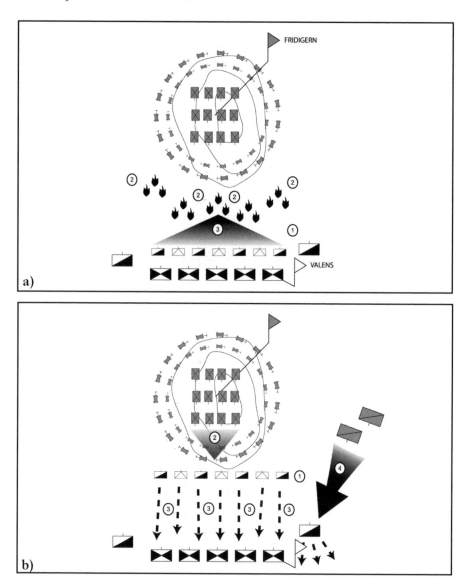

Map 5.6. The Battle of Adrianople, 378 CE. (a) Phase I: Valens encounters a Gothic wagon laager on a low hill and deploys his force from column into line behind a screen of infantry archers and heavy cavalry from the Imperial bodyguard (1). As the Romans form, Fridigern orders the grass between the forces set afire (2). Valens orders his skirmish line to attack in order to buy time to complete his deployment (3). (b) Phase II: Valens' skirmishers press their attack too closely (1), and the Goths counter-attack (2), throwing the Romans back into their own infantry (3). Returning from foraging, Gothic cavalry attack the Romans' right-flank horsemen (4). (c) Phase III: Outflanked by the

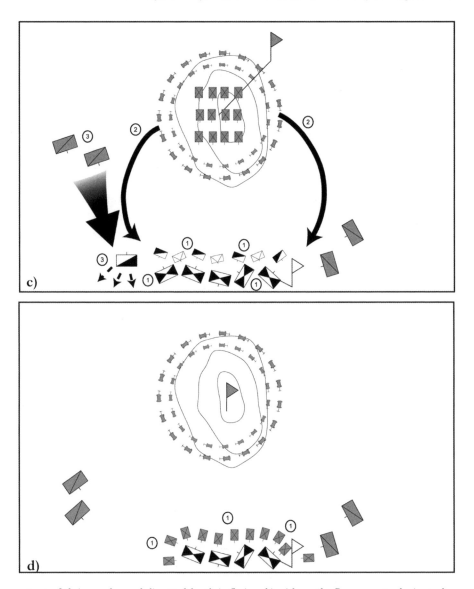

retreat of their cavalry and disrupted by their fleeing skirmishers, the Roman centre begins to lose cohesion (1). Seeing this, the Gothic infantry sally forth from the laager, encircling the Roman foot soldiers (2). Another contingent of Gothic horsemen arrives, driving off the Romans' left-flank cavalry (3). (d) Phase IV: The surviving Roman infantry are compressed into an immobile mass (1). Unable to wield their weapons, perhaps as many as two-thirds of the Romans are killed, including Emperor Valens, whose body is never recovered.

To adapt to the forests of central and western Europe, the Huns adopted the panoplies and infantry tactics of the Germanic tribes they assimilated into their confederation. The army Attila the Hun commanded would have more in common with the Visigoths and Romans than with the steppe nomads. Like the Germans and 'barbarized' Romans, the Hunnic infantryman wore no armour, at least no breastplate or helmet. Hunnic and Germanic nobles probably wore helmets, but mail armour was very uncommon.[64] Unencumbered by heavy armour, barbarian infantry was light and mobile.[65] When the Huns crossed the Rhine in 451, they faced a Roman army with similar characteristics.

The commander of the western Roman army in Gaul, Flavius Aetius (*c.*395–454), was a product of the new barbarization of the imperial army. Born of a Scythian father and Italian mother, Aetius rose through the ranks of the Roman army as a cavalry commander, becoming the most capable general the late Western Roman Empire produced and the de facto ruler of Gaul. Aetius' relationship with the Huns was not always antagonistic. The Roman general persuaded the Huns to attack the Burgundian *foederati* marauding along the lower Rhine, wiping out 20,000 of the invaders.[66] But Aetius' influence over Attila had waned by the late 440s, and the 'Scourge of God', as Attila was known to Christianized Europe, turned his attention toward the Western Roman Empire. Early in 451 Attila invaded the Rhine, supported by a large army of Huns and associated allies such as the Ostrogoths, Burgundians and Alans. This Hunnic confederation crossed the Rhine on a broad front stretching from Belgium to Metz and brought the city of Orleans in central Gaul under siege.

To meet this Hunnic confederation, Aetius allied himself with the Visigothic king, Theodoric I – son of the infamous Germanic ruler Alaric II, who sacked Rome in 410. The combined armies marched to the relief of Orleans. The Huns, unwilling to be caught between the walls of Orleans and a relieving army, abandoned the siege and withdrew northward. Here, a large battle developed near the city of Châlons on the Catalaunian plain in what is now the Champagne district of France. Known to history as either the battle of Châlons or the Catalaunian Plains, the engagement 'was one of the decisive encounters in the history of the western world'.[67]

On 20 June, the day of the battle, Attila was uncertain of victory. He maintained his forces behind a wagon laager until late in the day, presumably to delay the battle in order to use the cover of darkness for escape in case the battle went poorly. When Attila finally offered battle, he placed himself in command of his most reliable troops, the Huns, arraying them in the centre of the line in order to push through the enemy's centre. The Hun commander then placed the Ostrogoths on his left wing, and his other allies on the right.[68]

Aetius decided on an opposite strategy. The Roman commander placed his least reliable troops, the Alans, in the centre to take whatever attack Attila might launch, then arrayed his Visigoths on his right and his Romans and Franks on the left wings to execute a double envelopment on the flanks of the enemy. Like Adrianople seven decades earlier, the battle that would take place would be primarily an infantry rather than a cavalry engagement. Contemporary sources do not give us a reliable estimate of the belligerents' troop strengths, but an estimate of perhaps 25,000 to 30,000 troops on each side is not out of the question.[69]

The initial skirmish took place on Aetius' left, where the Romans seized the high ground, giving them the advantage for a planned flanking manoeuvre (Map 5.7(a)). When battle was finally joined, the Huns struck hard against the Alans in Aetius' centre, pushing the *foederati* back. Attila then wheeled to hit the Visigoths in the flank. In heavy fighting, King Theodoric was killed, but his Visigoths rallied and counter-attacked. Meanwhile, the Romans and Franks threatened Attila's weak right flank from their superior position on high ground. Witnessing a counter-attack on his left and the threat of envelopment on his right side, Attila called for a retreat to the wagon laager as Hunnic archers kept the Romans and Germans at bay (Map 5.7(b)). Under the cover of darkness, the Huns slipped away from the battlefield. Casualties on both sides were horrific, but in the end, the victory was Aetius'. Attila was forced to retreat beyond the Rhine.

The Roman victory at Châlons was a near-run thing, and the narrow margin of victory suggests parity in forces, both quantitatively and qualitatively. Aetius and Attila met on the battlefield with relative equality in numbers. It is not known for certain what role cavalry played in this engagement, but one can surmise that horsemen were present on the battlefield, though not in large numbers. The Hunnic confederation suffered great losses, enough to abandon the fight and withdrawal from Gaul. And while Aetius won the day, his forces suffered heavy casualties, including the loss of King Theodoric.

By the middle of the fifth century, the equipment and tactics of the Huns, Germans and Romans were very similar. Aetius' confederation of Romans and barbarians was essentially a mirror image of Attila's forces: poorly armed and armoured unarticulated infantry fighting with limited cavalry support. The battles of Adrianople and Châlons illustrated the decline of the Roman heavy infantry. Gone were the days of a Roman legion meeting and defeating a barbarian army three times its size.

Aetius' victory over Attila at Châlons did not end the Huns' threat to the Western Roman Empire. In 452 Attila crossed the Alps and pushed into Italy with a vengeance. The city of Aquileia was utterly destroyed, while Milan, Verona and Pavia were either bankrupted bribing the Huns or depopulated. The city of Rome was saved only by papal intervention. But western civilization was spared further deprivations when Attila asphyxiated on his wedding night, and the Hunnic confederation, without a strong personality to lead it, dissolved.

With the Huns gone, the power vacuum in western Europe was filled by a combination of *foederati* already present within the borders of the Western

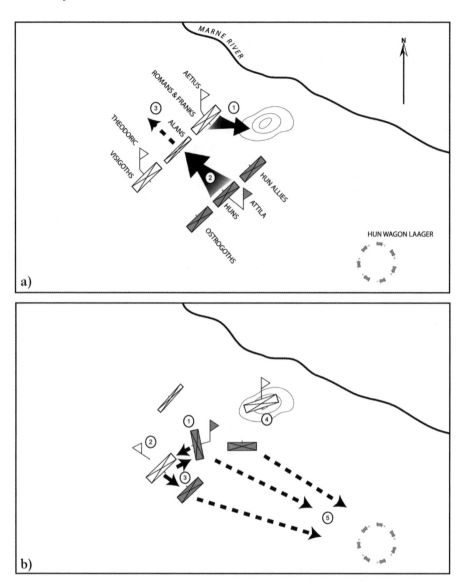

Map 5.7. The Battle of Châlons, 451 CE. (a) Phase I: Aetius' Roman and Frankish infantry open the action by occupying a piece of high ground on the Hun right flank (1). Attila launches an attack at Aetius' weak, unreliable Alan centre (2). The Huns press the attack as the Alans break and begin to rout (3). (b) Phase II: The Huns wheel to attack the Visigoths' flank (1). Theodoric is killed (2), but his troops rally and counter-attack the Huns on their flank and the Ostrogoths to their front (3). The Visigoth counter-attack and the Roman/Frankish threat to his right flank (4) convince Attila to order his army to retreat to the wagon laager (5), screened by Hunnic archers. After nightfall, Attila's army slips away from the field and ultimately beyond the Rhine.

Roman Empire or new tribes crossing the frontiers. No longer willing to live under the pretence of Roman hegemony, these barbarians carved up the Western Roman Empire into their own Germanic kingdoms. By 476 the last Roman emperor in the west, Romulus Augustulus, would simply be removed by a Germanic army commander, Odovacer, ending a millennium of Roman control in central Italy.

With the fall of the Western Roman Empire came the disintegration of the political and economic infrastructure needed to field a professional army. By the time the end came, centuries of 'barbarization' had eroded the combat efficiency of the Roman legion, and with the end of the professional army came the end of well-articulated heavy infantry, replaced by the Germanic militia system and its unarticulated battle squares. Though articulated heavy infantry would continue to exist in the Byzantine east with a greater reliance on cavalry, in western Europe the tactical dark ages had arrived.

Conclusion: The 'Western Way of War' and Decisive Battle
The first thirty-five centuries of warfare in western civilization witnessed the development of a characteristic 'western way of war' which emphasized a confrontational approach to warfare, with the objective of destroying the enemy on the field of battle. The elements that made this western-styled decisive battle possible took millennia to evolve, and involved lessons learned by both Near Eastern and European commanders and armies.

Between 3000 and 1000 BCE, Bronze Age Mesopotamian kings and Egyptian pharaohs fielded increasingly capable armies, supported by logistical trains that allowed generals to campaign hundreds of miles from their own borders. Standing armies emerged, complete with permanent arms industries, large-scale conscription, military training regimens and general staff structures. Martial technologies developed quickly too, with humans forging bronze daggers, swords, maces and socket spears, and wielding slings and armour-piercing composite bows. The art and science of military fortification also advanced. Bentwood construction allowed chariot wrights to construct light, manoeuvrable machines that served as ideal missile platforms for composite bowmen. Tactics advanced as well. Commanders learned how to orchestrate thousands of these chariots and infantry in well co-ordinated attacks, as the decisive battles of Megiddo and Qadesh illustrated. All of the elements historians associate with large-scale warfare were now in place.

But this 'Age of the Chariot' was successfully challenged during the late Bronze Age's 'Catastrophe' when chariot-hunting barbarians engaged the mounted aristocracy with devastating effects. The coming Iron Age and classical period (*c.*1000 BCE–*c.*500 CE) saw the rise of imperium on a new scale and a period of nearly constant warfare. Wide-scale use of iron increased the lethality of war, and the Assyrians became the first civilization to master the potential of this alloy. Assyrian kings were also the first rulers to incorporate cavalry in their armies in large numbers (to supplement their chariotry), and they mastered the science of siegecraft, reducing the cities of their Mesopotamian and Egyptian neighbours. Assyria's military heir, Persia, used its army and exceptional logistical support to expand westward across the Near East to north Africa and Europe and east to the Punjab, eventually to include a million square miles and 70 million inhabitants and the various military capabilities of its subject peoples.

Inexplicably, this military Goliath's expansion would be blunted in the west by the Greek *poleis* and their innovative and brutal heavy infantry tactical system, a system where hoplites fought side by side in a phalanx in a decisive and bloody scrum. This type of Hellenic warfare was forged on the anvil of Greek civilization at large, producing soldiers who possessed, in the words of Victor Davis Hanson: 'a sense of personal freedom, superior discipline, matchless weapons, egalitarian camaraderie, individual initiative, constant tactical innovation and flexibility and preference for shock combat of heavy infantry'.[70]

The amazing violence of this shock combat led to a distinctive 'western way of warfare', one where western armies consistently defeated numerically superior enemies not adept at this type of confrontational battle. The Persians experienced first-hand the violence of western arms during the Persian Wars at Marathon, Thermopylae and Plataea, while the Greeks learned the value of Persian logistics while serving as mercenaries for the Achaemenid super power. Now, western generals had the knowledge to project power far from home.

Alexander the Great at Granicus, Issus and Gaugamela, Julius Caesar in Gaul and centuries of legionary dominance in the Mediterranean basin demonstrate the efficacy of western tactics, discipline and the doctrine of decisive battle. Even in defeat, this type of combat inspired generations of western warriors, as shown by the Spartan king Leonidas and the fateful stand of his 'Three Hundred' at Thermopylae. In fact, so effective was western battle that wars between western states nearly led to ruin, as the Great Peloponnesian War and Roman Civil Wars illustrate.

But Europeans did not have a patent on brutality or the doctrine of decisive battle, as the Assyrian campaign against the Urartu, Hannibal's brilliant campaign against the Romans at Trebia, Trasimene and Cannae in Italy, and the Parthian victory over Roman legions at Carrhae show us. Many of the non-western armies faced by the soldiers of Europe were either heavily influenced by western technologies and tactics or included substantial numbers of western mercenaries within their ranks.

Western superiority at arms could also be cyclical. Alexander conquered much of the known world, but his Hellenistic successors had their kingdoms whittled away by the rise of Parthia in the east and Rome in the west. Heirs to the Persian military experience, the Parthians were successful partly because they married the 'hit and run' martial abilities of the steppe horse archer with the confrontational tactics of heavy cavalry cataphracts. This balance combined-arms warfare provided the Parthians with a potent army in open territory, as the Romans would find out at Carrhae in 53 BCE. In fact, the Romans themselves, long infatuated with the infantry tradition, adopted heavy cavalry to guard their eastern provinces against the mounted Parthian threat. Persian-styled heavy cavalry would become the primary tactical system of the Byzantine army during the medieval period.

The rise and fall of Rome as Mediterranean hegemon also exemplifies the cyclical nature of western power. At its best, the Roman military machine blended a long martial tradition with a willingness to adopt and adapt foreign military technologies and experiment with new fighting techniques and tactics. The product was a professional soldier, the Roman legionary, unmatched in the ancient world and routinely capable of defeating numerically larger enemy armies along all of Rome's frontiers, as the Roman victory at Verulamium shows us. But when these same legionaries fell prey to 'barbarization', they lost the drill and tactical discipline that produced superior warriors and enforced the doctrine of decisive battle, as the Roman defeat by Visigoths at Adrianople and relative parity with the Huns at Châlons exemplify. Still, despite some notable exceptions, the legacy of western warfare during the ancient period is one of decisive battle and lethality in arms, a legacy that continues in volume two, *Warfare in the Medieval World*.

Glossary of Military Terms

Agema: (4th century BCE) An elite 1,000-man Macedonian battalion of heavy infantry *phalangites*, part of the 3,000 strong *Hypaspists* or 'Shield Bearers' who made up the king's infantry guard. Because of their discipline and loyalty, the Hypaspists were often placed between the phalanx and the elite Macedonian heavy cavalry, entrusted with filling the inevitable gap that appeared when heavy infantry and cavalry operated together in offensive action.

ala, **pl.** *alae*: (1st–3rd centuries CE) A cavalry unit of the Roman army and allied *auxiliaries* during the imperial period. Caesar Augustus made a regiment of 120 cavalrymen organic to each legion during the 1st century CE.

alae milliariae: (1st–3rd centuries CE) Auxiliary cavalry units numbering 800–1,000 men who supported the Roman legion. These units date from the reign of Nero (d. 68 CE).

aquilifer: (3rd–1st centuries BCE) A Roman standard-bearer who carried the legion's standard (*aquila*), a gold statuette of an eagle. This standard was very important to the legionaries who fought to bring their legion honour, and to emperors who went to great lengths to recover the standard if it was lost in battle.

articulation (tactical): A military term describing the offensive capability of troops. Unarticulated troops usually lacked the drill and discipline to march and fight in close order, and therefore usually fought in static, defensive formations. Well-articulated troops were capable of offensive action in close-order combat.

aspis, **pl.** *aspides*: (7th–4th centuries BCE) A round wooden concave shield used by Greek hoplites in the phalanx. It was nearly 3 feet in diameter and weighed over 15 pounds, and was utilized in combat by holding a central grip behind the central boss. The round shield remained locked on the forearm with its weight being borne by the left shoulder. It was usually used in conjunction with a thrusting spear or short thrusting or slashing sword (*kopis*).

auxiliaries: (1st century BCE–3rd century CE) Non-citizen troops recruited to serve as valuable extra manpower for the Roman army, as well as in specialized tactical roles such as cavalry and light infantry. They were organized into *cohorts* and *alae*.

'barbarization': The infiltration of non-Roman peoples (typically Germanic tribes) into Rome's territory and political/military institutions, the crippling effects of which plagued the later years of the Roman Empire. It should be noted, however, that this was due as much to Roman policy as to the efforts of the Germanic tribes. Barbarization changed the concept of Roman citizenship, resulting in a weakening of the social, cultural and political foundations of the empire. After the defeat of the eastern Roman army at Adrianople in 378 CE, the Emperor Theodosius started the policy of accepting whole barbarian tribes into military service. Whole tribes would enter into Roman service under their own leaders. The barbarians would not follow Roman training and discipline.

barding: A protective covering for mounts. Barding could be of felt or leather or even form-fitted iron, and was designed to balance protection with mobility. Although horses were most often barded, camels and even elephants could be covered for war.

baritus: A Germanic war cry. Indo-European tribes often developed distinctive war cries when entering combat. The Roman army later adopted these battle cries after its 'barbarization'.

bentwood technologies: (early 2nd millennium BCE) A woodworking technique which allowed for the construction of the spoked wheel with a rim of curved felloes, and the manufacture of lightweight chariot bodies. These new-style chariots revolutionized combat in north Africa during the New Kingdom period by creating for the first time a fast, manoeuvrable machine, one that could be used as a firing platform for composite-bow-wielding archers.

bow (self- and composite): The self-bow was a bow made of a single piece of wood. The first bows in human history were self-bows. Perhaps the most famous self-bow is the English longbow. The composite bow was a recurve bow constructed of wood, horn and tendons from oxen, carefully laminated together to create a bow of superior strength, range and impact power. Composite bows were first used by steppe peoples from horseback, and by civilizations from chariots.

bucellarii: (4th–6th centuries CE) Units of armed retainers of Byzantine nobles who took an additional oath of fealty to the Byzantine emperors. They usually consisted of very high quality cavalry.

cataphracts: (7th century BCE–15th century CE) Chain- or scale-mailed heavy cavalrymen from the Near East who employed the two-handed *kontos* in shock combat. This kind of close-order heavy cavalry originated in Persia in the 7th century BCE and became the signature tactical system for later civilizations from that region (Persians, Parthians, Romans and Byzantines).

centurion: (1st century BCE–3rd century CE) A professional class of Roman officers who served for long periods of time (sometimes as long as twenty-five years) and provided the backbone of experience for the Roman army. There were sixty centurions per legion and each commanded a *century* of 60–80 men.

century: (4th century BCE–3rd century CE) The basic subunit of the Roman legion, consisting of between 60 and 80 legionaries. The century was commanded by a centurion and was eventually made up of ten *contubernia* (groups of eight men who shared a tent and messed together).

chariotry: A term used by historians to indicate a force of chariots.

clibanarii: Heavily armoured cavalry in the Roman and Byzantine armies. These lancers and mounts were protected by composite chain- and scale-mail armour. As the Roman Empire wore on, these units formed an increasingly higher proportion of Roman cavalry and would become the dominant tactical system of the later Byzantine Empire.

cohort: (2nd century BCE–3rd century CE) This term originally applied to troops allied to Rome in the early republic, but became the basic manoeuvre unit of the Roman army by the end of the second century BCE, creating the cohortal legion. It normally consisted of 480 legionaries in six 80-man centuries.

cohortes equitatae: Mixed auxiliary infantry and cavalry units numbering 800–1,000 men who supported the Roman legion. These units date from the reign of Nero (d. 68 CE).

comitatenses: (4th–6th centuries CE) Units of the late Roman and early Byzantine field army that comprised mixed regular and barbarian regiments not specifically tied to frontier provinces. They often supported *limitanei* and *bucellarii* on campaign.

'Companions': (4th century BCE) Elite Macedonian cavalry. Companions were divided into fourteen squadrons or *ilai* of 200 to 225 men each, with an elite *ile*, the Royal Squadron, comprising 300 horse, which the king led personally. Heavy cavalry units fought in a wedge formation as lancers, carrying long spears known as *sarissas* of cornel wood and a long single-edged curved sword or *kopis*.

corvus: (Latin for 'crow') A raised gangplank in the bow of the ship with a large spike on the underside. The *corvus* was Rome's secret naval weapon in the First Punic War (264–241 BCE). To overcome their naval inexperience, the Romans dropped the *corvus* on to one of the more manoeuvrable Carthaginian ships, and the spike held it in place. The Romans could then board the ship and use their superior marines to take the ship. In effect, they turned naval warfare into land warfare.

dathabam: (6th–4th centuries BCE) A Persian term for a ten-man file consisting of one shield-bearer protecting nine archers. Part of the *sparabara*. Persian shield-bearers were armed with short, 6 foot thrusting spears to better protect the file of nine archers behind them. This new arrangement enabled the ratio of archers to shield men to be significantly altered in order to give a heavier concentration of arrow fire. The *dathabam* was the smallest unit of the Persian army, consisting of ten men: see *myriad*.

decimation: A harsh form of Roman capital punishment administered by legionaries against their own soldiers. It was inflicted on those who had given ground without cause in combat or exposed their neighbours to flank attack. The process of decimation took place after the engagement, when a tenth of the offending unit was chosen by lot, then clubbed to death by their own comrades.

enomotiai: (5th century BCE) Spartan platoons consisting of twenty-five hoplites spread out into three files. See *lochos*.

exploratores: A term for Roman scouts, often mounted, who reconnoitred enemy movements.

foederati: (4th–6th centuries CE) Barbarian allies of Rome who retained their Germanic commanders and were allowed to roam within the boundaries of the empire. Eventually, these barbarian units became indistinguishable from regular Roman and Byzantine units, who adopted Germanic arms, armour and tactics.

gladius: (3rd century BCE–3rd century CE) A short thrusting-and-cutting sword, originally from Spain, which became the standard Roman infantry weapon for close-quarter combat.

hasta: (5th century BCE–5th century CE) A general term describing a thrusting spear used by Roman infantry from the beginning of the republic to the end of the empire.

hastati: (4th–2nd centuries BCE) The first line of heavy infantry in the mid–republican-era legion, recruited from younger men and armed with two *pila* and *gladius*, and protected by helmet, body armour and a large oval *scutum*. See *maniple*.

hazarabam: (6th–4th centuries BCE) A regiment of the Persian army consisting of 1,000 men. See *myriad*.

heavy cavalry: Well-armoured horsemen who use shock combat as their primary way of fighting. Heavy cavalry relied on collective effort to be effective, and collective effort required discipline and training. Famous examples of heavy cavalry from history are the *cataphracts* from Persia, *clibanarii* from Rome or Byzantium, or medieval knights.

heavy infantry: Well-armoured foot soldiers who use shock combat as their primary way of fighting. Heavy infantry relied on collective effort to be effective, and collective effort required discipline and training. Famous examples of light infantry are Greek hoplites, Macedonian *phalangites*, Roman legionaries, the Swiss *Auszug*, or German *landsknechts*.

hoplite: (7th–4th centuries BCE) A Greek heavy infantryman who fought beside his fellow citizens in a close formation called a *phalanx*. His name comes from his *hopla* (panoply), consisting of a thrusting spear and short sword, and a heavy metal helmet, breastplate, greaves and a wooden round shield (*aspis*).

host: A term used by historians to describe an army pulled together on a temporary basis.

hundred: An Indo-European infantry formation consisting of around 100 men and led by a war chief. It often fought in a wedge (*cuneus*) formation (sometimes referred to as a 'boar's head' wedge). The wedge placed the heaviest armoured and best-armed men in the front ranks, with lesser-armoured warriors filling in behind. This formation had limited offensive articulation, but presented plenty of impact power on a small frontage. The 'boar's head' array was launched at an enemy in order to break up opposing formations in a single movement.

Huvaka: (6th century BCE) An honorary title meaning 'kinsmen' given to Persian noblemen by the first Great King of Persia, Cyrus the Great. Cyrus gave land to 15,000 Persian nobles known as 'equals', and then required them to use this land to support the cost of cavalry.

Hypaspists: (4th century BCE) A 3,000-man Macedonian force of heavy infantry *phalangites*. The *Hypaspists* or 'Shield Bearers' made up the king's infantry guard. See *Agema*.

ile, **pl.** *ilai*: A Macedonian squadron of 200–225 heavy cavalrymen. See *'Companions'*.

'Immortals': A division (*myriad*) of 10,000 Persian heavy infantry so named because when a member of this elite group fell, he was immediately replaced by a previously selected man. They acted as the Great King's bodyguard, and he was never without them on the battlefield. These handpicked troops were taught horsemanship and Persian martial arts (skills with sword, lance and bow) between the ages of five and twenty. For the next four years, he was on active duty with his elite myriad, and was liable to serve until the age of fifty.

imperium: (4th–1st centuries BCE) The authority to command the Roman army entrusted by the Senate to the consuls, or to their junior colleagues, the praetors.

javelineer: A term historians use for a light infantryman who wields a javelin. Commanders often used these light troops as skirmishers or to screen the deployment of friendly heavier troops.

kontos: (1st century BCE–6th century CE) A long, two-handed thrusting spear used by heavy cavalry (*cataphracts* or *clibanarii*) from Parthia, Persia, Rome and Byzantium.

kopis: (6th–1st centuries BCE) A single-edged Greek sword similar in shape and function to the Gurkha *kukri*. Both the cutting edge and back were convex in shape, and it was used by *hoplites* and *phalangites* in close-quarter combat as a slashing sword, usually after their thrusting spear was broken or discarded.

laager: An encampment created by drawing an army's baggage wagons into a circle or square. This temporary fortification was often used when camping in hostile territory or served as a base of operations or refuge in battle.

lamellar armour: A type of composite armour consisting of a shirt of laminated layers of leather sown or glued together, then fitted with iron plates. This type of armour was popular with both barbarian warriors and the soldiers of civilization.

lance: A spear used from horseback as a shock weapon, usually in conjunction with a built-up saddle and stirrups.

legion: Originally a term meaning levy of troops. The legion was the basic battle group of the Roman army made up of predominately citizen infantry. From the 2nd century BCE it numbered ten cohorts of between 4,000 and 5,000 men. During the Principate the First Cohort was doubled in strength. By the late empire, the legion dwindled to around 1,000 men.

legionary: The name given to a Roman citizen soldier throughout the entire Roman republican and imperial periods. Although his equipment and fighting formation changed over this 1,000 year period, he remained the backbone of the Roman fighting force.

levée en masse: A mass conscription of able-bodied men for warfare.

light cavalry: Light armoured horsemen who use missile combat as their primary way of fighting. These lighter units were less armoured than their heavier counterparts, and consequently had greater tactical mobility. Famous examples of light cavalry are the various horse archers from the Eurasian steppe (Scythians, Parthians, Magyars, Turks and Mongols) and Spanish *genitors*.

light infantry: Light armoured foot soldiers who use missile combat as their primary way of fighting. These lighter units were less armoured than their heavier counterparts, and consequently had greater tactical mobility. Famous examples of light infantry are Thracian peltasts, Rhodian slingers and English longbowmen.

Limes: A Roman guarded and often fortified border in frontier regions. Roman grand strategy emphasized a fortified and guarded border, placing the legions in perpetual contact with the barbarians and ensuring that the Roman legionary was always in a high state of training and readiness. The *Limes* system also helped keep the legions far from the Roman capital and away from imperial politics.

limitanei: (4th–6th centuries CE) These units were a militia of retired legionaries mustered to defend their homeland. In times of emergency, *limitanei* could be promoted into the field army, receiving the title *pseudocomitatenses*. The complement of these new units was about one-third of a first-century legion.

lochos: (5th century BCE) A Spartan battalion consisting of 100 heavy infantry *hoplites*, the chief tactical unit of the Spartan army in the second half of the fifth century BCE. The *lochos* was divided into two companies or *pentecostyes* of fifty men each, while each *pentecostys* was further divided into two platoons or *enomotiai* of twenty-five hoplites.

long sword: A type of sword usually longer than 30 inches in length and usually wielded as a cut-and-slash weapon. It became popular at the beginning of the Iron Age for both infantry and cavalry.

lorica segmentata: (late 2nd century BCE–3rd century CE) A name invented by modern scholars to describe the banded armour of the Roman legionary. It offered excellent protection and distributed the weight of the armour more evenly than mail.

mace: One of the earliest weapons. Essentially a long-handled implement with a spiked or flanged ball at the tip. It was a very effective contusion weapon and became a weapon of choice against plate mail and full plate in the high and late medieval periods.

magister equitum and *magister peditum*: (4th–5th centuries CE) Titles for Roman field marshals of a large army (perhaps 100,000 men). The *magister equitum* commanded the cavalry, while the *magister peditum* commanded the infantry.

maniple: (4th–3rd centuries BCE) The basic fighting formation of the republican Roman legion until the end of the Second Punic War. There were thirty maniples per legion. Each maniple consisted of two centuries and was organized into three heavy infantry lines (the *hastati* or first line, the *principes* or second infantry line, and the *triarii* or third infantry line).

'Marius' mules': (late 2nd century BCE–3rd century CE) A name given to Roman legionaries after the reforms of Consul Marius. Marius improved the mobility of the Roman army by allowing only one pack animal for every fifty men, and requiring every legionary to carry his own arms, armour, entrenching tools, personal items and several days' rations on the march. Each of 'Marius' mules' was capable of travelling up to 20 miles a day over good roads and then fortifying the army camp as a precaution against nocturnal attack, a standard Roman practice when in hostile territory

missile combat: A form of warfare where participants use ranged weapons (slings, bows, javelins, throwing spears) against the enemy. Such combat is usually performed by light troops (infantry and cavalry).

mora: (4th century BCE) A Spartan unit comprising four battalions of between 100 and 150 men each. The later Spartan army consisted of six divisions or *morai* of between 400 and 600 men. It was commanded by a *polemarch*.

myriad: (6th–4th centuries BCE) A Persian division of 10,000 men. The most famous *myriad* was the 'Immortals', who served as the Great King's personal bodyguard. The Persian army was organized on a decimal system, with the largest manoeuvre unit being the *myriad*. The myriad consisted of ten *hazaraba* or regiments of 1,000 men, ten *sataba* of 100 men, and ten *dathaba* of 10 men.

palatini: (4th–6th centuries CE) Military units in the late Roman Empire and early Byzantine period which were of a higher status and prestige than the *comitatenses*. They often formed part of the field armies.

'Parthian shot': A standard nomadic light cavalry manoeuvre where horse archers break formation and gallop toward an enemy formation firing arrows, then wheel right and retreat, firing over their shoulders back at the enemy. The manoeuvre is named after the Parthians, though all steppe archers practised it. The 'Parthian shot' was often used in conjunction with the feigned retreat, pulling enemy cavalry into pursuit, then ambushing them far from their camp.

peltasts: (5th–4th centuries BCE) Light infantry skirmishers and screening troops, originally from Thrace, who fought with javelins or spears and who protected themselves with a small, crescent-shaped shield or *pelta*. The *pelta* was usually made of wicker and covered with goatskin. Peltasts were used by Greek commanders to harass enemy heavy infantry or provide protection as their own phalanxes deployed.

pentecostys: (5th century BCE) A Spartan company consisting of 50 *hoplites*. See *lochos*.

pezetairoi: (4th century BCE) Macedonian *phalangites* who were organized in battle squares sixteen deep and sixteen wide. This 256-man square, called a *syntagma*, was organized six to a battalion or *taxis*, usually just over 1,500 men strong. The Macedonian army contained twelve *taxeis*.

phalangite: (4th–1st centuries BCE) A specialized heavy infantryman in the Hellenistic period who differed from a hoplite in that he who wore very little armour and wielded a *sarissa* as his main offensive weapon.

phalanx: A close order heavy infantry formation with spearmen arranged in rank and file. This formation was capable of devastating offensive power through the collision and push of its soldiers. There is evidence that this formation dates back to Bronze Age Mesopotamia, though it was certainly perfected by the Greeks and Macedonians during the archaic, Hellenic and Hellenistic periods and resurrected in the late medieval period by the Swiss.

pikeman: A general term historians use for a heavy infantryman armed with a long-hafted thrusting spear (usually over 12 feet in length) who often fought in rank and file in a phalanx.

pilum: (3rd century BCE–3rd century CE) Either of two different kinds of weighted javelin used by Roman legionaries as a missile weapon designed to break up enemy formations before shock combat ensued. The light *pilum* was thrown first at around 35 yards, followed quickly by the heavy *pilum*.

polearm: A long-hafted heavy infantry weapon popular throughout the history of warfare, designed to be used with two hands against infantry and cavalry formations.

polemarch: (4th century BCE) The title given to a Spartan commander of a *mora*.

Praetorian Guard: (1st–3rd centuries CE) The military bodyguard of the Roman emperors, beginning with Augustus. Praetorians were originally recruited from Italian areas and received higher pay and donatives, and enjoyed far better service conditions than other legionaries.

principes: (late 4th–2nd centuries BCE) The second line of heavy infantry in the mid-republican legion, organized into *maniples*. These units were armed with sword and *pila*, and protected by helmet, body armour and *scutum*. They were recruited in the prime of their lives. They fought behind the *hastati*.

pseudocomitatenses: (4th–6th centuries CE) The title given to units of *limitanei* who were attached to field armies in the late Roman imperial and early Byzantine periods.

quincunx: (late 4th–2nd centuries BCE) The chequerboard formation used by the mid-republican legion in which three lines were deployed with wide intervals between the maniples, the gaps being covered by the maniples of the second line. This formation gave the legion great flexibility, especially in combat against the phalangeal formations from the Hellenistic East.

rhipsaspia: In Ancient Greece, the act of throwing away the *aspis* (shield) and running away. This was considered the ultimate act of cowardice in Greek society.

'Sacred Band': An elite group of Theban hoplites renowned as homosexual lovers. This unit usually fought at the place of honour on the right wing, but fought on the left wing opposite the Spartans at Leuctra in 371 BCE with great success. The Macedonians killed them in this place of honour in 338 BCE at the battle of Chaeronea.

sarissa: (4th–1st centuries BCE) A Macedonian pike used by phalangites in a phalanx. Made of cornel wood and tipped with a heavy iron tip and bronze butt-spike, the *sarissa* ranged from 14 feet to 20 feet in length and was ideally suited for frontal assault.

satabam: (6th–4th centuries BCE) A unit of the Persian army consisting of 100 men. See *myriad*.

scutum, pl. *scuta*: (3rd century BCE–3rd century CE) A large shield used by Roman legionaries. The early *scutum* was semi-cylindrical and oval in shape. Later, the shape would change to a rectangle, ideal for closed formations. The shield was held by a single transverse handgrip behind a central boss, and was ideally suited to protect the Roman soldier as he wielded his *gladius* in battle.

shock combat: A form of warfare where participants use close-quarter weapons (swords, axes, maces, thrusting spears) against the enemy. This combat is usually performed by heavy troops (infantry and cavalry) and most often in well-articulated formations.

short sword: A type of sword usually shorter than 30 inches in length and usually wielded as a thrusting weapon. It is the first sword design in history and became popular at the beginning of the Bronze Age for infantry.

sparabara: A term meaning 'archer-pairs' used by both Assyrians and Persians. The Assyrian *sparabara* were composed of two different units of troops of equal strength, operating together in a tactical formation comprising only a single line of archers behind a single line of shield-bearers. Persian *sparabara* operated in the same ten-man file or *dathabam* at a ratio of one shield-bearer for every nine archers.

spatha: (1st–6th centuries CE) A long sword originally used by Roman and auxiliary cavalry and, later, infantry. Though the *spatha* was pointed for thrusting, it was usually utilized for cut-and-slash strikes, emulating the favoured tactics of the Germanic tribes.

spearman: A general term historians use to describe a warrior who uses a spear. A spearman can be heavy infantry if he uses his spear as a shock weapon or light infantry if he throws his weapon as a missile.

strategos: A Greek term for general. It dates back to the archaic period when the *strategos* actually fought in the front rank of the phalanx.

synaspismos: (4th century BCE) A term meaning 'locked shield order'. In the Macedonian phalanx, each man occupied a space less than 3 feet in width, but when receiving an enemy attack, it closed up still further into *synaspismos* or 'locked shield order', in which each heavy infantryman presented a front equal to the width of his shoulders.

syntagma: (4th century BCE) A Macedonian phalanx consisting of a 256-man square. There were six *syntagmata* in a battalion or *taxis*.

taxis, pl. *taxeis*: (4th century BCE) A 1,500-man Macedonian battalion consisting of six *syntagmata*, phalangites who were organized in battle squares sixteen deep and sixteen wide. The Macedonian army contained twelve *taxeis*.

triarii: (late 4th–2nd centuries BCE) The third and senior line of heavy infantry in the mid-republican legion. This line was recruited from veteran soldiers who were armed with the long *hasta* or thrusting spear and protected by helmet, body armour and oval *scutum*. See *maniple*.

trireme: (7th–4th centuries BCE) A sleek and fast Greek war galley with a crew of around 200 sailors. Highly manoeuvrable and capable of sinking an enemy vessel with its bronze and wood ram, this type of warship dominated the Mediterranean during the archaic and Hellenic periods.

velites: (late 4th–2nd centuries BCE) Roman light infantry of the early- and mid-republican legion. These troops were recruited from the *capite censi* (urban poor) or those too young to serve as heavy infantry. Armed with light javelins and sword, and unprotected except for helmet and hide-covered wicker shield, these troops acted as a screen for their heavier armed and less mobile comrades, the *hastati* and *principes*.

Notes

Introduction

1. John Keegan, *A History of Warfare* (New York: Alfred A. Knopf, 1993), 179–180.
2. Adrian Keith Goldsworthy, *The Roman Army at War, 100 BC–AD 200* (Oxford: Oxford University Press, Clarendon Press, 1996), 224. J.F.C. Fuller estimates that ancient warriors became fatigued after only 15 minutes of shock combat (*Julius Caesar: Man, Soldier and Tyrant*, London: Eyre and Spottiswoode, 1965, 90–91), while Carl von Clausewitz suggests soldiers in the Napoleonic Wars became exhausted after 20 minutes (*On War*, translated by Michael Howard and Peter Paret, Princeton: Princeton University Press, 1984, 291–313).
3. Clausewitz, *On War*, 119–121.
4. Peter Paret, 'Clausewitz', in *Makers of Modern Strategy from Machiavelli to the Nuclear Age*, ed. Peter Paret and Gordon A. Craig (Princeton: Princeton University Press, 1986), 202.
5. Clausewitz, *On War*, 121.
6. Ibid.
7. Ibid., 75.
8. Keegan, *History of Warfare*, 12.

Chapter 1. Warfare in the Ancient Near East

1. Arther Ferrill, *The Origins of War: From the Stone Age to Alexander the Great*, rev. edn (Boulder, CO: Westview, 1997), 38.
2. For an in-depth treatment of the evolution of Bronze Age weapons and armour in the ancient and classical periods (*c.*3500 BCE to 500 CE) see Richard A. Gabriel and Karen S. Metz, *From Sumer to Rome: The Military Capabilities of Ancient Armies* (Westport, CT: Greenwood, 1991), ch. 3.
3. Ibid., 51. The first recording of body armour appears on the Stele of Vultures (*c.*2500 BCE) which shows Sumerian soldiers protected by leather cloaks with sewn spined metal disks. The victory stele of Naram Sin appears to show bronze scale-armour, and, though it is impossible to be certain, bronze scale-armour may have been in use for a few hundred years. By 1700 BCE the comparatively unsophisticated armies of the Hyksos had this type of armour. After the Hyksos conquest of Egypt in the seventeenth century BCE, it became standard throughout the ancient Near East.
4. Ibid., 58.
5. Ibid., 4–6. Also see Trevor Watkins, 'The Beginnings of Warfare', in *Warfare in the Ancient World*, ed. John Hackett (New York: Facts on File, 1989), 19–20.
6. Georges Roux, *Ancient Iraq*, 3rd edn (New York: Penguin, 1993), 137.

7. Yigael Yadin, *The Art of Warfare in Biblical Lands in the Light of Archaeological Discovery*, trans. M. Pearlman, 2 vols (New York and London: McGraw-Hill, 1963), vol. 1, 135–136.

8. Roux, *Ancient Iraq*, 133, 140.

9. Gwynne Dyer, *War* (New York: Richard D. Erwin, 1985), 21. Naram Sin's victory over the Lullubi is commemorated by a rock sculpture showing the king armed with a composite bow, marking the first appearance of the composite bow in history and strongly suggesting that it was of Sumerian-Akkadian origin.

10. Gabriel and Metz, *From Sumer to Rome*, 9.

11. Ibid., 67. A self-bow of the fourth millennium required 30 or 40 pounds to pull to full length and could fire an arrow between 100 and 150 yards, easily penetrating an unarmoured human body. But as armour became more common on Near Eastern battlefields, commanders sought a more powerful bow.

12. Ibid., 67–68. Also see the excellent treatment of the construction, range and dimensions of Turkish, Persian and Indian composite bows in the appendix of Ralph Payne-Gallwey, *The Crossbow: Medieval and Modern, Military and Sporting* (London: Holland, 1903).

13. Gabriel and Metz, *From Sumer to Rome*, 69.

14. Yadin, *Art of Warfare*, vol. 1, 129–131.

15. Gabriel and Metz, *From Sumer to Rome*, 76.

16. Watkins, 'The Beginnings of Warfare', 27.

17. Erik Hildinger, *Warriors of the Steppe: A Military History of Central Asia, 500* B.C. to *1700* A.D. (New York: Sarpedon, 1997), 15–16. Also see Watkins, 'The Beginnings of Warfare', 28.

18. Watkins, 'The Beginnings of Warfare', 27–28.

19. Yadin, *Art of Warfare*, vol. 1, 87–89. Gabriel and Metz, *From Sumer to Rome*, 76.

20. Gabriel and Metz, *From Sumer to Rome*, 77. Watkins, 'The Beginnings of Warfare', 28.

21. T.G.E. Powell, 'Some Implications of Chariotry', in *Culture and Environment: Essays in Honor of Sir Cyril Fox*, ed. I. Foster and L. Adcock (London, 1963), 165–166.

22. Watkins, 'The Beginnings of Warfare', 31.

23. Robert Drews, *The End of the Bronze Age: Changes in Warfare and the Catastrophe, ca. 1200 BC* (Princeton: Princeton University Press, 1993), 127–129. Drews cites the numerous inscriptions and papyrus depictions of Egyptian warriors shooting over the heads of their teams. He also suggests all chariot-based armies in Eurasia used the machine in this manner, believing that the Hittites, Mycenaeans, Egyptian, Indian and Chinese used chariots similarly as missile platforms.

24. Ibid., 141–147.

25. There are two different dates for the battle of Megiddo, one in 1479 BCE and the other in 1458 BCE. I agree with the later date because it is known that Thutmose was prevented from assuming power because of the regency of the powerful Queen Hatshepsut, the widow of Thutmose II. After adolescence (aged sixteen), Thutmose spent sixteen years with the Egyptian army as an officer before he became pharaoh himself. The battle of Megiddo was fought in the first year of his reign, 1458 BCE.

26. For treatments of the battle of Megiddo see Ferrill, *Origins of War*, 54–57; J.F.C. Fuller, *A Military History of the Western World*, vol. 1, *From the Earliest Times to the Battle of Lepanto* (New York: Funk and Wagnalls, 1954–1957), 4–6; and Richard A. Gabriel and Donald W. Boose, Jr, *The Great Battles of Antiquity: A Strategic and Tactical Guide to Great Battles that Shaped the Development of War* (Westport, CT: Greenwood Press, 1994), 39–62.

27. Ferrill, *Origins of War*, 55–56. Ferrill estimates that Thutmose moved his army an average of 15 miles per day for nine days.
28. This quotation is taken from Yadin, *Art of Warfare*, vol. 1, 100–103.
29. Ibid.
30. Ferrill, *Origins of War*, 56–57.
31. Gabriel and Boose, *Great Battles from Antiquity*, 55.
32. Ibid., 57.
33. Ferrill, *Origins of War*, 57.
34. Gabriel and Boose, *Great Battles from Antiquity*, 59.
35. For an excellent account of the campaign between Ramesses and the Hittites, see Mark Healy, *The Warrior Pharaoh: Ramesses II and the Battle of Qadesh* (London: Osprey, 1993). Also see Yadin, *Art of Warfare*, vol. 1, 103–110; Ferrill, *Origins of War*, 57–60; and Gabriel and Boose, *Great Battles from Antiquity*, 64–87.
36. See Alan Gardiner, *The Qadesh Inscriptions of Ramesses II* (Oxford: Griffith Institute, 1960), R43 and R44, for the best estimate of Hittite troop numbers. The unusual size of the Hittite force is explainable because two previous monarchs had been successful in uniting the vassals of Anatolia and northern Mesopotamia and concluding treaties with the city-states of Syria. At the battle of Qadesh, the full manpower pool of the Hatti and their allies was available for the defence of the region (Gabriel and Boose, *Great Battles from Antiquity*, 71).
37. Gabriel and Metz, *From Sumer to Rome*, 77.
38. Robert Drews, *The Coming of the Greeks: Indo-European Conquests in the Aegean and the Near East* (Princeton: Princeton University Press, 1988), 120–122.
39. Ferrill, *Origins of War*, 58.
40. Ibid.
41. Gabriel and Boose, *Great Battles from Antiquity*, 79.
42. Gardiner, *The Qadesh Inscriptions of Ramesses II*, P80–90.
43. Gabriel and Boose, *Great Battles from Antiquity*, 82. Ferrill and Yadin believe the Egyptian force that arrived from the north was not the returning chariot reserve but mercenary troops that had been summoned earlier from the coast (Ferrill, *Origins of War*, 58; Yadin, *Art of Warfare*, vol. 2, 267).
44. Gabriel and Boose, *Great Battles from Antiquity*, 82.
45. Much of what is known about Mycenaean warfare comes from the Linear B tablets (a form of early Greek), discovered in the early twentieth century by the Englishman Sir Arthur Evans in his excavations, and deciphered by Michael Ventris in the 1950s.
46. Ferrill, *Origins of War*, 91.
47. Ibid., 99.
48. Homer's disdain for the bow can be seen in his portrayal of Paris the adulterer. Diomedes, friend of Achilles, speaks the mind of the Homeric warrior when he addresses Paris: 'You archer, lovely in your locks, eyer of young girls. If you were to make trial of me in strong combat with weapons, your bow would do you no good at all'. Homer, *Iliad*, trans. Richard Lattimore (Chicago: University of Chicago Press, 1951), 2.385–387.
49. John Chadwick, *The Mycenaean World* (Cambridge: Cambridge University Press, 1976), 159–179. See Chadwick for a detail of the chariot tablets at Knossos and Pylos. One document alone gives a total of 246 chariot frames and 208 pairs of wheels. Ferrill believes the estimate of an army of 200 chariots is conservative (Ferrill, *Origins of War*, 96).
50. Chadwick, *Mycenaean World*, 160–164. Also see A.M. Snodgrass, *Arms and Armor of the Greeks* (Baltimore and London: Johns Hopkins University Press, 1999), ch. 1, for a discussion on Mycenaean arms, armour and shields.
51. Ferrill, *Origins of War*, 97–98.

52. Ibid., 98. Also see Carol Thomas, 'A Dorian Invasion? The Early Literary Evidence', *Studi micenei ed egeo-anatolici*, 19 (1978), 77–87.

53. Robert Drews, *Coming of the Greeks*, 74–120. Drews believes the chariot was used for transportation and royal display as early as 1900 BCE, but did not become militarily important until 1700 BCE when it was combined with the composite bow, creating a stable missile platform.

54. For an excellent overview of the various theories concerning the cause of the Catastrophe, see Drews, *End Of the Bronze Age*, part 2.

55. See ibid., part 3, for a detailed explanation of barbarian military technologies and tactics at the end of the Bronze Age.

56. See ibid., ch. 13, 'Changes in Armor and Weapons at the End of the Bronze Age', for an excellent treatment of when and what changes in armour, shield, javelin, spear, lance and sword design took place during the Catastrophe.

57. Ibid., 193–194.

58. Ibid., 174–176.

59. Ibid., 176–177.

60. Ibid., 177–180.

61. Gabriel and Metz, *From Sumer to Rome*, 19.

62. Ibid.

63. R. Ewart Oakeshott, *The Archaeology of Weapons: Arms and Armor from Prehistory to the Age of Chivalry* (London: Frederick A. Praeger, 1960), 40–42.

64. Gabriel and Metz, *From Sumer to Rome*, 21.

65. D.J. Wiseman, 'The Assyrians', in *Warfare in the Ancient World*, ed. John Hackett (New York: Facts on File, 1989), 38.

66. Ferrill, *Origins of War*, 70.

67. Trevor. N. Dupuy, *The Evolution of Weapons and Warfare* (New York: Da Capo, 1984), 10.

68. Ferrill, *Origins of War*, 82. Arrian states that Alexander had 40,000 infantry and 7,000 cavalry at Gaugamela, numbers modern historians do not challenge (Arrian, *Anabasis*, III.12.5). Arrian places the number of Persian troops at a farcical 1 million men. Ferrill estimates the Persian army at between 100,000 and 250,000 (*Origins of War*, 208), while Warry places the number at around 100,000 men, with roughly equal numbers of infantry and cavalry (John Warry, *Warfare in the Classical World: An Illustrated Encyclopedia of Weapons, Warriors, and Warfare in the Ancient Civilizations of Greece and Rome*, New York: Salamander, 1980, 82). Devine is the most conservative, calculating 50,000 infantry and 25,000 cavalry (Albert Devine, 'Alexander the Great', *Warfare in the Ancient World*, ed. John Hackett, New York: Facts on File, 1989, 104).

69. Gabriel and Boose, *Great Battles from Antiquity*, 98.

70. Ibid., 100; Gabriel and Metz, *From Sumer to Rome*, 51.

71. The arms and armour found on Ashurbanipal's royal bodyguard are somewhat similar to those worn by a Greek hoplite. Guardsmen wore their characteristically long mail coats and conical helms and carried long, leaf-bladed spears and large, round shields similar to an *aspis*. (From bas-relief, South-West Palace of Ashurbanipal, Nineveh, *c*.640 BCE, British Museum, London.)

72. Gabriel and Boose, *Great Battles from Antiquity*, 99.

73. Wiseman, 'The Assyrians', 44–45.

74. Ibid.

75. Ibid., 45.

76. Gabriel and Boose, *Great Battles from Antiquity*, 102.

77. Wiseman, 'The Assyrians', 43.

78. Robert L. O'Connell, 'The Insolent Chariot', *Military History Quarterly*, vol. 2, no. 3 (1990), 81.

79. Gabriel and Boose, *Great Battles from Antiquity*, 103.
80. A bas-relief *c.*650 BCE shows a pursuit of Arab infantry and camel cavalry by Assyrian light infantry and light cavalry archers. The camel carries two riders: facing forward is a jockey with riding crop, and twisting his torso to fire behind him is a second mounted archer, firing at the pursuing Assyrians. North Palace of Ashurbanipal, Room L, British Museum, London.
81. Ferrill, *Origins of War*, 72.
82. Ibid., 73. Gabriel and Boose, *Great Battles from Antiquity*, 103.
83. For a very detailed explanation of Sargon II's Urartu campaign see Gabriel and Boose, *Great Battles of Antiquity*, ch. 5. Ferrill also spends a few pages discussing the campaign in his *Origins of War*, 77–79.
84. Ferrill, *Origins of War*, 77–78. All of the following quotes from Sargon's Urartu campaign are taken from the complete translation of Sargon's letter in Daniel D. Luckenbill, *Ancient Records of Assyria and Babylonia* (London, 1989), 73–99.
85. Gabriel and Boose, *Great Battles from Antiquity*, 111–112; Ferrill, *Origins of War*, 78.
86. Gabriel and Boose, *Great Battles from Antiquity*, 111–112.
87. Ibid., 115.
88. Luckenbill, *Ancient Records*, 81–82.
89. Ibid., 82.
90. Ibid.
91. Ibid., 99.
92. Gabriel and Boose, *Great Battles from Antiquity*, 117; Ferrill, *Origins of War*, 79.
93. Victor Davis Hanson, *Carnage and Culture: Landmark Battles in the Rise of Western Power* (New York: Doubleday, 2001), 32.
94. This inclusion of foreign soldiers in the Persian army included not only subject peoples, but also foreign mercenaries such as Greek heavy infantry hoplites.
95. Nick Sekunda, 'The Persians', *Warfare in the Ancient World*, ed. John Hackett (New York: Facts on File, 1989), 83–84.
96. Herodotus, *History*, VII.113. For more on the Immortals see Warry, *Warfare in the Classical World*, 29; Sekunda, 'The Persians', 84; Ferrill, *Origins of War*, 82.
97. Sekunda, 'The Persians', 84.
98. Ibid., 82–83.
99. Ibid., 85.
100. Ibid., 96.
101. Wiseman, 'The Assyrians', 36.
102. Gabriel and Metz, *From Sumer to Rome*, 23.
103. Robert Laffont, *The Ancient Art of Warfare* (New York: Time-Life, 1966), 45.
104. J.M. Cook, *The Persian Empire* (New York: Schocken, 1983), 108; Percy Sykes, *A History of Persia* (London: Macmillan, 1958), 164–165.

Chapter 2. Archaic and Hellenic Warfare

1. For an excellent treatment of the arms and armour of the Greek hoplite, see Snodgrass, *Arms and Armor of the Greeks*, ch. 3.
2. See Ferrill, *Origins of War*, 99–100, for the argument supporting Corinth as the origin of the phalangeal formation. See John Lazenby, 'Hoplite Warfare', *Warfare in the Ancient World*, ed. John Hackett (New York: Facts on File, 1989), 57, for the case supporting Pylos as the origin of the phalanx.
3. Archer Jones, *The Art of War in the Western World* (Urbana and Chicago: University of Illinois Press, 1987), 3. Also see Antonio Santosuosso, *Soldiers, Citizens, and the Symbols of War from Classical Greece to Republican Rome, 500–167 BC* (Boulder, CO: Westview, 1997), 99.
4. From Victor Davis Hanson's translation of Xenophon's *Hellenica* IV.3.19, in *The Western Way of War: Infantry Battle in Classical Greece*, 2nd edn (Berkeley: University of California Press, 2000), 169–170.

5. Ferrill, *Origins of War*, 102–103.
6. Hanson's translation of Plutarch in his *Western Way of War*, 64.
7. Victor Davis Hanson, 'Hoplite Technology in Phalanx Battle', *Hoplites: The Classical Greek Battle Experience*, ed. Victor Davis Hanson (London and New York: Routledge, 1991), 68–69. Also see Snodgrass, *Arms and Armor of the Greeks*, 53–54.
8. Lazenby, 'Hoplite Warfare', 55.
9. Thucydides, *History of the Peloponnesian War*, trans. C.F. Smith, Loeb Classical Library (Cambridge: Harvard University Press, 1920), IV.2.18.
10. J.K. Anderson, 'Hoplite Weapons and Offensive Arms', *Hoplites: The Classical Greek Battle Experience*, ed. Victor Davis Hanson (London and New York: Routledge, 1991), 22.
11. Hanson, *Western Way of War*, 27–28.
12. Hanson, 'Hoplite Technology in Phalanx Battle', 75–76.
13. See sections 3, 4 and 5 in Victor Davis Hanson's *The Western Way of War* for the definitive discussion of how Greek hoplites prepared, charged, collided and pushed their way to victory on the battlefield. He also describes how and why Greek soldiers routed, and the aftermath of battle.
14. Ibid., 114–115.
15. Ibid., 140.
16. Ibid., 144–145.
17. See section 4 in Hanson's *The Western Way of War*.
18. *Plutarch's Moralia*, trans. Frank Cole Babbitt, vol. 3 (Cambridge, MA, 1949), 241.16.
19. Hanson, *Western Way of War*, 210–218.
20. John Lazenby, 'The Killing Zone', in *Hoplites: The Classical Greek Battle Experience*, ed. Victor Davis Hanson (London and New York: Routledge, 1991), 101.
21. Ibid.
22. Ferrill, *Origins of War*, 102.
23. Ibid., 102.
24. Xenophon, *Hellenica* VII.4.8, as cited in *The Greek Historians*, ed. Francis R.B. Godolphin and trans. Henry G. Dakyns, 2 vols. (New York, 1942), vol. 2, 216.
25. Robert L. O'Connell, *Of Arms and Men: A History of War, Weapons and Aggression* (Oxford and New York: Oxford University Press, 1989), 48–49. Archery did continue on the island of Crete and Cretan archers were sometimes used as mercenaries (Warry, *Warfare in the Classical World*, 8).
26. Herodotus, *History* IX.68. Herodotus tells us that the Thebans screened their retreating infantry at the battle of Plataea in 479 BCE.
27. Hanson, *Western Way of War*, 60–63.
28. Josiah Ober, 'Hoplites and Obstacles', in *Hoplites: The Classical Greek Battle Experience*, ed. Victor Davis Hanson (London and New York: Routledge, 1991), 174–175.
29. N.G.L. Hammond, 'The Campaign and Battle of Marathon', *Studies in Greek History: A Companion Volume to a History of Greece to 322 BC* (Oxford: Oxford University Press, 1973), 203, 210. Hammond places the number of Persians at 77,000 for the Persian expedition, with 25,000 men a minimum number for fighting forces.
30. Ferrill, *Origins of War*, 108.
31. For an explanation of the Persian plan see Santosuosso, *Soldiers, Citizens, and the Symbols of War*, 33.
32. Ferrill, *Origins of War*, 108.
33. Ibid., 109.
34. Ibid., translation of Herodotus, *History* VI.112.
35. Ferrill, *Origins of War*, 110. Although Herodotus does not mention the presence of cavalry at Marathon, Ferrill believes that there may have been some Persian light cavalry present.
36. In the decade between the two Persian expeditions, the Athenians had discovered

silver and used the wealth to acquire a powerful fleet which they intended to use in defence of their *polis*. For more on the rise of the Athenian thalassocracy, see Chester G. Starr, *The Influence of Sea Power on Ancient History* (Oxford and New York: Oxford University Press, 1989), 30.

37. Ferrill, *Origins of War*, 113.
38. Herodotus, *History* VII.211.
39. This passage is taken from Santosuosso's reconstruction of Herodotus' account of Persian tactical capabilities at the battle of Thermopylae in his *Soldiers, Citizens, and the Symbols of War*, 46.
40. Lazenby, 'Hoplite Warfare', 62.
41. Starr, *Influence of Sea Power*, 32.
42. Ibid., 33. For another interpretation of fleet strengths and a remarkable account of the battle of Salamis and its aftermath, see Hanson, *Carnage and Culture*, ch. 2. Hanson believes that the Persians possessed a fleet of over 600 ships at Salamis, while the Greek alliance put to sea between 300 and 370 vessels (p. 43). Many historians do not subscribe to the story of Themistocles' defection. I agree with Professor Ferrill's explanation that the ruse was indeed possible. 'Athens had fallen, and the Persian high command undoubtedly knew of the dissension among Greek commanders on matters of strategy. Many Greek states and leaders had already defected to Persia, and with Athens in ruins Xerxes might easily have believed that Themistocles preferred Medizing (defecting) to a strategy of defence of the Peloponnesus' (*Origins of War*, 117–118).
43. Starr, *Influence of Sea Power*, 33–34.
44. The numbers are Ferrill's estimate (*Origins of War*, 120). Herodotus claims the Greeks faced an army of 300,000 Persians and 50,000 allied Greeks (IX.33). Santosuosso believes the Persian host to have been around 100,000 combatants, including Greek allies (*Soldiers, Citizens, and the Symbols of War*, 59).
45. Ferrill, *Origins of War*, 120.
46. For a very detailed treatment of the battle of Plataea see Santosuosso's *Soldiers, Citizens, and the Symbols of War*, 58–66. Also see Ferrill, *Origins of War*, 119–121.
47. Herodotus, *History* IX.69.
48. Ferrill, *Origins of War*, 120. Traditionally, the finest Greek soldiers had a place of honour on the right wing. This usually meant that the best soldiers on the battlefield never faced each other. Professor Ferrill speculates that the reason Pausanias switched wings was because the Athenians had had experience against the Persians at Marathon.
49. Herodotus, *The History*, trans. Henry Cary (New York: Harper, 1873; reprint: Prometheus, 1992), IX.59.
50. Santosuosso, *Soldiers, Citizens, and the Symbols of War*, 65.
51. Herodotus claims the Greeks lost only 600 Megarians and Phliasians from the centre, 91 Spartans and 17 Tegeans from the right wing, and 52 Athenians from the right wing (IX.70). Plutarch puts Greek casualties at 1,360 men (*Vitae, Aristides* 19).
52. Starr, *Influence of Sea Power*, 38.
53. L. Casson, *The Ancient Mariners* (New York: Macmillan, 1959), 87.
54. Ferrill, *Origins of War*, 105–106.
55. J.K. Anderson, *Military Theory and Practice in the Age of Xenophon* (Berkeley, CA: University of California Press, 1970), 225–251.
56. Thucydides, *Peloponnesian War* IV.32.1, IV.40.
57. On the Thracian peltast, see J.G.P. Best, *Thracian Peltasts and Their Influence on Greek Warfare* (Groningen: Wolters-Noordhoff, 1969).
58. For an excellent treatment of the battle of Sphacteria, see Santosuosso, *Soldiers, Citizens, and the Symbols of War*, 93–96.
59. Thucydides, *Peloponnesian War* IV.8.9.
60. Ibid., IV.38.

61. Ibid., IV.40.2.
62. Ferrill, *Origins of War*, 133.
63. Ibid., 139.
64. Ferrill, *Origins of War*, 145.
65. Ibid.
66. Ibid., 152. See George Cawkwell's assessment of the battle of Cunaxa in his introduction to Rex Warner's translation of Xenophon, *The Persian Expedition* (Harmondsworth: Penguin, 1972), pp. 36–38.
67. For a modern reconstruction of the battle of Cunaxa, see Warry, *Warfare in the Classical World*, 56–58, and Ferrill, *Origins of War*, 151–156.
68. Xenophon, *Persian Expedition* III.3.
69. Ibid., IV.2. Xenophon's appeal to the Rhodians to come forward and utilize their skills as slingers was accompanied by an offer of improved pay and conditions.
70. Ferrill, *Origins of War*, 155.
71. From Paul A. Rahe, 'The Military Situation in Western Asia on the Eve of Cunaxa', *American Journal of Philology*, vol. 101 (1980), 88. I agree with Ferrill's indictment of the simplicity of Rahe's statement.
72. Ferrill, *Origins of War*, 165.
73. For a very detailed reconstruction of the battle of Leuctra, see Santosuosso, *Soldiers, Citizens, and the Symbols of War*, 102–109.
74. Warry, *Warfare in the Classical World*, 60.
75. Ferrill, *Origins of War*, 166–169. Also see John Buckler, *The Theban Hegemony, 371–362 BC* (Cambridge, MA: Harvard University Press, 1980), 62–69.

Chapter 3. Warfare in the Hellenistic Era

1. Devine, 'Alexander the Great', 104.
2. For an excellent treatment of the composition of Alexander the Great's army and his campaigns, see Santosuosso, *Soldiers, Citizens, and the Symbols of War*, ch. 5.
3. Warry, *Warfare in the Classical World*, 82.
4. Devine, 'Alexander the Great', 105–106; Ferrill, *Origins of War*, 176–177.
5. Ferrill, *Origins of War*, 176.
6. Arrian, *Tactics* 16.6–7. This excerpt is taken from Michael M. Sage's very informative collection of primary sources entitled *Warfare in Ancient Greece: A Sourcebook* (London and New York: Routledge, 1996), 176.
7. Alexander deployed his cavalry in the centre of his formation at the battle of Gaugamela and on the wings at Granicus River and Issus.
8. A.B. Bosworth, *Conquest and Empire: The Reign of Alexander the Great* (Cambridge: Cambridge University Press, 1988), 272. Horse archers were recruited at least in part from the nomadic Dahae in Iran, who were regularly employed alongside Macedonian troops.
9. See Jones, *Art of War*, 21–16, for the definitive explanation of the Alexandrian combined-arms tactical system.
10. Devine, 'Alexander the Great', 119.
11. Warry, *Warfare in the Classical World*, 72–73.
12. Ibid., 73–74.
13. Devine, 'Alexander the Great', 105.
14. Ferrill, *Origins of War*, 178.
15. Donald Engels, *Alexander the Great and the Logistics of the Macedonian Army* (Berkeley: University of California Press, 1978), 15. This is the best treatment of the Alexandrian logistical system.
16. Ibid., 15.
17. Richard A. Gabriel, *The Culture of War* (Westport, CT: Greenwood, 1990), 96–99.
18. Engels, *Alexander the Great*, 153.

19. Ibid., 123–126.

20. Ibid., 145.

21. Warry, *Warfare in the Classical World*, 146; Bosworth, *Conquest and Empire*, 259; Ferrill, *Origins of War*, 194.

22. For treatments on Alexander's victory over the Persians at Granicus River, see Warry, *Warfare in the Classical World*, 76; Ferrill, *Origins of War*, 194–199; Devine, 'Alexander the Great', 109–113; and Gabriel and Boose, *Great Battles of Antiquity*, 240–246.

23. Arrian, *Anabasis Alexandri*, trans. P. Brunt, Loeb Classical Library (1954), I.16.2.6.

24. Ferrill, *Origins of War*, 196.

25. Bosworth, *Conquest and Empire*, 42–43.

26. Ferrill, *Origins of War*, 196.

27. Ibid., 201. Arrian claims that Darius had 600,000 men, including 100,000 cavalry, though no modern historian accepts this claim. The number cited is Ferrill's and represents a fair estimate, considering the numbers present at Issus.

28. For various accounts of the battle of Issus please see Ferrill, *Origins of War*, 201; Warry, *Warfare in the Classical World*, 80; Devine, 'Alexander the Great', 112–116; and Gabriel and Boose, *Great Battles from Antiquity*, 246–255.

29. Ferrill, *Origins of War*, 202.

30. Bosworth, *Conquest and Empire*, 63.

31. Warry, *Warfare in the Classical World*, 79–81; Ferrill, *Origins of War*, 204–205; Devine, 'Alexander the Great', 117; Bosworth, *Conquest and Empire*, 64–67.

32. For excellent treatments of the battle of Gaugamela, see Ferrill, *Origins of War*, 206–210; Warry, *Warfare in the Classical World*, 81; Devine, 'Alexander the Great', 120–124; Santosuosso, *Soldiers, Citizens, and Symbols of War*, 129–135; and Gabriel and Boose, *Great Battles from Antiquity*, 255–264.

33. See Chapter 1, note 68, for a discussion of the controversy concerning the strength of the Persian army at Gaugamela.

34. Devine, 'Alexander the Great', 120.

35. Warry, *Warfare in the Classical World*, 81–83; Ferrill, *Origins of War*, 206–211.

36. Ferrill, *Origins of War*, 210. The term 'hammer and anvil' tactic is taken from Ferrill's account of the battle of Gaugamela.

37. Albert Devine, 'The Battle of Gaugamela: A Tactical and Source-Critical Study', *Ancient World*, vol. 13 (1986), 108. Arrian states that 300,000 Persians were killed at Gaugamela, but a more realistic figure is a few thousand men.

38. Bosworth, *Conquest and Empire*, 94–96.

39. Ibid., 271–273.

40. Warry (*Warfare in the Classical World*, 84–85) and Gabriel and Boose (*Great Battles of Antiquity*, 264–273) place Indian infantry strength at 30,000 men, while Devine ('Alexander the Great') places the number of Indian infantry at 20,000 (pp. 124–127). Devine and Warry believe King Porus had around 80 elephants at his disposal, where Ferrill and Gabriel and Boose claim 200 pachyderms.

41. Gabriel and Boose, *Great Battles of Antiquity*, 266.

42. Ferrill, *Origins of War*, 212.

43. Ibid., 212–213. Porus originally had 300 chariots, but lost 120 machines in the first phase of the battle. The remaining 180 chariots were formed into two squadrons of equal strength, 90 machines apiece.

44. Ibid., 213. See also J.R. Hamilton, 'The Cavalry Battle at the Hydaspes', *Journal of Hellenic Studies*, vol. 76 (1956), 26–31. Also see Fuller's treatment in his *Military History of the Western World*, vol. 1, 180–199.

45. Ferrill, *Origins of War*, 214.

46. Ibid. Ferrill differs from Hamilton in his belief that Porus' left wing crossed in front of, rather than behind, the Indian infantry formations.

47. Quote taken from Arrian, *The Campaigns of Alexander*, trans. Aubrey de Selincourt (New York, 1958), V.17.

48. Devine, 'Alexander the Great', 127; Gabriel and Boose, *Great Battles of Antiquity*, 272.

49. See ch. 2 of Bosworth's *Conquest and Empire* for an excellent brief account of Alexander's life from accession to death.

50. Ferrill, *Origins of War*, 192.

51. Santosuosso, *Soldiers, Citizens, and the Symbols of War*, 149.

52. Sage, *Warfare in Ancient Greece*, 198.

53. H.W. Parke, *Greek Mercenary Soldiers: From the Earliest Times to the Battle of Ipsus* (Oxford: University of Oxford Press, 1930), 207. During the Hellenistic period, one of a general's chief responsibilities was safeguarding his mercenaries' wagon laager. If it was captured the loyalty of the army would cease, and might actually transfer to the holder of the treasure. A mercenary deprived of his laager was as undependable as a farmer-militiaman whose fields were in danger.

54. Warry, *Warfare in the Classical World*, 92–93.

55. Parke, *Greek Mercenary Soldiers*, 208.

56. See the diagram in Warry (*Warfare in the Classical World*, 96) for an excellent description of the evolution of Greek tactics from the battle of Marathon to the Hellenistic period.

57. Warry, *Warfare in the Classical World*, 96.

58. Ibid., 94.

59. Ibid., 95.

60. Ibid.

61. Santosuosso, *Soldiers, Citizens, and the Symbols of War*, 149.

62. Ibid., 93.

63. Ibid.

64. Nick Sekunda, 'Hellenistic Warfare', in *Warfare in the Ancient World*, ed. John Hackett (New York: Facts on File, 1989), 132.

65. Ibid.

66. Ibid., 133.

Chapter 4. Republican Rome at War

1. Lawrence Keppie, *The Making of the Roman Army from Republic to Empire* (New York: Barnes & Noble, 1984), 14.

2. Ibid., 14–15.

3. Chester G. Starr, *The Emergence of Rome*, 2nd edn (Westport, CT: Greenwood, 1982), 9–10.

4. Peter Connolly, *Greece and Rome at War* (London: Macdonald, 1981), 95. Also see Connolly's chapter 'The Early Roman Army' in *Warfare in the Ancient World*, ed. John Hackett (New York: Facts on File, 1989), 136.

5. Connolly, *Greece and Rome at War*, 95.

6. Ibid., 95.

7. Peter Connolly, 'The Early Roman Army', 136; Warry, *Warfare in the Classical World*, 109.

8. Connolly, 'The Early Roman Army', 136.

9. H.M.D Parker, *The Roman Legions* (Cambridge: W. Heffer, 1958; reprint, New York: Dorsett, 1992), 10.

10. Warry, *Warfare in the Classical World*, 109–111; Connolly, 'The Early Roman Army', 136.

11. Robert L. O'Connell, *Of Arms and Men*, 74.

12. Michael Grant, *The Army of the Caesars* (New York: Scribner, 1974), xxx.

13. Warry, *Warfare in the Classical World*, 109.

14. Ibid., 113; Connolly, *Greece and Rome at War*, 220–221; Parker, *Roman Legions*, 199–205.

15. Grant, *Army of the Caesars*, xxxi.

16. Julius Caesar, *Gallic War*, trans. H.J. Edwards, Loeb Classical Library (Cambridge: Harvard University Press, 1919), IV.25.
17. Taken from H.H. Scullard, *From the Gracchi to Nero: A History of Rome from 133 B.C. to A.D. 68* (London: Methuen, 1970), 267. Varus was the commander of Roman forces in Germania.
18. Robert L. O'Connell, 'The Roman Killing Machine', *Military History Quarterly*, vol. 1, no. 1 (1988), 38.
19. Connolly, 'The Early Roman Army', 138.
20. Parker, *Roman Legions*, 11.
21. Warry, *Warfare in the Classical World*, 112.
22. Ibid., 112.
23. For an excellent illustrated account of the organizational changes associated with the reforms of Camillus, see the diagrams in John Warry, *Warfare in the Classical World*, and Peter Connolly, *Greece and Rome at War*, 126–128.
24. See Adrian Goldsworthy's thoughtful defence of the *quincunx* formation in his *Roman Warfare*, ed. John Keegan (London: Cassell, 2002, 55–60). Goldsworthy maintains the Romans fought in this chequerboard formation because 'the maniples of the line behind covered the intervals in front' (p. 57).
25. Many scholars believe that the distance between maniples was equal to the frontage of the maniple itself (Keppie, *Making of the Roman Army*, 33–40; Connolly, *Greece and Rome at War*, 128), but Livy states that the maniples were 'a small distance apart': *Ab urbe condita*, Loeb Classical Library (Cambridge: Harvard University Press, 1919), 8.8.5.
26. F.E. Adcock, *The Roman Art of War under the Republic* (New York: Barnes & Noble, 1960), 8–13; Gabriel and Metz, *From Sumer to Rome*, 34–35.
27. Warry, *Warfare in the Classical World*, 111.
28. Gabriel and Metz, *From Sumer to Rome*, 65.
29. Jones, *Art of War*, 27.
30. Gabriel and Metz, *From Sumer to Rome*, 34–35. Vegetius tells us that Roman recruits trained both morning and afternoon against wooden posts with shields and swords twice the weight of normal *scuta* and *gladii* in order to build strength and endurance: from Roy Davies, *Service in the Roman Army*, ed. David Breeze and Valerie Maxfield (New York: Columbia University Press, 1989), 77–78.
31. Warry, *Warfare in the Classical World*, 100–108. For a concise treatment of the Tarentine and Punic Wars, see John Boardman, Jasper Griffin and Oswyn Murray, *The Roman World: The Oxford History of the Classical World* (New York and Oxford: Oxford University Press, 1988), 26–33.
32. Warry, *Warfare in the Classical World*, 114–116; Connolly, *Greece and Rome at War*, 143–147.
33. W.L. Rodgers, *Greek and Roman Naval Warfare* (Annapolis: Naval Institute, 1964; reprint, 1986), 275.
34. Warry, *Warfare in the Classical World*, 114–124.
35. For an excellent concise account of the battle of Trebia River see Santosuosso's *Soldiers, Citizens, and the Symbols of War*, 172–176.
36. Polybius, *The Histories*, trans. W.R. Paton, Loeb Classical Library (Cambridge: Harvard University Press, 1920–1927), III.72.12–13.
37. Jones, *Art of War*, 65–68. Jones describes the anatomy of the original Fabian strategy and the difficulty faced by the Carthaginian army while operating in Italy.
38. Polybius, *Histories* III.114.5.
39. Hanson, *Carnage and Culture*, 107. Hanson notes that the Roman infantry formation was the deepest since the Theban victory over the Spartans at Leuctra in 371 BCE.
40. Ibid., 108.
41. Polybius, *The Histories* III.117.

42. Peter Connolly, 'The Roman Army in the Age of Polybius', in *Warfare in the Ancient World*, ed. John Hackett (New York: Facts on File, 1989), 163. The 'tumbling effect' was coined by the military historian John Keegan.

43. Hanson, *Carnage and Culture*, 110.

44. Warry, *Warfare in the Classical World*, 121.

45. Santosuosso, *Soldier, Citizens, and Symbols of War*, 191.

46. Warry, *Warfare in the Classical World*, 121; Connolly, 'The Roman Army in the Age of Polybius', 164.

47. Polybius, *Histories* XV.14.9.

48. Livy, *History of Rome* XXXI.34.4. Taken from Livy's description in O'Connell, 'The Roman Killing Machine', 36.

49. Gabriel and Metz, *From Sumer to Rome*, 64–65.

50. O'Connell, 'The Roman Killing Machine', 38.

51. Livy, *History of Rome*, trans. B.O. Foster, F.G. More and R.M. Feer, Loeb Classical Library (Cambridge: Harvard University Press, 1939–1959), XXXIII.4.6.

52. For a description of the battle, see Warry, *Warfare in the Classical World*, 124–125; N.G.L. Hammond, 'The Campaign and the Battle of Cynoscephalae in 197 B.C.', *Journal of Hellenistic Studies*, vol. 108 (1988), 60–82.

53. Livy, *History of Rome* XXXIII.10.18.

54. Edward Luttwak, *The Grand Strategy of the Roman Empire: From the First Century AD to the Third* (Baltimore and London: Johns Hopkins University Press, 1976), 2.

55. For treatment of the Marian reforms see Keppie, *Making of the Roman Army*, 57–79.

56. Hans Delbrück, *History of the Art of War*, vol. 2, *The Barbarian Invasions*, trans. Walter J. Renfroe, Jr (Westport, CT, and London: Greenwood, 1980), 21, 31, 41–43.

57. Philippe Contamine, *War in the Middle Ages*, trans. Michael Jones (Oxford and New York: Basil Blackwell, 1984), 11; Jones, *Art of War*, 64.

58. Hugh Elton, *Warfare in Roman Europe, AD 350–425*, Oxford Classical Monographs (Oxford and New York: University of Oxford Press, Clarendon Press, 1996), 82.

59. Antonio Santosuosso, *Storming the Heavens: Soldiers, Emperors and Civilians in the Roman Empire* (Boulder, CO: Westview, 2001), 20–21; Keppie, *Making of the Roman Army*, 63–67; Warry, *Warfare in the Classical World*, 131–136.

60. Keppie, *Making of the Roman Army*, 67–68.

61. Ibid., 65; Warry, *Warfare in the Classical World*, 153; Brian Dobson, 'Army Organization', in Connolly, *Greece and Rome at War*, 213–227.

62. Warry, *Warfare in the Classical World*, 99, 193; Dobson, 'Army Organization', 223–224.

63. Keppie, *Making of the Roman Army*, 152.

64. L. Keppie, 'The Roman Army of the Later Republic', in *Warfare in the Ancient World*, ed. John Hackett (New York: Facts on File, 1989), 170.

65. Ibid., 172.

66. Connolly, *Greece and Rome at War*, 233.

67. Gabriel and Metz, *From Sumer to Rome*, 26.

68. John Peddie, *The Roman War Machine* (Conshohocken, PA: Combined, 1994), 59–79; Davies, *Service in the Roman Army*, 125–139. Davies describes the anatomy of Roman practice camps in Britain in some detail. Troops were able to construct camps of different layouts to suit different circumstances.

69. Michael Grant, *History of Rome* (New York: Scribner, 1978), 264.

70. The Roman marching order is taken from Josephus' account of Vespasian's march into Galilee during the Jewish revolt (66–73 CE). See Goldsworthy, *Roman Army at War*, for two different marching orders (pp. 105–11). Also, for an excellent illustration of the Roman army on the march, see Connolly's *Greece and Rome at War*, 238.

71. Goldsworthy, *Roman Army at War*, 30–32.

72. Peddie, *Roman War Machine*, 29–30.

73. Robert F. Evans, *Soldiers of Rome: Praetorians and Legionnaires* (Cabin John, MD: Seven Locks, 1986), 78. Peddie, *Roman War Machine*, 12–13.

74. Keppie, *Making of the Roman Army*, 61–63.
75. Brian Dobson, 'The Empire', *Warfare in the Ancient World*, ed. John Hackett (New York: Facts on File, 1989), 192. Also see R.E. Smith, *Service in the Post-Marian Army* (Manchester, 1958), 1–26.
76. Keppie, 'The Roman Army of the Later Republic', 173.
77. Starr, *Emergence of Rome*, 55–58.
78. Ibid., 58–59.
79. Julius Caesar, *Gallic War*, trans. H.J. Edwards, Loeb Classical Library (Cambridge: Harvard University Press, 1919), I.24–27. Also see the account of the unnamed battle in Fuller, *Julius Caesar*, 100–105; Ramon L. Jimenez, *Caesar against the Celts* (New York: Sarpedon, 1996), 45–57; and Keppie, *Making of the Roman Army*, 82–83.
80. Caesar, *Gallic War* I.25.
81. Ibid.
82. Ibid.
83. Ibid., I.26.
84. Larry H. Addington, *The Patterns of War through the Eighteenth Century* (Bloomington, IN: Indiana University Press, 1990), 35.
85. Caesar, *Gallic War* I.26.
86. Nick Sekunda, 'Hellenistic Warfare', 100; Dobson, 'The Empire', 200.
87. See the excellent diagram of the 'Parthian shot' tactic in Warry, *Warfare in the Classical World*, 154–155.
88. Hildinger, *Warriors of the Steppe*, 42–47.
89. Plutarch, *Crassus* 20.1.
90. Ibid., 21.3.
91. Ibid., 24.4. This translation is taken from Sage, *Warfare in Ancient Greece*, 213.
92. Plutarch, *Crassus* 25.1.
93. Ibid., 25.2.
94. Ibid., 28.1.
95. Ibid., 31.1.
96. Jones, *Art of War*, 38.
97. Starr, *Emergence of Rome*, 59–62.
98. For a complete description of the battles of Dyrrhachium and Pharsalus, see Fuller, *Military History of the Western World*, vol. 1, 176–193.
99. See the diagram of the circumvallation in Keppie, *Making of the Roman Army*, 106–108.
100. Caesar, *The Civil Wars*, trans. A.G. Peskett, Loeb Classical Library (Cambridge: Harvard University Press, 1914), III.45.
101. The exact site of the battle of Pharsalus has been under dispute for centuries, with some ancient sources (Hirtius, Frontinus, Eutropius and Orosius) placing it north of the Enipeus River near Palaepharsalus (modern Farsala), and others south of the river near Pharsalus (Appian, Plutarch, Polyaenus and Suetonius).
102. Caesar, *Civil Wars*, III.93.
103. Appian, *Roman History*, 'The Civil War', vol. 2, trans. Horace White, Loeb Classical Library (Cambridge: Harvard University Press, 1913), XI.82, quoting Polli, who was one of Caesar's officers at Pharsalus.
104. Jones, *Art of War*, 43.
105. Starr, *Emergence of Rome*, 62–64.
106. See John Warry's treatment of the battle of Actium in his *Warfare in the Classical World*, 185, 187.

Chapter 5. The Roman Empire at War

1. Grant, *Army of the Caesars*, 40.
2. Ibid., 42, 68, 71.
3. Ibid., 55.

4. Dobson, 'The Empire', 192.
5. Ibid., 192.
6. Ibid.
7. Warry, *Warfare in the Classical World*, 187.
8. Keppie, *Making of the Roman Army*, 182. The term *ala* had been applied under the republic to the allied contingents, both infantry and cavalry, which operated on the flanks of the legions. Under the empire, it was restricted to cavalry.
9. Goldsworthy, *Roman Army at War*, 241.
10. Elton, *Warfare in Roman Europe*, 114; Warry, *Warfare in the Classical World*, 200–201.
11. Goldsworthy, *Roman Army at War*, 241; Arther Ferrill, *The Fall of the Roman Empire: The Military Explanation* (New York: Thames and Hudson, 1986), 78–79.
12. Keppie, *Making of the Roman Army*, 182.
13. Ibid., 184.
14. Luttwak, *Grand Strategy*, 78–79.
15. Ibid., 19.
16. Evans, *Soldiers of Rome*, 2; Dobson, 'The Empire', 205.
17. Evans, *Soldiers of Rome*, 4.
18. Ibid., 5.
19. Gabriel and Boose, *Great Battles of Antiquity*, 419; Delbrück, *History of the Art of War*, vol. 2, 75. Delbrück estimates perhaps 12,000 to 18,000 combatants in the army, with another 8,000 to 10,000 non-combatants tagging along.
20. Velleius Paterculus, *The Roman History*, trans. Frederick W. Shipley, Loeb Classical Library (Cambridge: Harvard University Press, 1924), II.118.2.
21. Velleius, *Roman History* II.69.
22. Santosuosso, *Storming the Heavens*, 138–143. Also see Warry, *Warfare in the Classical World*, 192.
23. Gabriel and Boose, *Great Battles of Antiquity*, 422.
24. Ibid., 424.
25. Julius Caesar, *Gallic Wars*, IV.33. This translation is from Arther Ferrill's article 'Rome's British Mistake', *Military History Quarterly*, vol. 7, no. 1 (1994), 95.
26. Tacitus, *The Annals of Imperial Rome*, trans. Michael Grant (New York, 1989), 328.
27. Ibid., 329.
28. Ibid., 329–330. Warry places the Roman strength at 5,000 to 6,000 legionaries, 4,000 auxiliaries and 1,000 cavalry (*Warfare in the Classical World*, 194–195).
29. Tacitus, *Annals of Imperial Rome*, 330.
30. Ibid., 331.
31. Ibid., 331.
32. Luttwak, *Grand Strategy*, 55–60. Dobson, 'The Empire', 212–220.
33. Grant, *Army of the Caesars*, 232. Also see Roger Tomlin, 'The Late Roman Empire', *Warfare in the Ancient World*, ed. John Hackett (New York: Facts on File, 1989), 222.
34. Grant, *Army of the Caesars*, 75–76; Dobson, 'The Empire', 195.
35. Grant, *Army of the Caesars*, 257–261.
36. Ibid., 274.
37. Ibid., 276.
38. Elton, *Warfare in Roman Europe*, 106. Also see Ferrill, *Fall of the Roman Empire*, 79.
39. Ferrill, *Fall of the Roman Empire*, 42. For estimates on the size of the Roman army during Diocletian's reign see table 3.1 in Luttwak, *Grand Strategy*, 189. Also see R. MacMullen, 'How Big Was the Roman Army?', *Klio*, vol. 62 (1980), 451–460.
40. Luttwak, *Grand Strategy*, 78–79.
41. Ferrill, *Fall of the Roman Empire*, 43–50.
42. Ibid., 42, 47, 66.
43. Pat Southern and Karen Ramsey Dixon, *The Late Roman Army* (New Haven and London: Yale University Press, 1996), 12.

44. Ferrill, *Fall of the Roman Empire*, 49. Also see Elton, *Warfare in Roman Europe*, 94.

45. Ferrill, *Fall of the Roman Empire*, 47.

46. Ibid., 140.

47. Ibid., 96.

48. See the section on Roman organization in Elton, *Warfare in Roman Europe*, ch. 3.

49. Ibid., 110.

50. Ferrill, *The Fall of the Roman Empire*, 50.

51. Ibid.

52. Warry, *Warfare in the Classical World*, 200–201.

53. The eminent German military historian Hans Delbrück comments about the decline of the Roman army: 'With the disappearance of Roman discipline there had also disappeared the peculiar Roman combat technique, the skillful combination of the throwing javelin (*pilum*) with the use of the sword, a method that is only possible with a very well trained unit.' Delbrück continues with comments concerning the 'barbarization' of the Roman Empire in the fourth and fifth century: 'now the Romans too, utilized as their battle formation the Germanic square, the boar's head. The barbarian auxiliaries, who had formerly constituted a supporting force in the Roman organization, now formed its cadre and strength. Now the legate with senatorial rank disappeared, and a full-time soldier was commander of the legion and sometimes he was no longer a Roman but a German.' *History of the Art of War*, vol. 2, 220.

54. See Ferrill, *Fall of the Roman Empire* (pp. 52–56), for a discussion of Julian the Apostate's campaign in Persia.

55. For realistic estimates of the size of the Roman and Gothic armies, see Thomas S. Burns, 'The Battle of Adrianople: A Reconsideration', *Historia*, vol. 22 (1973), 336–345, and Santosuosso, *Storming the Heavens*, 196–207. For accounts of the battle of Adrianople using Ammianus' troop estimates of 50,000 Romans and 70,000 Goths, see Ferrill, *Fall of the Roman Empire*, 56–64, and Warry, *Warfare in the Classical World*, 207. Delbrück, *History of the Art of War*, vol. 2, takes a more conservative stance, placing the Roman strength at between 15,000 and 18,000 men, and the Gothic compliment at between 12,000 and 15,000 troops (pp. 269–284).

56. Ferrill, *Fall of the Roman Empire*, 63.

57. Ammianus Marcellinus, *The Roman History of Ammianus Marcellinus During the Reigns of The Emperors Constantius, Julian, Jovianus, Valentinian, and Valens*, trans. C. D. Yonge (London: G. Bell, 1911), XXXI.13.18.

58. Ibid., XXXI.13.19. This comment may not be true in regards to Romans killed, but the loss of two emperors in a generation against barbarians must have been traumatic, and Ammianus' statement probably reflects a historian's lament over the destruction of a Roman field army and the condition of the Roman strategic position.

59. Burns, 'The Battle of Adrianople', 336–345; Ferrill, *Fall of the Roman Empire*, 60.

60. Jones, *Art of War*, 93.

61. Herwig Wolfram, *History of the Goths*, 2nd edn, trans. Thomas J. Dunlap (Berkeley: University of California Press, 1988), 131–138.

62. Hildinger, *Warriors of the Steppe*, 61–65.

63. Rudy Paul Lindner, 'Nomadism, Horses and Huns', *Past & Present*, vol. 92 (1981), 14–15. If one assumes that the Huns used ten horses per cavalryman for a large-scale campaign, then the restricted size of the Hungarian plain (42,400 square miles) could support about 150,000 grazing horses or approximately 15,000 cavalry.

64. Hildinger, *Warriors of the Steppe*, 65.

65. Otto J. Maenchen-Helfen, *The World of the Huns* (Berkeley: University of California Press, 1973), 241–251.

66. Ferrill, *Fall of the Roman Empire*, 146.

67. Ibid., 147.

68. For an excellent account of the battle of Châlons, see Ferrill, *Fall of the Roman Empire*, 145–151; Fuller, *Military History of the Western World*, vol. 1, 282–301.

69. Hildinger, *Warriors of the Steppe*, 70. See Hildinger for a modern interpretation of troop strengths. Cassiodorus, who was born some thirty years after Châlons, places the Hunnic confederation at 500,000 troops total, a fantastical estimate: *The Gothic History of Jordanes*, ed. and trans. Charles Christopher Mierow (Princeton: University Press, 1915), XXXVI.105. The lack of reliable contemporary troop estimates has led some historians to shy away from reconstructing the battle of Châlons. Delbrück refuses to discuss the battle because of unreliable sources.

70. Hanson, *Carnage and Culture*, 4.

Selected Bibliography

Adcock, F.E. *The Roman Art of War under the Republic*. New York: Barnes & Noble, 1960.

Addington, Larry H. *The Patterns of War through the Eighteenth Century*. Bloomington, IN: Indiana University Press, 1990.

Anderson, J.K. 'Hoplite Weapons and Offensive Arms', in *Hoplites: The Classical Greek Battle Experience*, ed. Victor Davis Hanson. London: Routledge, 1991.

——. *Military Theory and Practice in the Age of Xenophon*. Berkeley, CA: University of California Press, 1970.

Best, J.G.P. *Thracian Peltasts and Their Influence on Greek Warfare*. Groningen: Wolters-Noordhoff, 1969.

Boardman, John, Jasper Griffin and Oswyn Murray. *The Roman World: The Oxford History of the Classical World*. Oxford: Oxford University Press, 1988.

Bosworth, A.B. *Conquest and Empire: The Reign of Alexander the Great*. Cambridge: Cambridge University Press, 1988.

Buckler, John. *The Theban Hegemony, 371–362 BC*. Cambridge, MA: Harvard University Press, 1980.

Burns, Thomas S. 'The Battle of Adrianople: A Reconsideration', *Historia*, vol. 22 (1973), 336–345.

Chadwick, John. *The Mycenaean World*. Cambridge: Cambridge University Press, 1976.

Chandler, David G. *The Art of Warfare on Land*. New York: Penguin, 1974.

Connolly, Peter. 'The Early Roman Army', in *Warfare in the Ancient World*, ed. John Hackett. New York: Facts on File, 1989.

——. *Greece and Rome at War*. London: Macdonald, 1981.

——. 'The Roman Army in the Age of Polybius', in *Warfare in the Ancient World*, ed. John Hackett. New York: Facts on File, 1989.

Cook, J.M. *The Persian Empire*. New York: Schocken, 1983.

Davies, Roy. *Service in the Roman Army*, ed. David Breeze and Valerie Maxfield. New York: Columbia University Press, 1989.

Delbrück, Hans. *History of the Art of War within the Framework of Political History*, trans. Walter J. Renfroe, Jr. Vol. 1: *Warfare in Antiquity*. Vol. 2: *The Barbarian Invasions*. Vol. 3: *The Middle Ages*. Vol. 4: *The Dawn of Modern Warfare*. Westport, CT, and London: Greenwood, 1982.

Devine, Albert. 'Alexander the Great', in *Warfare in the Ancient World*, ed. John Hackett. New York: Facts on File, 1989.

——. 'The Battle of Gaugamela: A Tactical and Source-Critical Study', *The Ancient World*, vol. 13 (1986), 87–113.

Dobson, Brian. 'The Empire', in *Warfare in the Ancient World*, ed. John Hackett. New York: Facts on File, 1989.

Dodge, T.A. *Hannibal.* New York: Da Capo, 1995.

Drews, Robert. *The Coming of the Greeks: Indo-European Conquests in the Aegean and the Near East.* Princeton: Princeton University Press, 1988.

——.*The End of the Bronze Age: Changes in Warfare and the Catastrophe ca.1200 BC.* Princeton: Princeton University Press, 1993.

Dupuy, Trevor N. *The Evolution of Weapons and Warfare.* New York: Da Capo, 1984.

Dyer, Gwynne. *War.* New York: Crown, 1985.

Eggenberger, David. *An Encyclopedia of Battles: Accounts of Over 1,560 Battles from 1479 B.C. to the Present.* New York: Dover, 1985.

Elton, Hugh. *Warfare in Roman Europe, AD 350–425.* Oxford and New York: University of Oxford Press, Clarendon Press, 1996.

Engels, Donald. *Alexander the Great and the Logistics of the Macedonian Army.* Berkeley: University of California Press, 1978.

Evans, Robert F. *Soldiers of Rome: Praetorians and Legionnaires.* Cabin John, MD, and Washington, DC: Seven Locks, 1986.

Ferrill, Arther. *The Fall of the Roman Empire: The Military Explanation.* London and New York: Thames and Hudson, 1986.

——. *The Origins of War: From the Stone Age to Alexander the Great*, rev. edn. Boulder, CO: Westview, 1997.

Fuller, J.F.C. *Julius Caesar: Man, Soldier, and Tyrant.* London: Eyre and Spottiswoode, 1965.

——. *A Military History of the Western World.* Vol. 1: *From the Earliest Times to the Battle of Lepanto.* New York: Funk and Wagnalls, 1954–1957.

Gabriel, Richard A. *The Culture of War.* Westport, CT: Greenwood, 1990.

—— and Donald W. Boose, Jr. *The Great Battles of Antiquity: A Strategic Guide to Great Battles that Shaped the Development of War.* Westport, CT: Greenwood, 1994.

—— and Karen S. Metz. *From Sumer to Rome: The Military Capabilities of Ancient Armies.* Westport, CT: Greenwood, 1991.

Gardiner, Alan. *The Qadesh Inscriptions of Ramesses II.* Oxford: Griffith Institute, 1960.

Goldsworthy, Adrian Keith. *The Roman Army at War: 100 BC–AD 200.* Oxford Classical Monographs. Oxford: Clarendon, 1996.

Grant, Michael. *The Army of the Caesars.* New York: Charles Scribner, 1975.

——. *History of Rome.* New York: Charles Scribner, 1978.

Hammond, N.G.L. 'The Campaign and Battle of Marathon', in *Studies in Greek History: A Companion Volume to a History of Greece to 322 B.C.* Oxford: Oxford University Press, 1973.

——. 'The Campaign and the Battle of Cynoscephalae in 197 B.C.', *Journal of Hellenistic Studies*, vol. 108 (1988), 60–82.

Hanson, Victor Davis. *Carnage and Culture: Landmark Battles in the Rise of Western Power.* New York: Doubleday, 2001.

——. 'Hoplite Technology in Phalanx Battle', in *Hoplites: The Classical Greek Battle Experience*, ed. Victor Davis Hanson. London and New York: Routledge, 1991.

——. *The Western Way of War: Infantry Battle in Classical Greece*, 2nd edn. Berkeley: University of California Press, 2000.

Healy, Mark. *Warrior Pharaoh: Ramesses II and the Battle of Qadesh.* London: Osprey, 1993.

Hildinger, Erik. *Warriors of the Steppe: A Military History of Central Asia, 500 B.C. to 1700 A.D.* New York: Sarpedon, 1997.

Jimenez, Ramon L. *Caesar against the Celts.* New York: Sarpedon, 1996.

Jones, A.H.M. *The Later Roman Empire, 284–602.* Vol. 1. Norman: University of Oklahoma Press, 1964.

Jones, Archer. *The Art of War in the Western World.* Urbana and Chicago: University of Illinois Press, 1987.

Keegan, John. *Face of Battle.* New York: Viking, 1976.
——. *A History of Warfare.* New York: Alfred A. Knopf, 1993.
Keppie, Lawrence. *The Making of the Roman Army: From Republic to Empire.* New York: Barnes & Noble, 1984.
——. 'The Roman Army of the Later Republic', in *Warfare in the Ancient World*, ed. John Hackett. New York: Facts on File, 1989.
Laffont, Robert. *The Ancient Art of Warfare.* New York: Time-Life, 1966.
Lazenby, John. 'Hoplite Warfare', in *Warfare in the Ancient World*, ed. John Hackett. New York: Facts on File, 1989.
Lindner, Rudy Paul. 'Nomadism, Horses and Huns', *Past & Present*, vol. 92 (1981), 14–15.
Luttwak, Edward. *The Grand Strategy of the Roman Empire: From the First Century AD to the Third.* Baltimore and London: Johns Hopkins University Press, 1976.
Maenchen-Helfen, Otto J. *The World of the Huns.* Berkeley: University of California Press, 1973.
Oakeshott, R. Ewart. *The Archaeology of Weapons: Arms and Armor from Pre-History to the Age of Chivalry.* New York: Frederick A. Praeger, 1960
Ober, Joshua. 'Hoplites and Obstacles', in *Hoplites: The Classical Greek Battle Experience*, ed. Victor Davis Hanson. London: Routledge, 1991.
O'Connell, Robert L. 'The Insolent Chariot', *Military History Quarterly*, vol. 2, no. 3 (1990).
——. *Of Arms and Men: A History of War, Weapons and Aggression.* Oxford and New York: Oxford University Press, 1989.
——. 'The Roman Killing Machine', *Military History Quarterly*, vol. 1, no. 1 (1988).
Parke, H.W. *Greek Mercenary Soldiers: From the Earliest Times to the Battle of Ipsus.* Oxford and New York: Oxford University Press, 1933.
Parker, H.M.D. *The Roman Legions.* Cambridge: W. Heffer, 1958; reprint, New York: Dorsett, 1992.
Peddie, John. *The Roman War Machine.* Conshohocken, PA: Combined, 1994.
Rahe, Paul A. 'The Military Situation in Western Asia on the Eve of Cunaxa', *American Journal of Philology*, vol. 101 (1980), 79–96.
Rodgers, W.L. *Greek and Roman Naval Warfare.* Annapolis: Naval Institute, 1964; reprint, 1986.
Roux, Georges. *Ancient Iraq*, 3rd edn. New York: Penguin, 1993.
Sage, Michael M. *Warfare in Ancient Greece: A Sourcebook.* London and New York: Routledge, 1996.
Santosuosso, Antonio. *Soldiers, Citizens, and the Symbols of War from Classical Greece to Republican Rome, 500–167 BC.* Boulder, CO: Westview, 1997.
——. *Storming the Heavens: Soldiers, Emperors, and Civilians in the Roman Empire.* Boulder, CO: Westview, 2001.
Sekunda, Nick. 'Hellenistic Warfare', in *Warfare in the Ancient World*, ed. John Hackett. New York: Facts on File, 1989.
——. 'The Persians', in *Warfare in the Ancient World*, ed. John Hackett. New York: Facts on File, 1989.
Snodgrass, A.M. *Arms and Armor of the Greeks.* Baltimore and London: Johns Hopkins University Press, 1999.
Southern, Pat, and Karen Ramsey Dixon. *The Late Roman Army.* New Haven and London: Yale University Press, 1996.
Starr, Chester G. *The Emergence of Rome*, 2nd edn. Westport, CT: Greenwood, 1982.
——. *The Influence of Sea Power on Ancient History.* Oxford and New York: Oxford University Press, 1989.
Sykes, Percy. *A History of Persia*, 2 vols. London: Macmillan, 1958.
Tomlin, Roger. 'The Late Roman Empire', in *Warfare in the Ancient World*, ed. John Hackett. New York: Facts on File, 1989.

Warry, John. *Warfare in the Classical World: An Illustrated Encyclopedia of Weapons, Warriors, and Warfare in the Ancient Civilizations of Greece and Rome*. London: Salamander; New York: St Martin's, 1980.

Watkins, Trevor. 'The Beginnings of Warfare', in *Warfare in the Ancient World*, ed. John Hackett. New York: Facts on File, 1989.

Wiseman, D.J. 'The Assyrians', in *Warfare in the Ancient World*, ed. John Hackett. New York: Facts on File, 1989.

Wolfram, Herwig. *History of the Goths*, 2nd edn, trans. Thomas J. Dunlap. Berkeley: University of California Press, 1988.

Yadin, Yigael. *The Art of Warfare in Biblical Lands in the Light of Archaeological Discovery*, 2 vols. New York: McGraw-Hill, 1963.

Index